HMS GANGES DAYS

HMS GANGES DAYS

From Nozzer to Dabtoe in 386 Days

PETER BROADBENT

CHAPLIN BOOKS

www.chaplinbooks.co.uk

Copyright © Peter Broadbent
First published in 2013 by Chaplin Books
Sixth impression

ISBN: 978-1-909183-13-1

A CIP catalogue record for this book is available
from The British Library.

Design by Michael Walsh
at The Better Book Company
Printed by Imprint Digital

Chaplin Books
1 Eliza Place
Gosport PO12 4UN
Tel: 023 9252 9020
www.chaplinbooks.co.uk

CONTENTS

AUTHOR'S NOTE

I wrote this book to commemorate the 50th anniversary of my joining *HMS Ganges* and to answer the following questions:

1. Why did a relatively introverted Grammar School boy join the Royal Navy at the tender age of 15?

2. Why did I elect to 'join-up' at the extreme bottom of the Naval pile as a Junior Seaman Second Class?

3. How in the world did I, a boy with little ambition and no resolve, sail through my time at the Royal Navy's toughest and most notorious training establishment?

I hope that this book answers all these questions and that my children (Paul and Helen), my grandchildren (James and Oscar) and those who may come after them will curl up on a warm, comfortable chair – and enjoy my story.

ACKNOWLEDGEMENTS

I happily start by acknowledging the support and understanding of my wonderful wife Margaret. For years, I tapped away at my keyboard while she gardened, washed, cooked and did a hundred and one other things that I should have helped with.

While my story draws mainly on my personal experiences, I have used fragments of information gleaned from a multitude of memories which other ex-*Ganges* boys have posted on the Internet. I have never purposefully plagiarised anything written by others and I offer heartfelt thanks to everyone who has written about *HMS Ganges* and placed it in the public domain. I have tried to make the book entertaining as well as being an accurate description of *HMS Ganges* training methods and UK life in 1960. I have purposefully avoided any individual references, and have invented characters and dialogue in order to give the book some depth. Individually none of the book's characters, in any way, represent actual Hardy or Keppel mess members or Instructors of the time.

Cheers to all my actual messmates and Instructors: in a multitude of ways you helped me through my *Ganges* Days.

I grew up with the archaic pounds shillings and pence monetary system and I've used it throughout this book. If anyone wants to find out the decimal equivalents (or, indeed, to convert the amounts into any currency) there are plenty of websites that will do this for you.

Peter Broadbent
Ex Junior Seaman, Second Class, P/053653
Hondón de Las Nieves, Spain
January 2013

A BRIEF HISTORY OF *HMS GANGES*

The first *HMS Ganges* came into service in 1779 when the Honourable East India Company presented three vessels to the Royal Navy. One of the vessels, the *Bengal,* was re-named *HMS Ganges* and broken up in 1816. Her successor, also named *HMS Ganges*, was built in Bombay, launched in November 1821 and arrived in Portsmouth in October of the following year.

After various commissions, she became the flagship of Rear Admiral R L Bayes and left for the Pacific in September 1857, the last sailing ship to be a sea-going flagship. In 1866 she became a boys' training ship, firstly in Falmouth harbour and then transferring to Harwich harbour in 1899. For seven years *HMS Ganges* served her purpose but a severe winter confirmed that better conditions were necessary to ensure the well-being of the boys. It was decided in 1905 to move the boys ashore onto land adjacent to the village of Shotley Gate. The move encountered fierce opposition from 'Their Lords at the Admiralty' who could not imagine sailors being trained on dry land. The following year, at 4am on the first Thursday of July 1906, the ship *HMS Ganges* was towed away by Government tugs to be scrapped.

When the boys first moved ashore there were around 500 of them. As the establishment developed, the numbers increased and by the end of the 1940s there were 2,000 boys under training, with a new batch of boys arriving every five weeks.

The raising of the school leaving age from 15 to 16 marked the end of *HMS Ganges* and on 16 January 1973 the final recruitment (No 41) of Junior entrants joined. On 6 June 1976 *Ganges* closed. The White Ensign was lowered for the last time at sunset on 28 October 1976.

Between 1905 and 1976 some 150,000 boy recruits had passed through her gates. Most had gone on to enjoy a full and active Royal Naval career. Many made it to the Wardroom. None of us ever forgot the place.

1

A NOSTALGIC VISIT

It's 16 February 1989, my 45th birthday. I'm sitting in my car, parked on a short, unremarkable Suffolk road staring at a pair of imposing black iron gates and smoking a cigarette.

Instead of driving all the way home after a late business meeting in Great Yarmouth yesterday, I'd decided to stay overnight and drive home to Stubbington in the morning. As I approached the outskirts of Ipswich, I made a spur-of-the-moment decision to re-visit Shotley Gate.

I've been to all corners of the world but not to this part of rural Suffolk for 28 years. I wind my window down: I can smell it. Caledonia Road, Shotley Gate, leads to only one place, the place that now sits silently behind those gates.

I recall how I had felt when I'd first marched down this road 29 years ago as a 15-year-old 'Nozzer'. The gates look less daunting now. The large anchor plaques, the huge figureheads and the flanking field-guns have gone. All those years ago, the place behind those gates had determined the course of my life and had turned a feckless, unremarkable schoolboy into ME!

Shotley Gate is a small village at the southern tip of the Shotley Peninsular, a piece of East Anglia bounded on the north east by the river Orwell, and to the south by the river Stour. The wind and rain whip mercilessly across this part of Suffolk which has an air of brooding isolation about it. If I had known the reputation of this place back in 1959, I wonder if I would have taken the 'Queen's Shilling', and subjected myself to what went on here.

I stub my cigarette out in a half-full ashtray and stroll towards the gates for a closer look. One of the small personnel side gates is unlocked. I give it a push and for the first time in many years I'm onboard *Her Majesty's Ship Ganges*, a brick-built barrack of a place. The hairs on the back of my neck stand to attention.

A smiling gentleman wearing a dark grey duffle coat emerges from what I remembered as the Gatehouse. He pulls his hood up to protect himself from the wind and greets me politely. I'm pleasantly surprised: I associate these gates with bellowing, strutting, unsmiling Regulating Petty Officers, brandishing swagger-sticks and crunching gravel under their well-shined boots.

I explain that I had spent time here as a young boy and am interested in seeing what has become of the place.

'No problem sir. Would you like to bring your car in?' he asks.

Bring my car in indeed! That's unexpected.

He opens the two large gates for me. I drive in and wind my window down. Still smiling, and gripping his hood tight, he explains that a company called Eurosport now owns the site and they provide sporting facilities for, amongst others, the police. Most of the original buildings are still here but some are in a sorry state of repair and any exploring I do will be at my own risk. I nod understandingly.

I park 50 yards inside the gate alongside the mast. There are a handful of cars parked on the Quarterdeck away to my right. I shake my head. Astonishingly, it looks as though that once sacred stretch of ground is now a car park.

Close up, the once impressive mast is rotting away. It's badly in need of some serious repair work. The ratlines and shrouds are frayed in places. The sheer pole, that first step of the mast-climb, is cracked. The safety net is frayed and threadbare in places, whippings have unravelled, blocks, bottle-screws, shackles and other hardware are rusting and in desperate need of a wire brush and some lubrication. The mast's white paint, that had looked dazzling from a distance, is cracked and peeling. I gaze up at the 'Devil's Elbow' and the 'Half Moon': still a good distance away.

Did I really climb up there?

I stare at the vast expanse of the Parade-Ground. I clearly remember it packed with 2,000 uniformed and upright young boys; the Bugle Band over to my right and the saluting dais in front of Nelson Hall to my left. The surface is cracked in places: this once most disciplined of places is now freckled with disrespectful tufts of East Anglian weeds. I can see some of the small faded grey circles that were once the bright white markers used to align classes for morning Divisions.

From somewhere in the far distance I can hear that unforgettable, stentorian voice ... *'The Only Two People Allowed To Walk On My Parade-Ground Lad Are Me And God ... And He Can Only Get Away With It ... Because I Can't See Him!'*

I'm back: a middle-aged ex-*Ganges* boy shuffling over your now-aging Parade-Ground, hands stuffed disrespectfully in his pockets. A zephyr of cold Shotley air whips around my ankles: it brings back memories of dull, dismal mornings standing unprotected and bitterly cold against the Suffolk wind. It was rumoured that Nelson Hall, the vast open-sided building on the west side of the Parade-Ground, was built to accommodate 2,000 boys on wet, inclement days, but I don't remember using it during my time here. We had paraded outside in the snow, hail, sleet and rain. Apparently, braving the elements was a character-building part of Royal Naval training back then.

HMS Ganges had closed as a training establishment 13 years ago, but the Royal Navy had not taken everything with them when they 'abandoned ship'. The large figureheads that had once flanked the Main Gate now look down from the inside corners of Nelson Hall, their paint flaking and dulled. Underneath one is a descriptive plaque: it had originally belonged to *HMS Caledonia*, a boy's training ship on the Firth of Forth in Scotland, which I suppose explains the Scottish name of the road outside. On the walls, hanging at precise intervals, are ageing, wooden-framed inspection mirrors where Instructors would have stood to inspect and preen themselves before Daily Divisions. Yellowed posters of Admiralty Instructions and Queen's Regulations in large uncompromising text glare at me as though they still have something relevant and important to say.

Standing in Nelson Hall's main entranceway, out of the wind, I take a deep breath and look out over the vast open expanse. All the surrounding buildings are still here: messdecks, the Senior

Rates mess, the NAAFI canteen, the Wardroom, the entrance to the Short Covered Way and further to my left, the ornate swimming pool building. The Central Mess Galley that had fed us three calorie-filled meals every day, now stands forlorn and unkempt, its well-dressed rows of broken windows, stretching dirty and forlorn.

I kick at a particularly healthy weed as I walk back towards my car and stop to read notices taped to the windows of what used to be the NAAFI Canteen. One asks for money to preserve the *Ganges* mast.

I drive around the Quarterdeck car park, and round again just for the pure hell of it. As Trainees we weren't allowed to march across this piece of ground ... we had to double. The reason that Royal Naval Quarterdecks were so sacred would only become apparent to me when I joined my first real ship: the Battle Cruiser *HMS Bermuda*, flagship of the Home Fleet. Leading off the Quarterdeck is the Long Covered Way, so named because it is a covered 'way' that is longer than the Short Covered Way. I halt facing the entrance arch. The legend 'FEAR GOD, HONOUR THE KING.' is still there: a bit faded now, but still legible beneath an ornate light-bracket. The large round clock that used to be under the light is gone.

I drive slowly down the Long Covered Way, passing my old mess on the left. On my right is the small post box. Further down on the left is where I learned to 'sling' a hammock. To the right there is the door to the small shop where I bought my tobacco and my dhoby-dust. To my left, the bricked rubbish compound and the road to the gym. To my right is the way to the infamous Laundry Hill.

At the bottom of the Long Covered Way, I look out over the windswept grey waters of the River Stour towards Harwich and decide against lighting another cigarette. Instead, I drive back up the Long Covered Way and screech to a disrespectful halt outside the doors of Keppel 9 mess, the fifth mess from the top. I get out of my car, stand and look around me: I can see myself 30 years ago. As a manipulated boy I had been tormented, insulted, yelled at, criticised, harassed and given my mail ... right here. This was where I had mustered three or four times a day, every day, to be marched or doubled somewhere. It was where we were yelled at and where we awaited the official results of mess inspections. In this exact spot I had drunk gallons of wonderfully, rich and invigorating Kye (hot chocolate) and smoked hundreds of sneaky, hand-cupped cigarettes during Stand-Easy. I had laughed and been on the verge of tears here, but I had never actually cried. In those days, 15-year-old boys from my part of West Yorkshire didn't cry, no matter how much they wanted to.

The double entrance doors and the windows of Keppel 9 mess are all closed. I can see through the grubby door glass and the inside looks long abandoned but invitingly familiar. It's obvious that these now derelict and neglected structures have little life left in them: they will either fall down or be demolished one day, and I don't want this particular bit of *Ganges* to disappear without one last look inside. I could be the very last Keppel 9 mess member to walk through these doors.

An application of shoulder proves sufficient to open the main doors and I stumble inside. I take a deep breath: it's a weird feeling. To my left is the bathroom, the filthy sinks slightly more contemporary than those I remember. The drying-room is unchanged: the central framework of black painted steel bars, over which I had hung my damp washing, still spans the hot water pipes that once provided a comfortably warm perch for an 'after lights' cigarette on those freezing cold winter nights. The night heads (toilets) now have full-length doors on the cubicles. I make a silent, dismissive gesture and say to nobody in particular, 'Not like it was in my day!'

I push my way through the blue swing doors into the messdeck proper: it looks exactly as I remember it, maybe a little smaller. The old cream and green paintwork is now covered by a Department of Trade shade of magnolia. It smells musty and stale, but surprisingly I can still detect the familiar whiff of a tallow-based deck polish. The windows on both sides are a grimy, dusty grey but unbroken and the metallic roof rafters span starkly naked, exactly as I remember them. Surprisingly there are no cobwebs anywhere.

I have a sudden desire to remove something from here. I want something to take home with me, something physical that I can hold and touch and that I know comes from my *Ganges* mess. I see the Tannoy speaker: it's exactly where I remembered, but set too high and too well bracketed to remove. My steps echo as I walk the parquet floor up to the top of the mess and back down again. I think about lighting a cigarette, but don't. Then I remember that we could never smoke in the mess, so I light an impertinent fag and look around me. I decide what piece of this place I want. I make a quick estimation as to where my bed-space used to be and I check it by squatting down and gazing at the roof rafters and the Tannoy. Satisfied that I've got the position about right, I return to my car for a tool. I grind the remains of my cigarette into the deck of the Long Covered Way.

The flat end of my wheel brace and a pocketknife do the trick and eventually I'm back in my car with my piece of Keppel 9 mess hidden under my seat. As a final act of devilment, I consider leaving the main doors open, but don't. Instead, I make sure they are secure against any further intrusion.

I spend the next hour or so driving and wandering around the rest of *Ganges*. The Seamanship school, down by the foreshore, is in a particularly decrepit state. I ponder a moment outside the main entrance doors. The small patch of grass where 173 class had 'skylarked', and earned themselves their first serious punishment session up and down those dreaded series of steps, is now strewn with old wooden pallets. Inside I wander from room to room but there is little I remember. I hope that the wonderful brass scuttle, a beautiful piece of maritime memorabilia, doesn't end its life unappreciated in a Suffolk landfill.

There is little left of the Assault Course. Only a small crenelated section of that dreaded wall remains, the nets and the pipework have gone and only straggly bits of rope hang limply on a rusty framework spanning pits of weed-encrusted, stagnant green water. I amble up and down those dreaded series of concrete steps, known to every *Ganges* boy, as Faith, Hope and

Charity: encroaching vegetation now overhangs and blunts the sharp, toe-busting edges.

The gymnasium and swimming pool are locked. The place where my 'log' used to lie, against the Shooting Range boundary wall, is impossible to find as there has been some development work in the area. As I walk up Laundry Hill, I pass the small, blue wooden shack: it still looks like a badly neglected garden shed. I recall how I had felt on the day I discovered the delights of Jayne Mansfield inside there. I wipe a circle of grime away and peer in through the window hoping that the desk is still there, but it isn't. The little blue shack is full of building materials.

Time to go. I've seen enough and I have a long drive back to Stubbington and a birthday cake to look forward to. At the Main Gate I acknowledge the gentleman's sloppy salute with a very civilian thumbs-up and slowly drive down Caledonia Road. I feel great: it may only be a dull and unloved block of wood under my seat, but it's now my part of *Ganges* ... mine. In my day, that deck had shone like glass.

Before leaving Shotley Gate I visit the Annexe, about a quarter of a mile from the main complex. This was where I had spent the first four weeks of my Naval Service and where my 15-and-a-bit years of youthful know-how and experience had been forcibly extracted. Within a small isolated compound, enclosed by a green metal fence, I had been cleansed, examined, drilled, insulted, punished, maimed, photographed, made to fight, kitted out and taught some basic Naval skills. Unfortunately, all that now remains of the Annexe is a lonely piece of tarmac surrounded by a wire mesh fence on which are wired notices explaining that it remains Government Property, 'No Entry and No Ball Games'.

On the edges of this very ordinary piece of cracked asphalt, were once buildings full of boys coming to terms with their first Naval experiences. One day, houses will probably be built here, on this unremarkable piece of Suffolk real estate, where so much youthful enthusiasm was tempered.

2

ITCHY FEET

I had a wonderfully happy childhood. I was brought up by my mother who, as well as looking after two sons single-handed after her divorce from my father, ran a Pudsey Off-Licence which, by law, was open 14 hours a day, six days a week and eight hours on a Sunday.

For reasons completely beyond me, I passed my Eleven Plus and went to the local Grammar School which offered me a first-rate education. The latter years of the 1950s were, however, full of distractions: music, girls, Leeds United, cigarettes, rock and roll, girls, cricket, drainpipe trousers, girls ... and I rejected anything academic, merely 'attending' my way through school. I was not a badly behaved pupil: far from it. I was only caught misbehaving once: for writing nicknames on the girls' hockey team-sheet on the noticeboard, and was given an enthusiastic 'six of the best' by the headmaster himself. By the time I was 15, I was the school's breaststroke champion swimmer, I'd had a crush on a girl or two and had a short-term girlfriend who went to a Grammar School in Bradford and wore an attractive pink uniform blazer. In my opinion I had experienced absolutely everything that Pudsey, West Yorkshire, had to offer me. I was bored ... bored stiff.

I've often wondered what made me, a relatively shy, academically stilted boy, sign up for nine years' service in the Royal Navy just months before I was due to sit my all important GCE 'O' level exams. After much reflection I think I've figured it out. Not only was I an enthusiastic stamp collector, I was also fascinated by maps and would spend hours searching atlases to discover where in the world my latest piece of perforated paper had come from. My fascination with maps was encouraged by my geography master, Mr George Parry, a wonderfully inspiring teacher. He also allowed me to borrow copies of his extensive collection of *National Geographic* magazines and I discovered, within those colourful glossy pages, photographs of semi-naked women. Consequently, my satchel bulged with George's magazines most nights. So, that's probably the answer: what made my feet 'itch' was a combination of philately, cartography and semi-naked women.

'Join The Navy And See The World' was a prominent advertising blurb run every day in the *Daily Mirror*. The 'See the World' bit hooked me completely and in the early summer of 1959 I wrote a letter of inquiry to the Maritime College at Hull, asking them what I had to do to join the Navy and 'See the World'. They told me to stay on at school to obtain the greatest number of GCE 'O' level passes that I could before re-applying. I was too impatient: staying on at school was out of the question. I was desperate to see what lay beyond my grimy West Yorkshire boundaries. If I was to believe the *National Geographic* there was a colourful world out there where the sun shone, palm trees grew, the oceans were blue ... and women wore very little.

At the time, I didn't understand the difference between the Merchant Navy and military service in the Her Majesty's Royal Navy, and there was nobody I knew who could explain it to me. So it was that in the early summer of 1959, I found myself being welcomed into the Royal Naval Recruitment Office on a dingy back street round the back of Leeds City railway station. My mother and I seated ourselves opposite an elderly uniformed gentleman with two and a half rows of medal ribbons above his left breast pocket. He had the lined, bronzed face of a traveller, a man who had seen everything and had been everywhere. Behind him were posters of suntanned, happy looking young men in Naval uniform gazing out over turquoise waters and golden beaches under a cloudless blue sky. My wanderlust buttons were being well and truly pressed. My wrinkled friend on the opposite side of the desk didn't tell me to stay on at school: he answered all our questions, gave us some literature and explained to me that if I wanted to become Captain of my own ship, I should join the Seaman Branch, as that was the only Branch from which it was possible.

Once my mother had signed all the preliminary documents and I had agreed that the Seamanship Branch was for me, all I had to do was go home, relax and wait for notification of my medical. Assuming that I had no physical problems, I should be on my travels before the end of the year.

I officially left school on the day that the long 1959 summer school holiday started in late July. My mother had already paid for a school trip to Switzerland that year ... so I went. I stayed in a lakeside Youth Hostel in a small place called Thun: stared at glaciers, travelled in chair-lifts and small Swiss trains, swam in the freezing waters of Lake Thun and met a blonde-haired beauty called Christina from Berne whose parents had a summer chalet on the banks of the Lake.

Back home, I spent the remainder of the summer loafing around, secure in the knowledge that shortly my life was about to change and my horizons broaden. I swam a lot, hung around town, occasionally met up with friends after school and exchanged letters with Christina.

It wasn't long before the first buff envelope emblazoned with the words 'ON HER

Look at the hair. My girlfriend told me to put my collar up

MAJESTY'S SERVICE, OFFICIAL PAID', fell on our linoleum floor. It instructed my mother to accompany me for my medical examination.

On the prescribed day, Mum stuck an explanatory notice on the door and closed the shop. We eventually found the Dickensian building in a gloomy area of Leeds that neither of us had visited before. Mother and I waited alone in a dimly lit room where the marks left by the recently removed gas mantles were evident on the walls. Eventually I was ushered into a large, darkened room, seated in front of a dark glass screen and told to press a red or green button whenever I saw a small red or green light. This wasn't easy: the lights were very small and it was sometimes impossible to tell what colour they were. Then a pair of uncomfortable headphones were clamped over my ears

Mum

and I was instructed to press a button whenever I heard a 'beep'. When these tests were complete, I was taken into another room where shelves full of glass jars containing strange shapes filled the walls. In the centre, behind a large, well-used wooden desk, sat a man wearing a stained white coat, with a stethoscope draped over his sloping shoulders. Without looking up he instructed me to remove all my clothes. As my underpants hit the floor, I suddenly felt less confident about everything. But the underpants were clean on this morning, thanks to Mum, and I had also bathed in copious amounts of hot, Radoxed water the previous evening. The man at the desk checked my name and other particulars, writing copious notes as I stood there naked, my clothes in a disorganised bundle at my feet. I was asked what diseases or illnesses I had suffered from. Put on the spot, I couldn't remember anything apart from a recent bout of Spanish flu. I was a reasonably fit young man, a good competitive swimmer, I played football, cricket and tennis to an acceptable standard and I didn't smoke much or drink alcohol ... despite living in an Off-Licence. In the cold uncarpeted room I was examined by the bloke with a stethoscope who obviously had no real interest in me as a person or as a future member of Her Majesty's Royal Navy. My hair was examined for anything microscopic, a light was shone in my ears, mouth and nose. My spine was scrutinised, my instep measured, my arms pulled and rotated, fingers individually counted and checked. I was told to take deep breaths and to say 'Aaaaggghh' more than once while an ink-stained ruler was thrust into my mouth. Then I was invited to sit on the edge of the desk and to cross my legs whilst he attacked my knee with a toffee hammer before counting my toes and giving both my legs a lengthy check. As I was told to stand my naked bottom stuck briefly to the desktop and I wondered how many young backsides had sat in the exact same spot. The final examination was the most embarrassing: with an elderly hand cupping my 'tackle' I was instructed to perform a series of coughs while I stared at a point above the top shelf on the facing wall. Before my first-ever blood pressure test I had to perform a series of star jumps while facing a darkened window: it was the first time my unsupported tackle had been subjected to such gravitational forces, and it wasn't a pleasant experience.

As I fished for my underpants with my feet, my examiner sat down behind his desk and wrote more notes. I stood there shivering until eventually he waved a hand at me and told me to get dressed. Once I was clothed, he invited my mother in and asked what illnesses or diseases I had contracted as a child. I was surprised to learn that I had suffered from chicken pox, German measles, mumps and a moderate bout of whooping cough. The man in the white coat said that the combination was quite normal for Pudsey, West Yorkshire.

A week or so later we received another buff envelope which contained the results of my medical. I was classed A1 which was the grade for Pudsey boys with no apparent health problems. I was not colour-blind, my hearing was exceptionally good and I was of average build and above average height at a touch over five foot ten inches. I had good lungs, my feet weren't flat, my eyes and hair were brown and I had no distinguishing marks. At the top of the letter were three boxes marked Royal Navy, Army and Royal Air Force, with a big tick in the Royal Navy box.

It wasn't long before my mother received an envelope of official documents and a hardback book called 'Your Navy Past and Present'. A separate letter gave me details of my official joining date: surprisingly, I wasn't to report to Portsmouth, Plymouth or anywhere nautical, but to the Manchester Recruiting Office at 10am on Monday 4 January 1960. I was a little disappointed.

As an avid reader, I immersed myself in the semi-glossy pages of 'Your Navy Past and Present', compiled by Lt-Commander S G Clark RN and published by *HMS Ganges* Juniors' Training Establishment. Among many other things, I read about the War of both the English and Spanish Succession, The War of Jenkins' Ear, Austrian Succession, The War that went on for Seven Years and The Quarrel with the American Colonists. It took me on a literal journey from the beginnings of the Royal Navy to the present day.

A bloke called Captain R D Franks DSO OBE RN, in his foreword to the book, wrote:

> 'It is worth knowing something about the Royal Navy for many reasons. For one thing you will meet Royal Marines or Soldiers or Airman or foreigners who will be rightly proud – and knowledgeable – about their own service histories. But we in the Royal Navy have a more famous story than any of them, and we should be able to tell them so.'

At the end of the book there was the following statement:

> 'This is your heritage, this tradition has to be maintained and your training at **HMS Ganges** is but the first step. The Royal Navy has had a glorious past: it is your job to ensure that it has an equally glorious future.'

My job? No pressure there then.

Sometime in December my parents organised and paid for a farewell dinner at a restaurant over a large garage on the Leeds Ring Road: for the first time I was allowed to drink wine, but didn't like it much. At home, I had some friends around for a farewell party above the shop. I recall a free-for-all to one of the most popular tunes of the day *Seven Little Girls Sitting In The Back Seat* by The Avons. I was DJ on my recently acquired multi-play Dansette Record Player. As shindigs go it was quite a tame affair. Colin, my older cousin, took my ex-girlfriend home at the end of the evening: I was a little peeved about that.

Mum and Dad bought me a zipped leather writing case as a going-away present, which was to serve me well throughout my Naval career. I still have it 50 years later. Inside are the names of long forgotten girlfriends along with the places I'd visited.

My last visit as a civilian to the home of my local football team, Elland Road, was on a cold and windy Boxing Day to watch Leeds United lose 2-4 to Tottenham Hotspur. That day we fielded an unenthusiastic team: we were having a crap season.

Christmas was a particularly snowy affair. West Yorkshire December snows were traditionally lengthy and severe, and having to shovel our way out of the front door wasn't unusual. It began to thaw as the New Year came and we all bade farewell to the 1950s. I didn't know it at the time but before the 60s were over, I would have travelled the world and been promoted many times. I would have married, bought a house on the south coast overlooking Portsmouth harbour and played a noteworthy part in my wife's first pregnancy.

Early on the dark, cold morning of Monday 4 January 1960 I left my comfortable Pudsey home. I kissed my tearful Mum goodbye, promising that I would look after myself. I pledged to keep my underwear and myself clean and to avoid any trouble. I said goodbye to my younger brother Tony. I don't remember tears: West Yorkshire teenagers and Off-Licence owners in those days were a stoic lot.

My youthful longing for independence took a dip or two during the cold, dark trans-Pennine journey to Manchester in Dad's campervan. In the back was my suitcase containing the small number of items that the Royal Naval Recruiting Service had told me to bring, along with my electric razor, changes of underwear, all the shirts I owned, my football boots and my swimming trunks. Where was I going? What would it be like? Would I be alone? Would there be anyone I liked? Would they like me? What was the Royal Navy going to be like? Like the Cubs or the Boy Scouts? What the hell, I had to keep telling myself, I was going to travel the world, see exotic places and hopefully, meet many mysteriously glamorous girls.

The drive was relatively conversation-free. I didn't get much in the way of last-minute fatherly advice or, if I did, I don't remember it. I was on the verge of a major life-change, about to go headlong into an environment that I didn't understand and which I certainly wasn't prepared for. During the forthcoming years I was going to encounter criminals, sadists, homosexuals, prostitutes, alcoholics, bullies, pathetic individuals, and many good friends. And I wasn't ready for any of them.

We ran over a black cat somewhere between Pudsey and Manchester.

3

A SCHOOLBOY DECIDES

Dad and I arrived at the Manchester Recruiting Office early in the murk and drizzle of a very cold January dawn, long before it was open. We waited, joined by a steady trickle of other arrivals, accompanied by a large contingent of mums, dads, brothers, sisters and girlfriends. Dad made tea on the campervan stove whilst I got stuck in to the cheese sandwiches that Mum had made.

The Recruitment Office doors were opened at exactly ten-o-clock and we were all invited inside. Collectively we were given a last opportunity to change our minds. Nobody did. Along with all the other civilians my father had to leave: our goodbye was a manly pat on the back and his heartfelt 'Good luck son.'

The joining formalities took most of the day. I signed pieces of paper that I didn't read or understand, I was talked to by a variety of men in blue uniforms, but my inherent inability to concentrate on anything for longer than a couple of minutes meant that most things went in one ear and out of the other. At one stage, I lowered my trousers so that an elderly Manchester gentleman in an off-white coat could examine my tackle once again.

I spent much of the day sitting on a series of burgundy coloured, tubular framed chairs in a waiting-room where the walls were decorated with recruitment posters extolling the virtues of life in the Royal Navy. Gone were the photographs of suntanned sailors in blue uniforms gazing out over turquoise seas.

I was given a booklet to read. Here was real Naval information ...

There are a number of privileges available in the Navy, which are considerable assets in themselves or mean an appreciable saving in a man's personal expenditure. Some of the privileges have been enjoyed for so long that they are almost taken for granted; others have been gained in recent years. The main ones are as follows:-

1. Leave. Minimum rate of 30 days' paid leave each year.
2. Free rail travel. Three free return railway warrants in the UK each year to go on leave.
3. Rail travel at reduced rates. Cheap railway fares in the UK for yourself and family for distances over 30 miles.
4. Duty-free 'smokes'. Each tobacco coupon represents about 15s duty.
5. Grog.
6. Reduced rates of National Insurance contributions. Naval men pay 3s 11d a week instead of 6s 9d.
7. Postal concessions.
8. Cheap clothing.

Note: It is fair to add about £3 0s 0d to your weekly pay total to allow for what you get free in the Service, such as food and accommodation, and for what you get cheaply.

During the last 10 years, probably more changes have taken place in the Royal Navy than in any other similar period of its long history. Scientific developments have revolutionised Naval tactics and weapons. New types of ships and aircraft and much new equipment have had to be designed and built and work is in hand on still newer projects.

In the personnel field, too, many changes have been introduced. Pay and pensions have been increased; a new officer structure has been announced; the period of family separation has been shortened; many more married quarters have been built; amenities afloat and ashore are being improved; and centralised drafting, which will go far towards equalising advancement prospects throughout the Service, has been decided upon.

The traditional role of the Navy in peace-time is, as it always has been, to sustain our foreign and colonial policy.

Use is made of the newest training devices and courses range in standard from the elementary to that required for a University degree.

Showing the flag is one of the most pleasant duties of the peace-time Navy. In the course of a year, there are few countries with a coast-line which do not receive at least one visit from an HM ship ...

The Navy needs many skills to man its ships and aircraft and to operate and maintain the vast amount of equipment which they carry. In a ship, officers and men of all branches are of one company. Each fulfils an essential purpose and in war all face action together.

Seaman Department. Responsible for the operation and safety of the ship and her boats, for fighting the greater part of the armament, for communications, the operation of radar, etc.

As the equipment in Naval ships and aircraft increases in complexity, so does the work of each officer and rating become more important and responsible.

Everyone in the Service, or who is connected with it, realises that there are hardships involved in Navy life. Living conditions afloat are necessarily cramped. The Navy does however, offer its compensations. Everyone in the Service belongs to a corporate body, with its well defined duties to perform and possessing its own customs, traditions and individuality.

There are opportunities of seeing much of the world and of meeting people of many types and races ...

According to the latest figures, the current strength of the Royal Naval fleet is 5 Fleet Aircraft Carriers, 5 Battleships, 21 Cruisers, 9 Light Cruisers, 1 Guided

Weapon Trials Ship, 1 Aircraft Repair Ship, 1 Aircraft Maintenance Ship, 1 Royal Yacht/Hospital Ship, 4 Depot Ships, 77 Destroyers, 163 Frigates, 261 Minesweepers, 61 Submarines and 206 other Naval manned Support vessels. Under construction are an additional 1 Light Fleet Cruiser, 3 Cruisers, 19 Frigates, 13 Submarines, 69 Minesweepers and 17 Support vessels.

I was going to join the world's second largest Navy with a force of 102,000 men and a significant number of WRNS ... Women's Royal Naval Service ... women!

In addition to all the wonderful opportunities outlined above, Her Majesty was going to pay me 6 shillings per day less charges. I wondered if I was being paid for today.

We were eventually ushered outside to a waiting blue Naval bus and taken to a YMCA Hostel somewhere in the back streets of urban Manchester where we were fed and told that we were to spend the night. For me, and I suspect most of the others, it was the first time I'd set foot inside such a place and a YMCA Hostel, particularly the Manchester branch, was not the place I had expected to spend my first night in the Service of Queen and Country.

Lying under a tickly blanket on a lumpy mattress without a sheet and with a badly stained pillow in an echoing, cold dormitory was a shock to my system. A man in uniform switched the lights off and told us to get a good night's sleep as we had a busy day tomorrow. I was more than a little overwhelmed by everything: as well as trying to come to terms with a strange smelling, uncomfortable bed I had to try and ignore the noises made by 40 other lads. Bodily reverberations that only nervous, recently fed, healthy young men could muster filled the dank, dormitory air. At home I had shared a bedroom with my younger brother and I am ashamed to admit that I would complain bitterly if he as much as breathed heavily while I was trying to get to sleep. Normally I needed quiet ... and I wasn't going to get it tonight.

The same uniformed bloke switched the lights on in the morning. After dressing and a slow walk past the washbasins (a typical teenager's winter-wash) we boarded a blue bus and were taken to the railway station to catch a train to a place called Ipswich in Suffolk. I had travelled extensively with the school – Holland, Belgium, Switzerland, France – and I collected stamps from every corner of the world, but exactly where was Suffolk? Like most of the others, I kept myself to myself, grunting or speaking only when spoken to. There were, however, a few who were less shy and friendships, as well as individual dislikes, were beginning to develop. I began to understand that we were all in this together, whatever it was.

By the time we arrived in London there had been a scuffle which had resulted in a cracked carriage window. We lounged on the platform at Euston Station while the two culprits were interviewed by police. Eventually everything was sorted and we were ushered on to yet another blue Naval bus and whisked across London to Liverpool Street Station for the last leg of our journey.

From what I could see as we approached Ipswich, Suffolk was a flat and uninspiring place. Where were all the hills and dales? Suffolk looked as though all its wrinkles and undulations had been ironed out. There was snow on the ground.

Once off the train, we boarded our last blue bus of the day while a team of men dressed as sailors tossed our suitcases into the back of a canvas-backed lorry. Our journey through the narrow winding roads took about three quarters of an hour. If I had known how long it was going to be before I would see these narrow roads again, the houses, shops and people – particularly girls – I would have taken more notice.

4

INDOCTRINATED INTO THINGS ROYAL NAVAL

Solid, green gates opened in a tall corrugated-iron fence. We entered and the gates closed behind us with a solid scraping sound signalling the end of our journey. It was Tuesday 5 January 1960 and my Naval Service was about to begin. Recruitment number 28, the first of the decade, had arrived at *HMS Ganges*. To be perfectly accurate we hadn't yet arrived at *Ganges* proper: for the first four weeks of our Naval Service we were to be quarantined in a place called the Annexe, a self-contained intensive training compound situated about a quarter of a mile north west of the main establishment.

The Annexe was a depressingly ugly place. Low buildings, clad in corrugated iron, enclosed a square Parade-Ground. On opposite sides were the entrances to three messdecks. On one other side was the Galley, the Dining Hall and the bathrooms. Opposite, behind the mast, was the Main Clothing Store and Administration Offices.

After locating our cases we were roll-called and allocated our accommodation: I was in a group who were taken to a place called Hardy mess, a long room with metal-framed beds arranged down both sides. We were told to find ourselves a bed and then, in the best tradition of the Royal Navy, to line up and drop our trousers. My tackle was then re-examined, I suppose just in case any constituent part had deteriorated during the train journey south from Manchester. This was the second time in so many days that a bloke had cupped my bits and told me to cough, and I wondered if this was to be a regular occurrence: if so, it was a bit of a worry. I had never seen so many skinny white legs in one place before, nor had I seen such an assortment of tackles. I was pleasantly surprised to realise that I was probably about average in that department. After hoisting our trousers we were each given a postage-paid postcard and told to write our home address on it and, in a few brief words, inform our nearest and dearest that we had arrived safe and sound at *HMS Ganges*. Our official address was rubber-stamped in one corner. Surprisingly some of the lads didn't know, or couldn't immediately remember, their home address.

There were about 30 of us in Hardy mess. We each had a bed and a small metal locker alongside. The floor was polished brown linoleum, the walls were painted cream and green, the windows were un-curtained and permanently open. At the end of the mess, by the main entrance door, was a night toilet and a washroom. Tomorrow, we would discover that our main mess bathroom and toilets, used during the day, were located outside and a good distance round the corner.

We were instructed to prepare ourselves for bed. Personalities were gradually beginning to emerge: talkative ones, silent ones, smiling ones, morose ones, quick ones and slow ones. My bed was in the middle of those down the left side of the mess. My neighbour to my left was a slim, fair-haired boy called George. To my right was a lad who introduced himself as Cliff Barker from no fixed abode and who had a look of the travelling community about him.

Our Mess Instructor was a weather-beaten elderly man with greying hair sprouting out of his nostrils and ears. On his left chest he had a double row of medal ribbons. His movements and dress were precise and he stood squarely and easily erect, his facial expression controlled and steady. 'My Name Is Petty Officer Payne!' He scanned our faces as he paraded up and down the centre of the mess. 'At All Times ... At All Times You Will Address Me As Sir. Individuals In This Man's Navy Who Are Fortunate Enough To Share My Family Name Are Commonly Known As Whacker. Behind My Back Or Out Of Earshot You May Be Tempted To Refer To Me As Whacker ... But If I Hear Any Of You Refer To Me As Anything Other Than Sir ... With A Capital S ... You Will Suffer The Full Force Of My Displeasure. Understand?'

A few feet shuffled and there was a rumble of a mumble from somewhere near to the top of the mess.

'Do You Understand?'

A rather shy chorus of 'Yes ... err, sir' stopped him in his tracks for a moment.

'I Can't Hear You! DO YOU UNDERSTAND ME?'

'Yes sir.' Slightly louder this time. But still a touch uncertain.

'I Am Petty Officer Payne ... Known To You As Sir.'

'Yes sir,' most of us replied for the third time. At this stage of our young lives we weren't about to disobey a man brandishing a stick and two rows of medal ribbons.

Petty Officer Payne stopped in front of Cliff Barker and pointed his stick at Cliff's right ear. 'Is That An Ear-Ring, Darling?'

'Yes sir.'

'Unhitch It! Take It Off! Only Girls Wear Ear-Rings In My Man's Navy!'

Cliff nodded.

'Well? Remove The Bloody Thing Then!'

Cliff removed it, with some apparent difficulty, and placed it in Petty Officer Payne's outstretched hand.

'If Anyone Else Is Wearing Earrings Or Any Other Jewellery ... Remove It NOW!' He slapped the end of a metal bed-frame with his stick.

Petty Officer Payne, standing at the end of the mess with his cap under his arm, explained a variety of *Ganges* rules and regulations. There were definitely many more don'ts than do's. To summarise: as from tomorrow morning we were expected to be active, alert, athletic, attentive, conscientious, determined, diligent, energetic, enthusiastic, interested, keen, loyal, obedient, persevering, perceptive, respectful, sensible, tenacious and willing. Was that all? I didn't know what half the words meant. Apparently the most important rule was how to address people. To keep it simple, we were told that everybody, apart from other mess members and any Annexe rodents, were to be called 'sir'.

It was explained to us that the Annexe of *HMS Ganges* was a nursery. We would spend four weeks here during which time we would learn the very basic elements of Naval life in preparation for our transfer to The Main Establishment. During our time in the Annexe we would be subjected to a series of tests and examinations and anybody who didn't achieve the required Naval standard would remain behind and do the whole Annexe training routine again and again until they were considered ready to join the real Navy ... that was just down the road.

We were ushered over to the Dining Hall where we experienced our first Naval meal dished out by unsmiling, white-uniformed chefs. I was lucky: I was one of those peculiar individuals who enjoyed school meals and happily consumed most anything that was plonked on my plate, except yellowed cauliflower and fatty meat.

At the end of a long, and sometimes confusing day, Whacker told us to 'Turn-In!' and the mess lights were switched out. It was already pitch black outside and flurries of Suffolk snow wafted in through the now partially closed windows. At the end of the mess, near to the main entrance door, was a Junior Instructor who slept in the mess. He had a distinctive blue and white counterpane on his bed to distinguish him from the rest of us. Although our Junior Instructor, named Hawthorne, appeared to be very old, he had only just finished his training at *Ganges* and was probably no more than 16. In the absence of Petty Officer Payne, who slept elsewhere, Junior Instructor Hawthorne ensured that we maintained a reasonable degree of good order. My mattress, uncovered pillow and hairy blanket were similar to those of last night: irritatingly uncomfortable.

'Excuse me mush, can we close our windows?' one of the more outspoken of us asked.

'You what!' screamed Junior Instructor Hawthorne.

'Can we close our windows?'

'Can you close your window WHAT?' JI Hawthorne leapt out of his bed and scuttled up the mess.

'Can we close our ferkin windows?'

'Call me sir!'

'Can we close our ferkin windows sir?'

'No! Now get your head down. That's an order.' He stood in

the centre of the mess until he was sure that the subject was closed. Obviously the Royal Navy considered it healthy to leave windows wide open. Even at home, Mum had left bedroom windows open whenever possible, but not when it was snowing. I believed it had something to do with the post-war treatment and prevention of TB.

My second night away from home was worse than the first. For some, the reality of the situation was beginning to sink in. Shortly after JI Hawthorne got back into his bed, the sniffles and coughing started. I felt isolated and cold: there was a different feel to the cold of a January night this far south. I was apprehensive about what was going to happen the following day and hadn't yet developed a 'take each day as it comes' attitude. I didn't succumb to tears but it was difficult not to feel a little home-sick when the sniffles and the snorting started. During my time at *Ganges*, I spent many hours lying awake staring at the angular steel roof rafters pondering the events of the day, thinking about what I had done wrong, why I had been yelled or screamed at, and wondering what I was doing in such a God-forsaken and unfriendly place.

Today I had learned a smattering of Navy-speak: 'Turn In!' meant 'Go to bed', and 'Pipe Down' meant 'Shut your gob'.

My second morning in the service of Queen and Country was a shock. It was dark. Snowflakes were wafting in through the open windows and settling on my blankets and according to my wristwatch with the luminous hands, it was half past five: half past ruddy five! Whacker was strutting up and down the mess banging the ends of our beds with his stick and bellowing at us to 'Show A Leg'. That obviously meant we should get out of bed and show him at least one of our legs. I clearly understood the meaning of 'Hands Off Cocks ... On Socks!' I wasn't that naive, despite never having heard such an early morning rhyming-couplet before. The freezing, morning wind blasted into every corner of the mess. I crawled, bleary-eyed out of my bed and sat there with my head in my hands.

A number of things happened very quickly that morning. We all washed, after a fashion, and dressed, before being taken over the Parade-Ground to the Dining Hall for our first Naval breakfast. We were allowed to heap as much as we liked on our plates but we weren't allowed to 'Go Round The Buoy!' (queue for second helpings). That morning I discovered the delights of Naval deep-fried bread. There were bowls full of cereals and buckets brimming with watered-down milk ... for those few who wanted that kind of breakfast. We all continued to size up our fellow messmates: more characters were emerging. There were groups of boys who obviously knew each other already and they naturally grouped together. The rest of us sat where there was space and made conversation when we thought it appropriate. I suppose we all had an inbuilt social disposition that enabled us to communicate and bond with boys who we thought were similar in nature to ourselves. It would take weeks before I would begin to establish my individual position in the mess hierarchy. There were the inevitable personality clashes, but they were short-lived explosive affairs that were soon quashed and forgotten. Living together 24 hours a day with 30 other boys was, for the majority of us, a strange new experience that we were all adapting to in our own way and at our own pace.

After breakfast we were taken to a building on the side of the Parade-Ground as the watery Suffolk sun began to colour the green tin Annexe buildings. There, along with those from the other messes, we queued up and waited our turn for a group of elderly men in brown coats to give us an array of clothing and a white enamelled tin mug with a rolled blue rim containing a tube of toothpaste, a razor and a pack of Government-issue razor blades.

In the mess, Whacker told us to stow our newly acquired items of stuff in our lockers and to remove all the civilian clothing that we were wearing, along with any rings, jewellery and watches.

'Does that mean everything sir?' someone with a strange accent asked.

'Everything!' bellowed Whacker.

'Including my ... err underpants ... sir?'

He marched up the mess and stood, ramrod straight, facing the lad who had asked the question. 'Everything, Lad. I Can See That We're Going To Have Trouble With You. What Don't You Understand About The Word Every ... Ferkin ... Thing!'

'Err, nothing ... nothing sir.'

That cleared that one up then. I immediately realised that in Suffolk they swore the same way that people in West Yorkshire did, but much, much louder.

'The Kit And Equipment That Her Majesty Has Been Kind Enough To Issue You With Today ... Will Be Enough For Your Immediate Needs!' Petty Officer Payne told us.

We rifled through the items, jamming them into our metal lockers. The sheets, pillowcases and striped pyjamas were easily identifiable, but some other items were more mysterious. Whacker strode the mess instructing us what to wear. The lad in the next bed but one appeared to know exactly what everything was. He wriggled into a pair of yellowy-grey underpants with a gusset that drooped almost to his knees. I heard the phrase 'Dung-Hampers' for the first time. I extracted what looked to be the same item and smelt it: it had a peculiar aroma, like something that had been in storage for many years. It was made from a peculiarly ruthless material that looked and felt unsociable. I struggled into my Dung-Hampers that fitted where they touched, then I wriggled into a vest made from the same remorseless material. Following the underwear I pulled on a heavy woollen jumper, a blue cotton shirt, thick woollen socks and dark blue trousers, that were designed to accommodate the underpants, and a pair of slippers called deck-shoes. We looked and felt strangely uncomfortable. Everything was uncommonly stiff and either far too big, too small, long in the arm or short in the leg. For someone whose tailored drainpipe trousers were his pride and joy, these naval trousers had far too much material. The standard Naval Shape was quite obviously not that of an average 15 year old. We were encouraged to swop any ill-fitting items of clothing with other taller, shorter, fatter mess members if possible. This, at least, gave us the opportunity to meet some of our messmates and was a reasonably enjoyable interlude in what was turning out to be a confusing exercise. We had shorts that were neither long shorts nor short longs, and a pair of brown Naval issue sandals that were totally unsuitable for delicate teenage feet.

All our civilian clothes and other removed bits and pieces had to be placed inside our suitcases. There were a couple of exceptions: we could keep our swimming costume, our writing equipment and our football boots if we had brought any. We should have realised what was about to happen once we were told to write our home address on a label and tie it securely to the handle of our case. Whacker spent some considerable time with each of us ensuring that we had kept nothing inappropriate. The Navy even issued us with handkerchiefs, three white ones, noses for the use of.

One surprising exchange when labelling our cases was when Whacker was leaning over one lad's shoulder watching him address his label. 'Where Is S-O-T Then, Lad?'

'It's just S-O-T ... sir.'

'But Where Exactly Is S-O-T. What Does It Stand For?' asked a ramrod straight Whacker.

'Just S-O-T ... sir.'

'But What Does It Mean, Lad?'

'It's where I live sir.'

'But What Does It Mean, Lad?'

'Just S-O-T sir.'

'OK! You're Obviously As Thick As Two Short Planks, Lad ... Let's Take It One Small Step At A Time Shall We?' He took a deep breath and tapped the end of the bed with his stick. 'When Your Mummy Goes Shopping, Where Does She Go?'

'Shop on the corner sir.'

'Doesn't She Sometimes Go Into A Big Town?'

'Sometimes.'

'Sometimes What?'

'Just sometimes.'

'Don't You Mean Sometimes SIR!'

'Sorry sir. Yes, sometimes sir.'

'And What Do You Call That Big Town She Sometimes Goes To?'

'Stoke sir.'

Whacker gazed at the roof rafters and exhaled. 'So S-O-T Could Actually Be Stoke-On-Trent Then?'

'Don't know sir.'

'Stoke On Trent. Have You Never Heard Of Stoke On Trent, Lad?'

'Yes sir ... yes.'

'Good! ... We'll Write Stoke-On-Trent On The Label Then Shall We?'

'OK then sir.'

'Go On Then Lad. There's A Clever Boy!'

'Did you say Trent ... sir?'

Whacker swiped every bed end with his stick as he strutted his way back down the centre of the mess. I thought I saw the glint of a tear in the corner of his eye.

Whacker and JI Hawthorne checked that our labels were tied in the correct Naval manner and the suitcases were then carried outside and left in a pile outside the mess. It was to be a long, long time before I saw my drainpipe trousers, my favourite shirt, my wristwatch, my Pifco electric razor and my comfortable underwear again. Years later my mother said that she had cried when my case arrived back home.

Once again we were told to strip. This was becoming an embarrassing Naval habit. It was however, to be our first messdeck lesson, albeit a strange and unexpected one. Whacker grabbed the nearest naked recruit and demonstrated, with some dexterity, how to wrap and secure a brand new white towel around the lower half of his skinny pale body, then quickly removed it. Our naked messmate quickly covered his tackle and blushed bright pink.

'You Don't Need To Cover Your Reproductive Equipment, Lad ... It's Not Going To Frighten Anybody!'

Our messmate nodded and very slowly removed his protective hands. I was shivering. I was standing naked between two open windows. The unfortunate lad, whose only offence was being within arm's reach of Whacker, stood with his arms reluctantly outstretched while Whacker, who stood behind him, wrapped a towel around his waist and tucked the top corner in. He repeated the procedure a few more times.

'Being Able To Secure A Towel Round Your Waist So That It Won't Fall To The Deck Will Be Very Important Once You Baby Sailors Eventually Go To Sea.' Pause for emphasis. 'With All Those Really Big, Hairy Arsed Sailors.'

How to secure a towel around the lower part of my body was second nature to me: I'd spent half my life in and out of swimming-pool changing rooms. We all wrapped our towels around our waist and stood at the end of our bed to be inspected before being ushered off to the bathroom.

As I muscled my way past the lad in front of me to get into the relative warmth of the bathroom, my towel slipped. I tried to slide past Whacker without being noticed, but failed.

'Ah Ah ... A Badly Secured Towel Is It, Lad?'

'Pardon sir.'

'Don't Pardon Me, Lad. What Did I Say?'

'Something about my towel sir.'

'Show Me How You Secured Your Towel, Lad.'

I completed the towel wrapping process swiftly in the hope that he wouldn't spot anything wrong with my technique. Thankfully at that exact moment there was a 'crack' as someone towel-flicked his mate.

Whacker turned. 'You There! ... You Lad! Lash Bloody Larue! Outside! Stand To Attention By The Door Until I Tell You To Come Back In!' He turned back to me, looked at my towel and waved me away.

All the bathroom windows were wide open. There were no baths, only showers: but today there was loads of piping hot water. The lad, now known as 'Lash', was blue with cold when he was eventually allowed back into the bathroom.

By the end of the day our beds and lockers were crammed full of foul-smelling equipment called kit. At the end of the mess a blackboard appeared with a list of chalked instructions and a small number of Naval expressions we were expected to learn.

Later that evening as we were turning-in, I was personally taught my first Naval term. I desperately needed the toilet, so I slipped into my deck shoes and with the legs of my striped pyjamas rolled up I clip-clopped down the mess towards the toilets.

I had passed the blackboard before I was rumbled. 'And Where Do You Think You're Going, Lad?' bellowed Whacker.

'Who me?'

'Who Me ... What?'

'Who me sir. Toilet ... sir. Me toilet sir.' I was stringing my words together like a three year old.

'WHERE?' Whacker glared at the blackboard.

'Err,' I couldn't see what was on the blackboard from where I was standing, but I had read it earlier and remembered that the Naval term for a toilet began with an 'H'. I went for it. 'Horses sir. I need to go to the horses.'

'The WHAT?'

I obviously hadn't got it right. 'Horses ... sir?'

'Wrong Lad. Hopelessly Wrong!' He tapped the blackboard. 'A Bit Bone Are We Lad?'

'No ... sir. Pardon sir?'

'What Part Of The Country Do You Come From?'

'Yorkshire sir.'

'That Makes Sense.'

'Thank you sir.'

'Refresh Your Memory Then Lad!' He tapped the blackboard again.

I looked quickly. Apparently, in the Navy, toilets were called heads. 'Heads sir. I need to go to the heads.'

'Quick As You Can Then Lad: Quick As You Can. Wouldn't Like You To Miss Out On Any Of Your Well Deserved Sleep Would We?'

'No sir. Thank you sir.'

I had the quickest slash of my life and made it back to my bed-space unnoticed.

I looked at the blackboard that had now been relocated to the centre of the mess. On it were strange words: bulkhead, deck, deckhead. This was going to be more difficult than I imagined: all I wanted to do was travel the world. In addition to Heads, I had also learned that 'Bone' was Navy-speak for being thick or unintelligent, which I obviously was ... in Whacker's opinion.

As he switched off the mess lights, Whacker bellowed his final series of instructions for the day, 'Pipe Down ... Keep Quiet! ... No Skylarking!'

Skylarking sounded amusing but what did it mean? It kept me awake for a while until, from the end of the mess, someone asked, 'What's skylarking then?'

'Playing around.'

'Thanks.'

'What's all that about piping down then?'

'Tell you in the morning.'

'Thanks.'

'Now shut your gob and go to sleep.'

'Cheers Oppo.'

'Oppo' was Navy-speak for friend. Bed springs creaked in the early hours of the night. Sniffles, snuffles, farts and badly disguised sobs were becoming commonplace. I placed my arms behind my head, stared at the roof rafters and considered the day just past, trying to explain things to myself. Wondering why it had been me that had been singled out on my way to the heads: what a stupid name for the bog.

Occasionally someone would shuffle barefoot down the centre of the dark mess towards the night heads. For two nights running it had been the same boy, a big, strapping lad from Wales, called Taff who obviously had a weakened bladder.

The third day, I was at my lowest: I'd been in the Navy long enough to realise that this training business wasn't going to be a picnic and deep down I was already longing for my home comforts. It started badly by having to make my bed before breakfast. A *Ganges*-made bed was unlike any other: it was completely stripped and both blankets were folded and placed at the head of the bed, both sheets were also folded and placed on top of the blankets and topped with the pillow. The mattress cover was then pulled taut so that no creases showed. We weren't allowed to sit on our beds once they were made. JI Hawthorne told us that this wasn't a special Thursday way of making our bed, this was the way that our beds were to be made every day. And, as from tomorrow both blankets, which were different sizes, had to be folded to the exact same dimensions ... and the sheets folded so that our name showed. Name showed? What name? JI Hawthorne, recently re-christened 'Spotty' because of his rampant acne, showed us how to fold our blankets and position them correctly at the head of the bed. Failure to do this correctly, as from tomorrow, would result in our bed being 'trashed'.

The day then went downhill. I had my hair butchered. An old guy named Shotley arrived to shear us. We queued in apprehensive silence as one by one we sacrificed our Brylcreemed and youthful hairstyles to the floor ... sorry ... deck. Sideboards, quiffs, DAs all ended up around our feet. As we lined up down the centre of the mess, Whacker assured us that we now looked like members of Her Majesty's Royal Navy and not pathetic Teddy Boys.

A rotund bloke in a sailor's uniform with a Red Cross badge on his left sleeve appeared in the mess and we were ordered to 'Drop 'Em!' This was the fourth time in four days: it was becoming embarrassing.

The man with the Red Cross badge strolled in front of us, glancing at our tackle as he passed.

Some were told to 'Take one step to the rear!'

This was a selection process of some kind: we were being split, and it was strangely unnerving. I remained in the front rank.

'Front Rank Grab Your Towels And Washing Gear And Double To The Outside Bathroom! ... On The Double! ... Off You Go!'

Something was going on: we had all washed this morning already.

Once we were all assembled, shivering in the bathroom, all was explained. 'Today, My Little Sparrows, Today Is Known Onboard Her Majesty's Ship Ganges As FMD ... Foreskin Manoeuvring Day. That Little Bit Of Skin On The End Of Your Reproductive Equipment Is Known In Medical Circles As A Foreskin. And Today ... Today My Little Sparrows ... Is The Day When You Will Demonstrate To The Sick Berth Attendant Here That You Have Nothing Untoward Hidden Beneath Said Foreskin!'

'We all looked at each other in complete disbelief.

'First Six Hynaaah Shower ... Gew!'

I was cold so I made sure that I was in the first six. The water was tepid.

'At The Order PULL ... You Will Pull Your Foreskin Back To Its Stand-By Position ... The Stand-By Position. If You Have A Problem Shout For The Sick Berth Attendant ... Understand? Hardy Mess ... Hardy Mess ... PULLLLLAAH!'

For me it was no problem: thanks to Dad it was part of my normal personal hygiene routine. After a nod from the expert on such matters, those of us who had successfully passed the test were instructed to dry ourselves off and wait in the corner by the door. I was surprised to see that a small number of my messmates had problems. We stood shivering by the draughty door wrapped in our damp towels while the lads remaining in the shower were re-encouraged.

'PULLLLLAAH!

George, my fair-haired neighbour, became the centre of much attention. 'Nar Then Lad. Pretend That Your Little Winkle Is A Deadly Bloody Weapon ... Your Weapon Lad ... Your Reproductive Stick ... Grab Hold Of The Thing Like You Mean Business ... Grab It Lad ... Take Charge Of The Damned Thing!'

George did as instructed, his eyes closed and mouth twisted in concentration.

'Now, Using All Your Fingers ... All Of Them! Try And Manoeuvre That Piece Of Skin ... Yes That's It! Move It Gently Back! It's Not Glued In Place Is It Lad? Give It A Good Tug Lad ...

Go On Give It A Tug … Tug The Damned Thing … TUG IT!'

'I'm trying sir.'

'Try Harder Then, Lad! Try Harder! Give It A Good TUG!'

Someone giggled, then others followed suit.

Whacker turned on us waving his stick 'The Rest Of You, Back To The Mess. Get Dressed In Shirts, Trousers, Socks, Boots And Cap… And 'Fall-in' Outside. Five Minutes!'

Once back in the mess one of the lads said 'We'll have to call him 'Tug' from now on then.' This was how Naval nicknames were bestowed.

Tug wasn't with us for dinner. It was rumoured that he had been taken to the Sick Bay.

The rest of the day was dedicated to kit: it kept our minds off our lost hair and, for some, their ill-treated foreskins. Whacker and Spotty stood in the centre of the mess and went through our kit, item by item, to ensure that we had everything in accordance with their lists. We were given a final opportunity to change any item of clothing that was too large or small. From a sewing thimble to a small brown case we checked everything. We watched as JI Hawthorne showed us how to fold everything and where to place each item in our lockers. I had never folded a shirt or a jumper in my life. It became clear that a book we had all been issued with, entitled B.R.1938 NAVAL RATINGS HANDBOOK 1954, was key. Of particular importance was Fig 6 on page 36 entitled 'Typical layout of kit for inspection'.

Underneath the illustration it said …

Note. All articles should be folded in such a way that the name is readily visible. The illustration shows the manner of laying out kits …

Our kit filled our lockers. According to Whacker we now had almost everything we needed. A small brown case, towels, sheets, pillow-cases, white fronts, sea jerseys, drawers (underpants), blue collars, pyjamas, scarf (called a comforter), toothpaste (unbranded), toothbrush, hairbrush, comb, hard boot brush, polishing boot brush, boot polish, socks, enamelled tin mug, action working dress shirts (No 8s), action working dress trousers (No 8s), belt, stockings (woollen), sports shirt blue, sports shirts white, housewife, sports shorts blue, sports shorts white, plimsolls (pumps), handkerchiefs, lanyards, silks, gloves, boots, sandals, deck shoes: but no ferkin shoes!

The item that raised a giggle was the housewife. This folded navy blue envelope contained needles, buttons, reels of cotton, a pack of needles and a thimble. The only thing missing was a pair of scissors. We were confused: why were we being given sewing stuff? Along with the NAVAL RATINGS HANDBOOK we were also issued with a thick blue hardback book entitled B.R. 67(1) ADMIRALTY MANUAL OF SEAMANSHIP 1951 Volume 1.

After tea the business of naming our kit was explained. A box full of wooden blocks, each with a single letter of the alphabet on one end and a slot in the opposite end, was placed on the mess table. We were each given a strip of wood, told to select the letters of our name and arrange them to produce a wooden type of our name.

'And Don't Forget The Full Stops!' instructed Whacker.

It wasn't that easy as I had to work my name back to front, but with help from Whacker and Spotty I eventually managed it. My name consisted of thirteen individual blocks, including full stops: P.N.BROADBENT. After we had all checked our 'types' for spelling we were allowed a short practice to check that we had arranged all our letters in the correct order and the right way round before dunking our types into black paint and stamping our name over the left breast pocket of both our Action Working Dress shirts.

If I had known what lay ahead I would have removed my middle initial and its associated full-stop. The only person with significantly more letters in his name than me was a boy called Magnus Fleming-Wainwright. After some negotiation he was allowed to mark his kit with only the last of his double-barrel names as the paint tray wasn't long enough to take all his letters.

Later that evening we were shown how to tie a cap tally on our caps with a little bow over the left ear. It took ages for most of us to master: bow-tying did not come naturally to teenagers of the time. A small group of lads, which the rest of us were beginning to know as Arry boys, had it mastered. There were four Arry boys in our mess who were far better than the rest of us at all things Naval. The rest of us didn't know exactly what an Arry boy was, until one of them took the time to explain to us that they had been at a place called *TS Arethusa* before joining the Navy. *TS Arethusa* was located on the river Medway and was home to young boys who were trained from a young age for a future career in either the Royal or Merchant Navy. It took a while, but eventually the rest of us began to appreciate how useful it was to be friends with an Arry boy who could explain things in a realistic, 15-year-old way. My Arry friend was called Garry Waters, otherwise known as 'Muddy'.

This was the day I discovered that my head size was six and seven eighths, but six and seven eighths what? Not even Muddy could explain that one.

Up until now I had lived my life in East and West Yorkshire surrounded by people who spoke with an accent similar to mine. Now I was surrounded by an array of accents and strange-sounding slang: Scots, Geordie, Brummie, Cockney and Valley-Welsh. Slowly, over the course of the following weeks we would all trade words and terms so that we could communicate effectively with each other. New Naval terminology was coming at us thick and fast too: mates became Wingers or Oppos. Whacker explained the meaning of the word 'Nozzer' to us: it meant brand-new recruit and had recently replaced the now unfashionable word 'Trog' that was an acronym of Trained Rating Of Ganges. Even the Dining Hall had a language all its own: chopped kidneys on deep-fried bread was known as 'shit on a raft'; 'train smash' was hot tinned tomatoes on a slice of fried bread; knives and forks were eating-irons; soup was loop and butter was called slide. The beautifully thick, hot cocoa drink made with shaved chocolate, sugar and evaporated milk, that we had mid-morning was called Kye.

I was a reasonably regular person and towards the end of the third day I couldn't put off a visit to the sit-down toilet ... heads, any longer as I hadn't enjoyed a good and satisfying movement since the Manchester YMCA. In the outside toilet I looked for a cubicle with a door, but there wasn't one: all four were completely open to the elements. The Navy had also decided that toilet seats were an unnecessary luxury. Cold, unyielding porcelain and no doors made a visit to the sitting-down facilities an embarrassingly swift and uncomfortable experience. I eventually found a roll of toilet paper in a locker by the side of the entrance door; just one roll. Each badly perforated, shiny sheet was clearly marked 'HM Government Property' no doubt to prevent theft. Under full operational conditions the sheets proved to be completely useless for the job in hand.

Messdeck rumour had two explanations for the lack of doors: one was that it prevented us young, healthy boys from abusing ourselves and ruining our eyesight. It was also rumoured that there had been a number of recent suicide attempts. I preferred to think that the first was the real reason.

In the early days I took to my bed as early as we were allowed. I found the cocooning effect of heavy blankets a comfort to me. Once in bed, the day's uncertain demands were at an end and for the next nine hours or so I no longer had to worry. Less than a week ago at this time I was sitting at home watching my mother preparing to close the shop. It had been a wretched day today. Tonight my mind was full of kit: in particular I was really annoyed that my electric razor, a last-minute leaving present from my Dad, had been in the suitcase I had sent home. I now had a Government-issue wet razor, a pack of five unbranded razor blades, a shaving brush and no shaving soap. How was I going to shave in the morning? With my electric Pifco, I had learned how to avoid slicing the tops off my acne spots; I didn't have many but those I did have were volcanic when disturbed.

Because I had nothing more entertaining to read, I opened the smaller of my two new books. The NAVAL RATINGS HANDBOOK at page iv ...

FOREWORD

This handbook has been published for the benefit of all ratings of all branches of the Service, and is issued to each rating when he joins the Navy. All ratings are sailors, whether they belong to the Seamen, Engineering, Supply and Secretariat, or any other branch.

No warship has room for passengers who are indifferent to what is going on around them. The sailor must develop sea sense, just as a driver of a motor vehicle develops road sense. He must be continually alert to visualise what and to anticipate what might happen next. An efficient sailor is always ready to act in time to avoid injury to his ship, to his messmates, or to himself. He does the right thing because he has learned how the sea behaves and how it affects a ship afloat. Read this book so that you may meet these requirements, and so that you will become familiar with the many terms that are used in everyday life onboard a ship.

Before a rating can become thoroughly efficient he must also have a sound knowledge of the Service as a whole and not be content with knowing all about his own 'part of ship' only. In this book there are brief descriptions of the administration of the Navy and its branches and reserves, and of the routine and organisation of a ship. So read this book also with the object of improving your general knowledge of the Service to which you now belong.

Nothing interesting there then! The new words I could remember from today were 'Zonk' which meant 'go to sleep', 'Humming' which meant 'smelly' and my favourite, because it sounded ridiculously different, was 'Berseyquack' which meant Frenzied ... or was it Annoyed?

There were occasions when I would wake suddenly, wondering where I was. I was always terribly disappointed when I realised that I was in Suffolk.

Friday 8 January. We were woken at 06:00 by something played on a bugle. Petty Officer Payne explained to us that the tune was officially called *Reveille*, but referred to throughout the Navy as 'Charlie'. I identified the strange looking funnel-shaped object up amongst the roof rafters as a loudspeaker ... because that's where Charlie came from. On future mornings, the static click of the Tannoy was enough to wake us from our deep Suffolk slumber.

Whacker had a wake-up routine that was becoming boringly repetitive. 'Rise And Shine!' he would shout as he swung open the main mess door and marched up and down the mess shouting, bawling and clattering the bed ends until we were all out of bed.

'Rise And Shine, The Morning's Fine!'

In reality, Suffolk's January mornings weren't fine, but dark, draughty and miserable. Outside, rain water overflowed from the gutters above the windows.

'Show A Leg ... Show A Leg ... Show A Leg ... Lash Up And Stow!'

This morning he examined all our chins and instructed anyone with the slightest sign of bum-fluff to 'Shave That Stuff Off. Who Do You Think You Are – Walter Ruddy Raleigh?'

Whacker, with a click of his heels, stopped at the end of a bed quickly vacated by a tall rangy individual who had uncommonly pale skin. 'What's Your Name, Lad?'

'Reynolds ... sir.' he said as he removed his towel from the bar on his locker door.

'What Does Your Mummy Call You Junior Seaman Second Class Reynolds?'

'Son ... sir.'

'Don't Be Funny With Me, Lad. What Is Your First Name?'

'Gene ... sir.'

'That's A Girl's Name.'

'Gene with a 'G'.'

'Gene With A 'G' WHAT!'

'Gene with a 'G' sir.'

'Like Gene The Singing Cowboy?'

'Yes ... sir.'

'What Happened To Your Chin, Reynolds?'

Gene stroked his chin. For the first time I noticed that it was rather an odd shape.

'I don't know what you mean sir.'

'What Has Happened To Your Chin? When And Where Did You Lose Your Chin, Reynolds?'

'I didn't know that I had lost it sir,' he pointed to his chin. 'It's right here ... sir.'

'Look Around You, Lad.' He swung his stick. 'Everybody Else In The Mess Has A Protuberance Between Mouth And Neck. But You ... Junior Seaman Second Class Reynolds ... Appear Not To Have One.'

'Sorry sir.'

'You're What We Call In This Man's Navy ... A Chinless Wonder.'

'Yes sir.' Gene rubbed his now shivering white chest with his towel.

'So You Won't Be Surprised If You Are Hereinafter Known As Chinless ... Chinless Reynolds, Will You?'

'Not really sir ... no sir.'

'You Are Hereby Renamed Chinless.' He tapped Gene's chest with the end of his stick.

'Thank you ... sir.'

Whacker waved an arm towards the bathroom and Chinless scuttled away.

I used my bar of unbranded Naval-issue soap to create a lather and shaved: the naval blades were rubbish and I sliced the tops of a number of my most active spots.

This was the first day that we were all dressed in our Number 8 shirt, trousers, cap, belt and horribly uncomfortable boots. Our individual name was clearly displayed in black paint above our left breast pocket. We had the 'A' of our GANGES cap tally in-line with the seam of our cap and our nose. We had also been issued with two very strange items of kit known as gaiters. These inflexible items were to be strapped around our ankles, I suppose to keep the trouser bottoms tidy. They were khaki in colour and were cleaned with some foul-smelling green stuff that was so tacky we were advised to use only one of our boot brushes to apply it. Whacker also wore khaki gaiters, but JI Hawthorne wore sparkly white ones.

The reason for our sudden uniformity was soon revealed. After breakfast we were ushered out onto the Parade-Ground where a series of benches and seats had been arranged for the official mess photograph. While we were waiting for a bloke called Mr Fisk to set up his camera I asked Muddy what Whacker's 'Lash Up And Stow' rubbish was all about.

'It's to do with hammocks.'

'Hammocks?'

'Yeah.'

Mr Fisk, who Whacker told us was the official *Ganges* photographer, quickly had us organised, clicked once, said thank you and left us standing there like idiots.

That afternoon we were herded onboard a blue Royal Naval bus and driven the short distance through the main *Ganges* camp to the Sick Bay. It was our first glimpse of the *Ganges* mast and a bewildering array of large Victorian brick buildings. We passed smartly marching groups of sailors. Inside the Sick Bay we were systematically subjected to a confusing series of tests and examinations, copious notes being taken at every stage. A sample of my urine was taken and a small globule of blood: I coughed as some bloke paid particular attention to my tackle ... yet again! My teeth were examined and notes taken. My eyes and hearing were tested and a series of personal measurements were taken: today my vital statistics were 5ft 10 inches tall with an impressive 34-inch expanded chest. I can't remember how much I weighed; not a lot probably. I was officially informed that I'd have to run round in the shower to get wet. Someone in authority called me a Racing Snake for the first time. Eventually, physically assessed and catalogued, we were taken back to the Annexe. On the way we passed the *Ganges* mast again, a monstrous combination of whitened wood and thousands of bits of complicated looking bits of string: an impressive and intimidating structure.

Back in the mess a blackboard was placed alongside the main mess door. On it was taped a sheet of paper listing all our names alongside which were two numbers, our official Naval number and a Ships Book number. These had to be learned by heart ... 'Today! The List Will Be Removed At Lights-Out This Evening!'

Fortunately my Ships Book number was similar to my Mother's Co-op Dividend number and was only four digits long so I found that easy to remember. My official number (P/053653) was also memorable as most of the numbers were repeated: all I had to remember was in what order. With our numbers, we were officially transformed from civilians into Junior Seamen Second Class.

We had our first session of drill later the same day. It was known in the Navy as Parade Instruction and was undertaken regardless of the weather. Today there was a biting cold wind coming at us from over the Dining Hall and it was raining. Our first manoeuvre was to line ourselves up in three rows (ranks) with the tallest on the flanks and the shortest in the centre. That was simple enough, though some lads considered themselves to be taller than they actually were. Then things became progressively more complicated. Whacker demonstrated the various commands and JI Hawthorne showed us what our expected response should be. Standing to attention ('Haar-Ten-Shun!') required us to stand with the heels of our boots together and our toes splayed at between ten and 15 degrees. Our shoulders were to be pulled well back, chest out, head up and arms straight down by our sides with our fingers clenched at the first knuckle and thumbs in line with the seam of our action working dress trousers.

Whacker walked up and down the ranks checking on our feet and general bearing. He stopped and faced someone at the end of the front rank and eyed him up and down. He snorted, swung to the side and snorted again. He tapped the back of the lad's knees with his stick and leaned over so that he spoke directly into his ear.

'Where's Your Horse, Lad?'

'Pardon sir?'

'Where's Your Horse, Lad. The Inside Of Your Knees Are Supposed To Be Together ... Together!'

'Sorry sir.'

'Pull Them In Then, Lad ... Pull Them In!'

'Can't sir. That's as far as they will go sir ... sorry sir.'

'You Could Drive A Bus Through There, Lad.'

'Yes sir ... sorry sir.'

'A Double Decker Bus!'

'Yes sir ... sorry sir.'

'You Are What Is Known In This Man's Navy As Bandy Legged Lad.'

'Sorry sir.'

'You Are, My Son ... What We Call In The Navy ... Severely Bandy Legged!'

'If you say so sir.'

'I Do Say So, Lad! And Don't You Answer Me Back!'

'Yes sir. Thank you sir.'

'When You Are In Your Stinking Pit At Night ... Instead Of Playing With Your Little Winkle You Can Do Some Exercises That Will Slowly, Very Slowly Bring Your Knees Together ... Understand Me?'

'I think so sir.'

'Good!'

'Thank you sir.'

'Hardy Mess ... Hardy Mess ... Stan Atta Heyse!' This was another complicated manoeuvre. One foot ... our right foot ... was moved about one and a half feet away from its partner maintaining the same heel/toe splay-angle. At the same time our hands were to be moved smartly to a location behind our back, the right hand clamped firmly on top of our left ... or was it the left hand firmly on top of our right? Shoulders remained pulled back, chest out and head up. For some unknown reason this was the command that took us the longest to master.

The most eagerly anticipated command was 'Stan daaah Eysay!' This command would normally follow 'Stan Atta Heyse!' and was the opportunity for us to relax whilst keeping our shoulders back, chest out and head up.

The Arry boys excelled and made up most of the front rank. Having been the type of person who always felt more comfortable in the back row of the classroom, I naturally located myself in the rear rank, farthest away from the Instructors who strutted back and forth along the front.

In an effort to make us feel better, immediately following a particular poor attempt at doing a series of class co-ordinated commands, we were brought to 'Haar-Ten-Shun!' and reminded exactly where we stood in the Naval pecking order. Not that we needed reminding: we were already getting the message loud and clear.

'You Are All Junior Seamen Second Class ... Junior Seamen Second Class In This Man's Navy Are The Lowest Of The Low. With One Exception There Is Nobody In This Man's Navy Lower And More Utterly Useless Than A Junior Seamen Second Class Under Training At HMS Ganges.'

My shirt and trousers were soaked through, rain was dripping from the end of my frozen nose and I was shivering. To be told that there was somebody lower than a Junior Seamen Second Class at *HMS Ganges* was an unexpected morale booster. I wanted to know more.

Whacker slapped his stick against his thigh. 'There Are A Small Number Of People In This Man's Navy Who Are Lower Than You ... A Very Small Number!' He paced to one end of the front rank and back to the centre. I pressed my concentration button, waited for Whacker to start speaking again and tried to blow a particularly annoying nose-drip onto the back of the lad in front of me.

Whacker took a deep breath. 'Lower Than You By A Very Small Margin Are The Junior Seamen Second Class Under Training At HMS St Vincent In Gosport Hampshire.' He smirked. 'They Are Slightly Less Important Than You. HMS St Vincent

Boys Are Not ... And Never Will Be ... In The Same Class As HMS Ganges Trained Boys.' He almost smiled.

Great, absolutely great!

I was beginning to appreciate that in every large group of boys our age there was a comedian, a fledgling hypochondriac, a number of natural leaders, a large number of followers, a manic depressive and someone who is continually 'trying it on'. Add to this the inevitable number of optimists and an equal number of pessimists, a stoic, a few masochists and at least one, really irritating 'Black-catter' and you have Hardy mess. Our differences were beginning to surface. Our compulsive 'Black-catter' was a lad called Bill Yardley from Preston, Lancashire, who had done everything that anyone else had done but better, faster, more often and with many more girls. If you had a black cat, he had a blacker one: according to Muddy that's where the term originated. In addition to his exaggerated claims, Blacky, as he quickly became known, turned out to be useless at most things and I was unfortunate to have him in the next bed but one to mine on the other side of Tug's empty bed.

Occasionally, we would run a check on Blacky.

'Where's the furthest you've ever travelled?' someone would ask the mess.

'France,' someone would reply.

'Switzerland,' I said.

'I've been to Spain,' announced someone from the far corner of the mess.

'I've been to the Isle of Man.'

'I've been to Scunthorpe,' added the mess comedian.

'What about you Blacky, where's the furthest you've been?' someone asked.

'Australia ... or was it New Zealand? I went with a girlfriend of mine at the time and her sister, a couple of ...' replied Blacky, interrupted by jeers and cat-calls. I quickly learned that Black-catters didn't know they were doing it.

I spent the evening with my wooden type marking every item of my kit with my name in either black or white paint depending on the colour of the article. We were allowed to mark handkerchiefs, socks and stockings with our initials only. We were allowed to drape items over our lockers and bed-ends so that the paint would dry.

Whacker was quietly strolling up and down the mess when 'Lugs', a skinny, pale-skinned lad over six foot tall with a protruding Adam's Apple and sticky-out ears, spoke to him.

'Can I ask you a question please sir?'

'Of Course You Can, Lad. That's What I Am Here For. Ask Away!'

'When do we get our rum sir?'

'WHAT?' Whacker spluttered and turned crimson.

'When do we get our rum sir?' Lugs repeated

'When Do You Get Your RUM?' Spittle spurted from Whacker's lips.

'Yes sir.'

Whacker looked up at him with one eye closed. 'How Did You Learn About Rum, Lad?'

'In the papers sir.'

'In The Papers?'

'Yes sir.'

'So You Read The Papers Do You, Lad?'

'Sometimes sir.'

'Well My Tall Little Sparrow, How Old Are You?'

'Fifteen sir.'

'And Your Sixteenth Birthday Is When?'

'March sir, the second of March.' Lugs proudly tried to expand his concave chest.

'Well Young Man,' Whacker puffed up his chest to its maximum, his gilded buttons straining on the front of his jacket. 'Your Rum Will Therefore Be Available To You In Approximately Four Years And Two Months Time!'

'Pardon sir?'

'Your Rum Will Be Available To You In About Four Years And Two Months!'

'Four years and two months sir?'

'Rum ... The Naval Tot ... Grog ... Is Only Issued To Those Men ... I Say Men ... Over Twenty Years Of Age. I Repeat: Men!'

'Right sir. I think I understand sir.'

'A Privilege Only Available To Members Of Her Majesty's Senior Service, Who Have Reached The Age Of Twenty Years!'

'Thank you sir.'

'Can You Imagine, Lad, What A Tot Of Strong Naval Rum Would Do To Your Young, Delicate Body?'

'No sir.'

'Exactly My Point, My Little Sparrow ... Exactly My Point!'

I was a little disappointed: I had expected my rum when I turned 18 ... when I was allowed into pubs and legally a boozer. Twenty was years away!

Later that evening we all stood at the foot of our bed wearing our badly fitting pyjamas and deck shoes while we each in turn recited our two recently issued numbers to Whacker. Inevitably there were a few lads who got flustered and couldn't remember them.

I stared at the ceiling rafters that night, secure in the knowledge that it was Saturday tomorrow: the weekend and the time to relax. There was a smell of kit-marking paint pervading the mess. Quietly and without due ceremony, the lad from Stoke on Trent had followed his suitcase back home today: something about him wasn't quite right and the Royal Navy had apparently decided that they could continue their worldwide, post-war peace-keeping operations without him.

My Naval phrase of the day had to be 'Haar-Ten-Shun!' Others were 'Belay That!' which meant 'Stop it', 'Cack Handed' which meant 'Clumsy' and 'Pit' which was a bed.

For the first time, Whacker had cracked a joke this evening. In an uncharacteristically humorous mood he'd said: 'When I Joined The Navy, Lad, There Were No Official Numbers, Because We All Knew Each Other!'

Saturday 9 January was the day that a few more basic truths began to sink in. *Ganges* was the kind of place where, from waking to sleeping, we were told when and how to do everything. To go anywhere or do anything, without being told to, was classed as initiative and definitely not allowed. There was a Naval method of shaving, brushing teeth, combing hair and a hundred other things. If we thought that we knew anything ... the Navy taught us otherwise. Today was also the day that I learned that the Royal Navy don't do weekends. Saturday was different from the previous five days: it was worse. Today we cleaned the mess. Individually we were allocated cleaning duties and it appeared that between us all we had to clean absolutely everything ourselves: windows, deck, sinks, doors, rafters, night heads, part of the colonnade outside, walls, outside heads and bathroom: absolutely everything that didn't move had to be scrubbed or polished.

'It's normal routine,' said Muddy. 'If it moves salute it, if it doesn't then clean it!'

I must have done something to upset Whacker. Along with a few others I was given the outside heads to clean. Our unfortunate group were shown how to use a mop and bucket, how to clean the windows with scrunched-up paper and vinegar-based cleaner, and how to clean in and around the rows of toilet bowls with a long-handled brush and some strong-smelling ammonia-based liquid. All we lacked was enthusiasm. I looked for signs of removed door hinges on the cubicle framework: maybe some poor sods had actually committed suicide in here, maybe they had been on cleaning duty. I noticed old hinge marks. During the course of the next few hours we were checked regularly; after all, none of us had cleaned anything like this before. Personally I couldn't remember having cleaned anything resembling a toilet before. For a fleeting moment I wondered how or who had cleaned our toilet at home. Maybe it had been Mum ... and maybe she'd done it every Saturday morning.

By mid morning, we'd attempted to clean everything and were fell-in outside on the Parade-Ground while some bloke with a couple of gold rings on his jacket cuff had a wander around

Hardy mess, in a strange procedure called 'Saturday Morning Rounds'. When he had finished with our mess he moved on to our neighbour's and then over to the messes on the other side of the Parade-Ground. It was cold and windy and just standing still was chilling us to the bone. We were eventually allowed back in to find that all our neatly folded bedding had been strewn over the deck. Apparently it hadn't been folded well enough. The contents of a few lockers had also been removed and scattered over the deck. Whacker read out a list of things that had to be re-cleaned: a couple of windows, a section of the wall by the main entrance door and the inside of some lockers.

He also warned us that if our beds weren't done correctly next Saturday we would be dragging them out on to the Parade-Ground. Thankfully the outside toilet made it through the inspection without comment.

Just when we thought there wasn't time to fit anything else into our overflowing schedule, *Ganges* threw something else at us. Having marked all our kit with our name we now had to over-sew our names in red silk thread, each stitch no more than one eighth of an inch long. None of the underlying paint had to show when we had finished. Each sewn article had to be inspected and approved by Whacker. Once again I didn't pay full attention and missed the bit on how to do a chain stitch. We had to start with our housewives and it took me ages to stitch over the first few letters of my name until Muddy showed me how to do it correctly. Lesson learned: pay attention to the important things! The length of my surname, all of a sudden, became a problem: including initials my name had eleven letters and two full-stops. Directly opposite me was a lad called 'J. Ray' (four letters and one full-stop) who was able to sew three items of his kit to my one. Boxes full of red silk hanks were placed on a table in the centre of the mess alongside which was one set of mess scissors with rounded blades. We had a mountain of kit that had to be sewn-in and we had to finish every item before we left the Annexe. To achieve this, we had to spend every available minute sewing. Strangely it did generate a sort of camaraderie as some of those with shorter names offered to help those of us who were not so fortunate.

I was suffering from scarred fingers and aching thumbs by the time I'd finished sewing my name on my housewife, but I'd mastered the chain stitch and I red-silked the initials on one of my hankies in no time at all. I quickly learned to ignore the full stops that saved me a little time. Throughout my time in the Navy, I either lost items of kit, grew out of them, or wore them out. However, my housewife I kept forever and whenever I used it, I could see the exact moment I learnt how to chain-stitch. Embroidered red silk names always indicated a *Ganges*-trained boy and that, towards the end of my career, was something I was proud of.

Later that afternoon Tug returned to the mess. He was walking a little strangely. Apparently he had been circumcised and he was excused everything for a week ... apart from sewing. He had a nine-letter surname so I suppose it was fair in a way.

'In your absence, we've decided to call you Tug ... is that OK?' Someone asked.

'Call me what you like.' Tug grimaced as he braced himself up against the bottom rail of his bed.

'What did they do to you then, Tug?' asked Muddy.

'Don't ask. Don't ask.'

'OK then.'

'Does it hurt then mate?'

'I'm numb from the waist down.'

'You're not are you?'

'Yep.'

'It's only pain,' Taff explained.

'That'll be alright then,' replied Tug.

'So you haven't got a foreskin thing then ... any more?' asked Derek from Bridlington.

'Nope.'

'Ferkin hell!'

Someone at the top of the mess said 'Give us a look then.'

'Ferk off.'

There was no clock in the mess and those of us who had arrived with wristwatches had sent them home in our suitcase.

We just guessed, or Whacker told us, what time of the day it was. We became quite good at working it out by the length of shadows, if there were any, and our stomachs told us when it was time to eat. Whacker never left us alone for very long ... and he had a watch. The military 24-hour clock was, until that day, a mystery to many of us.

'Fourteen Hundred Is Two-O-Clock In The Afternoon. The Royal Navy Uses The Mathematically Accurate Twenty Four Hour Clock!' we were told one evening as we sat on the edges of our beds, dressed in our pyjamas ready to turn in.

Whacker strolled up and down the centre of the mess. 'Unlike The Other Services ... The Army And The Royal Air Force, We In The Royal Navy Do Not Say Fourteen Hundred Hours As We Are Intelligent Enough To Know That When We Are Talking About Time We Don't Need To Mention Hours. The Royal Navy Is Both Brief And Accurate In All Things.' He pointed to a boy who was staring at the floor. 'What Time Is Eighteen Hundred, Lad?'

'Pardon?'

'Pardon WHAT!'

'Pardon sir.'

'What Time Is Eighteen Hundred My Little Sparrow?'

'Time sir?'

'Yes ... Time!'

'Er ...'

'Come On, Lad!'

'Err ..'

'Eighteen Hundred, Lad?'

'Don't know sir.'

'Think About It, Lad!'

'About six-o-clock sir. in the evening sir!'

'Not About! Eighteen Hundred Is Exactly Six-O-Clock In The Evening!'

'Thank you sir.'

'Don't You Back-Chat Me, Lad! What Time Is Twenty Three Fifty Nine Then?' He swung to face a bemused-looking Blacky.

Blacky shook his head.

'Tell Him Lad!' Whacker pointed his stick at one of the Arry boys.

'One minute to midnight sir,' Boydie confidently replied.

'One Minute To Midnight. Twenty Three Fifty Nine Is One Minute To Midnight! Do You All Understand Why?'

We all nodded because we were getting bored with this new method of telling the time ... we were tired teenagers and we just wanted to go to bed.

If there was one word that was guaranteed to upset Whacker it was the word just.

'What Are You Doing, Lad?'

'I was just going to try and ... '

'You Were Just ... You Were Just! Who Do You Think You Are, Lad, One Of The Three Just Men?'

Or even better, 'Where Are You Going, Lad?'

'I was just going to ... '

'You Were Just ... Just! Who Do You Think You Are, Lad, One Of The Three Just Travelling Men?'

It was a recurring problem for us all: trying to trot out an excuse without using the word just. I spent the remainder of my life avoiding the word.

Staring at the roof rafters I decided that Saturday had been a terrible day. Thank goodness tomorrow was Sunday: the Navy couldn't bugger up a Sunday could they? Words of today had been 'Chuffed' which meant pleased, 'Cock-up' that meant nothing more sexual than a mistake and 'Tough Titty' which meant hard luck. 'Chop Chop' apparently had nothing at all to do with pork.

Sunday began well enough. Reveille was quarter of an hour later than normal at 06:15. We knew this, because Whacker told us. We had learned yesterday, that 06:15 was exactly quarter past six in the ferkin morning.

After breakfast we were mustered on the Parade-Ground along with groups from the other messes. Although we had already met some of the lads in the Dining Hall, there was no interaction between us at this stage of our training.

Whacker was keen to demonstrate to the other classes our mastery of basic drill. We were teenagers, however, and many of us had forgotten what we had been taught. Consequently we were disappointingly sloppy, but no worse or better than any of the other messes. Eventually we were all standing to attention: shoulders back, heads up and thumbs in line with the seams of our Action Working Dress trousers while we were inspected by another bloke sporting a couple of gold rings. He spoke to a couple of the lads, but thankfully not to me.

On a small podium in front of us, there appeared a gentleman dressed in flowing, religious robes who spent some considerable time saying prayers and extolling the virtues of hard work, commitment, teamwork, obedience etc. He droned on and on, but I couldn't hear him properly: the Suffolk wind was at my back.

After dinner, which was a very acceptable roast followed by a substantial pudding smothered with loads of creamy custard, we were ushered back to the mess where we were told that the rest of the day was ours. However, it was suggested that we spent our free time 'Sewing Your Names In!'

It was today that I realised that as well as not having a clock in the mess we didn't have a radio or a television. We were completely cut off from the outside world. Anything could be happening out there. I didn't even know how Leeds United had done yesterday.

That night, not for the first time, I wondered how things were at home and how Mum and my brother Tony were getting on without me: splendidly perhaps. Tomorrow morning I would have been in the Royal Navy a few hours short of a complete week.

Today's new rafter words were 'Rumbled!' which meant found out and 'Hang Fire!' which meant wait a moment.

Day number seven. The start of my second week: surely now things would start to get easier.

Whacker was intent on instilling into us the plain and simple fact that the Navy could do anything to us, anything at all, and we just had to grin and bear it. 'Yours Is Not To Reason Why: Yours Is But To Do And Die!' was one of his favourite phrases; maybe it was an inspiring Shakespearian line.

As a mess, we became good at mustering, knowing who to stand next to and in what rank. I had moved myself to the middle rank, realising that it protected me to both the front and rear. Whacker had already pigeon-holed many of us. He had identified those with leadership potential, those who were enthusiastic, those who were going to survive life in the Royal Navy and those who weren't. I wondered briefly in which pigeon-hole I'd been put ... probably a special one for those unfortunates who had a lengthy name to sew in and displayed little initiative. In reality, I wasn't much interested in what the Navy thought of me because I was too busy figuring out what I thought of the Royal Navy.

Today was the day I was singled out for the first time. I had made the mistake of having a couple of ladles of musical beans for breakfast, and at the first muster of the day I farted with alarming clarity exactly at the moment when the rest of the world had fallen silent.

'Who The Hell Was THAT?' yelled Whacker.

I had learned at school that it was always best to own up at a time like this. I held my hand up. 'It was me sir. Sorry sir.'

'Well Well Then, Lad. Would You Do That If You Were On Parade In Front Of Her Majesty?'

'No sir.'

He strutted around to the flank of the middle rank, chin up. 'Put Your Hand Down, Lad, You're Not In The School Playground Now!'

'Yes sir.' It was difficult to get everything right.

He took up a position in front of me: his neck stretched so that our noses were only inches apart 'Face Your Front, Lad! Would You Do That If You Were On Parade In Front Of The Admiral Of The Fleet?'

'No sir.'

'And In Front Of The Captain Of Her Majesty's Ship *Ganges*?'

'No sir.' This was becoming repetitively boring.

'You Saved It Up For Me Then ... Specially For Me?'

'No sir. It just sort of ...' I knew what I had said wrong.

He leaned over my shoulder and bellowed in my ear. 'Another Just Man Are You, Lad? We'll Have To Pay Particular Attention To Your Dung-Hampers During Our Forthcoming Dhobying Session Won't We, Lad?'

'Yes sir.'

'Control Yourself In Future My Lad. Learn To Control Your Horrible Little Body!'

Little? I was five foot ten inches tall and had a 34-inch expanded chest!

Not only was Stand-Easy a Parade-Ground order, it was also a much appreciated 15-minute mid-morning break when we were given a drink of that wonderful Naval concoction called Kye, a sticky bun and the opportunity for the first cigarette of the day. The strange instruction 'Out-Pipes!' that signalled the end of Stand-Easy had traditional significance, according to Whacker: it was apparently an historic instruction for clay pipes to be doused before resuming work or duties.

Before dinner, we had our Paybook photographs taken. Individually we stood outside the mess with a folded towel wrapped around our chest so that our printed name showed and Mr Fisk took our photograph. My expression was a mixture of despair and misunderstanding. What was I doing with a towel wrapped around my chest having my photograph taken and what were Paybooks all about anyway?

Will someone please tell me what the heck is going on?

Monday was traditionally kit-washing day. We gathered all our dirty washing together and placed it on our removed bed-sheet at the bottom of our beds. Whacker walked up and down examining the piles: if a pile wasn't sufficiently large, we were given the opportunity to explain why. It was impossible for anybody to convince Whacker that they didn't have much dirty washing to do, and he would dive into an individual's locker, stick flailing, to unearth additional items he considered unclean. Once we all had an acceptable pile of washing, we were instructed to strip and put on a pair of blue sports shorts and black plimsolls and fall-in outside the mess with our washing scrunched up inside the bed-sheet. We were then marched 20 yards around the corner to the washroom: a large room with deep, square washbasins around three walls. The windows on all walls were wide open and the whipping, ice cold Suffolk wind was screeching in. We stood expectantly in front of our sink and open window with our pile of dirty washing at our feet.

'Make Two Piles: Separate Your Blue Washing From Your White Washing!' instructed Whacker as he pulled on a pair of Wellington boots. 'Over Each Sink You Will Find Two Strange Looking Items Of Naval Equipment. These Are Called Taps. The One Marked With 'H' Will Give You Hot Water And It's Opposite Number Marked With A 'C' Contains ...' He swung around and pointed his questioning stick at Lugs.

'Cold Water,' replied Lugs without a moment's hesitation.

'Cold Water WHAT?'

Lugs gulped. 'Cold water sir.'

'Correct!' Whacker wrapped his scarf around his neck and buttoned up his coat. 'When Instructed You Will Half Fill Your Sink With Water That Is Hand Hot ... That Means Water That You Can Comfortably Put Your Hands Into.' He tapped the edge of a vacant sink with his stick. 'Then You Will Insert Your White Coloured Washing Into The Water ... Your White Washing. Not Your Blue Washing!' He stomped around the room testing the water temperature and making sure that we accurately identified our white washing. 'Good Boys ... Now Give Your Washing A Good Dunking!'

We dunked our whites.

Whacker swung on someone in the far corner who was fiddling with his blue pile. 'Are You Taking The Piss, Lad?' He scuttled over to Derek Knight's sink and slashed the sink with his stick. 'Give Those A Dunking ... Those White Things In The Sink!'

'I didn't know what you meant by dunking sir.'

'Don't You Put Your Green Coat On With Me, Lad!'

'Pardon sir?'

'Never Mind. Give Your White Washing A Good Soaking! Get Your Hands And Elbows In The Water! ... All The Way In ... Go On!' He marched back to his central position alongside a large bath full of water.

Spotty arrived with a tray full of what looked like blocks of Cheddar cheese.

I was trying desperately to get the stains out of a soiled handkerchief.

'Make Sure All Items Are Well Soaked!' Whacker pointed his stick at Derek. 'Remind Me To Explain To You ... And Everybody Else About Green Coats Junior Seaman Knight!'

'Yes sir,' replied Derek.

I wondered about the tray of cheese. Maybe this was another strange Naval tradition.

'The Junior Instructor Will Issue You Each With A Block Of Pusser's Hard Soap!'

The penny dropped. The cheese is not Cheddar ... it's soap: hard something soap.

'Junior Instructor Hawthorne Will Demonstrate To You How To Use This Magic Cleansing Material To Soap Your Kit Items And Remove Any Ingrained Stains!'

Spotty issued us all with one yellow block. Then he extracted an item of kit from one of the sinks and slowly demonstrated how to identify those areas that attracted most dirt or stains and how to attack them with the yellow block.

'Who Was It Who Farted On Parade This Morning?'

I put my hand up ... and then quickly put it down again. 'Me sir ... I'm here sir ... me.'

'As Promised I Shall Pay Particular Attention To Your Dung-Hampers.'

'Thank you sir.'

Whacker coughed. 'This Is The Prescribed Naval Hand Washing Method.' He whirled on someone. 'Wait Lad ... Wait! I Hope That You Will All Have In Your Sink A Pair Of Naval Issue Underpants ... Bollocks For The Protection Of!' He glared at us all in turn. 'Now I Am Sure That You Will All Be Able To Identify Your Own Stains ... And Attack Them!' He tapped his stick on an adjacent sink. 'Get On With It ... Attack Those Stains!'

Thus commenced our first hand washing experience. Over the next quarter of an hour or so, with advice from a well wrapped-up Whacker and a morose looking JI Hawthorne, we all got to grips with the rudiments of hand washing with a block of Cheddar cheese type soap. For someone used to the sudsy properties of Pears or Imperial Leather, this foul-smelling, sturdy yellow stuff was absolute rubbish; it made little impression on my soiled items. After washing our whites we had to wring out most of the soapy water then empty our sink and fill it with clean water of the same temperature, rinse our items and repeat .. and repeat ... and repeat. Each item was then presented to Whacker for his inspection. He would examine those vulnerable parts for any staining and squeeze the material between his fingers to check that all the soap had been removed. Misty was the first person to fail this inspection more than once and was made to plunge himself into the large central bath that was full of ice-cold water. The sight of Misty emerging from the bath with dripping shorts, blue veined skin, shivering and goggle-eyed, improved our washing technique immediately. My Dung-Hampers passed inspection first time: one of my handkerchiefs didn't.

Whacker pirouetted and jumped up and down three times. 'What Are You Doing, Lad ... What The Hell Do You Think You Are Doing?' He yelled at Boydie in the next-but-one sink to me.

'Wringing out my pyjama trousers sir.'

'Am I Mistaken ... Or Do I See Your Pyjama Trousers Wrapped Around Her Majesty's Plumbing, Lad?'

'Yes sir.' He quickly unhooked his pyjama trousers from the cold water tap and tried to hide them behind his back. 'I didn't know it belonged to ...'

Whacker swung his stick towards the centre of the room. 'Through The Bath ... Slowly ... Very Slowly Through The Bath!'

Boydie strolled over to the bath and gently lowered himself into the now greying water. 'Before You Submerge Yourself, Lad ... Say Sorry To Her Majesty!'

'Sorry to Her Majesty ... sorry sir.'

'Sorry SIR?'

'Sorry sir ... sorry your ... her Majesty.'

'Junior Instructor Hawthorne, Give Him A Push, Get His Disrespectful And Ugly Face Under That Water!'

Spotty gave Boydie a push so that he was totally immersed.

'Hold Him There!' Whacker swung around. 'Let This Be A Warning To You All. Her Majesty The Queen Did Not Provide You With Taps Of Fresh Flowing Hot And Cold Water So That You Could Use Them To Wring Out Your Manky Washing!' He tapped the side of the bath. 'Let Him Up!'

Spotty released his grip and a purple, spluttering Boydie surfaced.

'Get Out!'

Boydie was blotched purple all over, but he managed a smirk as he walked smartly back to his sink, head held high.

That afternoon, on the Parade-Ground, we were congratulated on our pathetic performance the previous day. We learned how to march as a group: we spent some considerable time going over what we had already been taught and when Whacker was confident that we had hoisted-in sufficient information, we were given the order 'Tin To The Right In Threes ... Right-Aah-Tin!' In theory it was a simple enough instruction, but a number of us got it wrong, confusing our left with our right. The procedure was repeated, until we were reasonably coordinated, and then we were given the order 'By The Right Quick-Aaaah March!'

What followed was total confusion, 'Leyf ... Rye ... Leyf ... Rye!'

the Arry boys moved but most of us looked to our neighbour to see what to do ... and tripped over ourselves.

'Halt ... Halt! Stay Exactly Where You Are! Don't Move!'

Eventually after much cajoling, insulting, coaxing and colourful persuasion, most of us were able to march in step. 'Heads Up, Shoulders Back, Arms Swinging To Shoulder Height And Parallel With The Deck.'

For the first time we responded to numerous 'Right Wheels!' and 'Left Wheels!' that took us to all corners of the Parade-Ground. I was wet and my boots hurt my feet. I would be glad to get back into the mess and get my housewife out.

After Stand-Easy we were herded up a set of steel steps to a room with lots of uncomfortable bare wooden benches. At the front of the room was a screen and at the back a projector. I figured out that we were in a cinema of some kind. The lights were turned off and for a wonderfully relaxing hour, we watched a series of Naval Educational Films, starting with a film about the Women's Royal Naval Service (WRNS) and then a series of short black and white films showing enthusiastic sailors onboard ships doing all kinds of nautical things. The final film was one depicting the ravages of Venereal Disease in full Technicolor.

Back in the mess, we were shown how to spit and polish our boots. I wrapped a duster around my forefinger and, for half an hour, applied alternate layers of my personal spit and Pusser's polish in a vain attempt to produce an ultra shiny toecap surface. I couldn't get the hang of it, so I decided that gobbing on my boots was a total and unnecessary waste of 'sewing-in' time and didn't persevere with it.

We were also shown how to use an iron. I didn't have a problem with ironing because I'd ironed my drainpipe trousers many times at home. I'd become expert in producing a fashionable razor-sharp crease down the front and back of my trousers by means of a steam iron and a damp cloth or a sheet of crinkly brown paper. Unfortunately the Royal Navy had not yet discovered the benefits of the steam iron and had remained faithful to the old-fashioned, post-war model that relied on a combination of heat and weight to flatten clothing.

As we were all snuggling into our beds, Whacker asked. 'Where Is Junior Seaman Knight?'

'Here sir.' Kev held his hand up.

'Remind Me To Explain To You What A Green Coat Is .... Tomorrow.'

'Yes sir. Thank you sir.'

Staring at the darkened outline of the rafters that night I decided that there was obviously a *Ganges* Training Programme. We got out of bed each morning not knowing what the day had in store for us. If nothing else, it was instinctively teaching me not to worry about the unexpected.

Today's new phrases were 'Bollocky Buff' which meant naked and 'Dhoby Dust' which was washing powder, not that we had any.

Tuesday. To celebrate our first complete week in the service of Her Majesty we were to be allowed out of the Annexe again. We were instructed to dress in blue sports shirt, matching shorts and pumps. Sharp as a tack, I quickly realised that we were not going to be spending the first part of the day watching more instructional films. I clearly recall the exact moment, during our enforced run around the lanes of rural Suffolk, when I realised that cross-country running was not for me: it was within yards of leaving the Annexe Parade-Ground. Athletically I'm no slouch: at school I played basketball, football, cricket and was considered a better than average one hundred yard hurdler. However, I was not a runner for running's sake. Running bare-legged along frost-encrusted, ice-puddled lanes on a freezing cold morning, with no end in sight was not for me. All the messes were running. It was my first experience of real *Ganges* competition and my introduction to a group of over-enthusiastic individuals dressed in figure-hugging white jumpers and tracksuit trousers known as Physical Training Instructors (PTIs). These vigorous blokes pushed, cajoled, kicked and threatened us until we had all completed the run and were herded safely back inside our compound. I wasn't the last back, but I did stagger in behind most of the others and spluttered my name, mess and ships book number to one of the PTIs as I lurched in through the Main Gate. I was absolutely knackered, my new shorts, sports shirt and plimsolls had chafed me in the most peculiar places and the distance run had been many steps too far. I'd hated every minute of it and vowed never, never to do it again ... if I could avoid it. We fell-in and waited as all the mess Instructors and PTIs went into a huddle in the centre of the Parade-Ground. Once the results were compiled Hardy mess were adjudged to be second overall: Whacker wasn't impressed. I thought my performance had somehow let the mess down.

Cleansed and dressed in our Number 8s we were then taken to the Dining Hall that had been turned into a temporary inoculation theatre. A team of unenthusiastic blokes jabbed us with a variety of needles and presented us with certificates noting that we were now completely protected against yellow fever, cholera, smallpox and TAB, whatever they were. Maybe they were something we would pick up in China, or somewhere. Inevitably there were a few lads who didn't like the needle: they were kept behind and jabbed in private. One of the Arry boys fainted.

Most boys of our age, separated from their parents, smoked and the Navy actively encouraged it. *HMS Ganges* Annexe however, had loads of smoking rules. For instance, smoking was strictly forbidden in the mess or associated toilets, bathroom or drying room. It was also banned in the Dining Hall. A few days ago, someone from one of the other messes was spotted sneaking a crafty drag in the Dining Hall queue by one of the mess Instructors. The unfortunate individual was told to extinguish his cigarette and ordered to chew and swallow what was left of it as punishment. We watched as he gagged and spluttered in an attempt to do as instructed. He was even given a glass of lubricating water. Eventually he turned green, spewed over his nice, shiny boots and was removed from the queue. We didn't have to be told a second time that smoking in the Dining Hall was not allowed. The poor sod also missed dinner.

The remainder of day eight was spent on the Parade-Ground where we learned all about 'dressing'. This manoeuvre enabled us to form equally spaced straight lines and it proved to be a much more complicated business than it sounded. Unfortunately, the two individuals who couldn't march properly yesterday had forgotten their extra instruction and were once again swinging their arms in a strangely uncoordinated fashion. They were to undergo extra Parade instruction that evening whilst the rest of us were sewing our names in.

I'd been in the service of Queen and Country for over a week now, so I suppose my first taste of punishment was long overdue. I was about to understand how the Royal Navy managed to keep loads of incarcerated, energetic young boys in line: they did it by adopting a diverse and complicated range of instant punishments. After a few warnings to keep quiet after lights-out, Whacker appeared from nowhere and we were ordered out of bed. He told us to roll our mattresses back, grab our boots and stand on our bed springs in our bare feet. We were then told to hold a boot in each hand and to extend our arms. Sounds simple, but Navy boots were built to last and deceptively heavy. After a few minutes, even for relatively fit young boys, the exercise proved painful. If anybody lowered an arm, or dropped a boot, the whole process was repeated until everybody managed an unknown period of time without dropping an arm. Of course we all lowered our arms whenever Whacker's back was turned.

There was something in the air that night: our boot punishment was soon forgotten and it wasn't long before we were making a noise again. This time our punishment was more inconvenient. It was snowing and we had to fall-in outside under the colonnade overhang, wearing nothing but our pyjamas and deck shoes with our rolled-up mattress on our head. We stood silently to attention, arms straining to control a Pusser's mattress which had a life of its own and didn't like being outside in the elements any more than we did. Individually we were allowed to place our mattress on the deck and, as a penalty, double around the Parade-Ground if we wished. After an hour or so we were all allowed back to our cold beds where a semblance of warmth slowly returned to our shivering bodies.

My word of today was 'Cackle' which simply meant to talk. I also learned that 'Not Bashing The Bishop' meant keeping my hands outside my blankets.

My very first kit inspection took place on day number nine. Of all the new skills we were required to learn, probably the most difficult and lengthy one to master was the *Ganges* Kit Muster. The mess ironing board was in continual use as we tried to present each item of kit in the prescribed manner, folded wherever practical to the width of the Manual of Seamanship, a book I had not yet opened. Whacker and Spotty buzzed around helping, swearing, criticising, insulting and occasionally demonstrating.

We pulled our mattress cover extra tight and laid out our entire kit in strict accordance with the photograph on page 36 of the Naval Ratings Handbook. Our locker doors were left open so that it could be seen that no item of dirty or un-ironed kit was secreted away. We laid whites out down one side, blues down the other: all folded with our name visible on the top centre. Multi coloured items, like pyjamas, were placed in the centre along with sports gear, manuals, gloves, lanyards and our Little Brown Case. At the base of the bed we lined-up our footwear: boots, deck-shoes, white plimsolls, black plimsolls and our football boots if we had brought them from home. Those items that couldn't be folded were rolled and secured with two bands of tape: white for the blue items such as sea jerseys and black for the white items such as towels. The tapes had to be in line and the securing knots hidden from view. Even my handkerchiefs were ironed and folded in a triangular shape. When approached by Whacker we would stand to attention and give our rank and name followed by 'Kit ready for your inspection sir.' Then, unless we were told to move, we stood there while Whacker methodically pulled everything apart, unfolding, rummaging, sniffing and poking until our entire kit was scattered over our bed-space. He casually pronounced judgement before moving on to wreak similar havoc on the next in line. Name-sewing progress was noted: mine was probably worse than average. A well spit-and-polished pair of boots were held up as a lesson to us all as was a pair of plimsolls used on the cross-country yesterday with the soles scrubbed and whitened: they belonged to a snivelling Arry boy, of course. We were all glad when it was over and we'd replaced our kit in our lockers in the prescribed order. I don't think any of us, with the possible exception of the Arry boys, realised how many times we were to lay our kit out over the forthcoming 377 days.

Later in the day we were issued with our blue uniform suit, a two-piece combination of utter confusion. What shocked me most was the amount of material in the trousers. Fashion-conscious teenagers of the late 1950s wore narrow drainpipe trousers: now I was expected to wear bell-bottoms that were absolutely enormous. The civilised world, including West Yorkshire, had recognised the benefits of zip-fronted trousers many years ago, the buttoned fly having long been considered old fashioned and consigned to trouser history. The Royal Navy, however, had developed a third method of securing the front of trousers: a complicated flap-type mechanism. It looked neat but was problematical when you were desperate for a pee. Fortunately, the jacket design had recently incorporated zip technology and was a tight torso fit which gave the uniform suit a sleek shape. Now officially identified as Number 2s, it was the only item of kit that the Navy made a real effort to fit us and we were allowed to exchange items until we found a reasonably good fit. Once fully uniformed, we stood to attention at the bottom of our beds and were inspected. There were the obvious tweaks and criticisms before we gathered around an ironing board, where we were shown the ironing procedures for our uniform and attachments. The collar had to be pressed with three creases: the central one 'in' and the two outer creases 'out'. The black silk had to be folded to the standard Naval width and carefully ironed to avoid any scorching: it was real silk, after all. The ends of the black tapes used to secure the silk had to be cut in an inverted chevron: we didn't have scissors, so we had to use Whacker's. The lanyard had to be sparkly white ... we didn't have to iron that. The arms of the jacket had to incorporate a single ironed-out crease down the front. The bell-bottoms were a revelation: they were to be ironed inside out so that both outer seams were 'in'. Then came the crazy part: those of us 5 feet 10 inches or taller had to iron seven horizontal creases in our trousers at a spacing of exactly 3¼ inches. Those smaller than 5 feet 10 tall only had to iron five horizontal creases. The creases were done in a concertina fashion so that the trousers could be folded up and kept flat in our lockers.

Did the mess have a ruler? ... of course not. Already, friendly rifts were developing: between those 'five crease' short-arses and those of us who had seven. There was a short queue for the ironing board as those who wanted to get their trousers creased before turning-in formed a silent line.

Unusually, as we were turning-in that night, we were told what we were going to be doing the following day. 'Tomorrow My Little Sparrows. Tomorrow We Are Going To Climb The Mast! Not The Toy Mast We Have At The Annexe But The Real Mast In The Main Establishment ... Sleep Well!'

That wasn't the sky-scraping structure we'd seen briefly during our visit to the Sick Bay ... was it? Surely not!

There was a restlessness amongst us.

Today's words were 'Bubble' which meant to inform on someone and 'Shambolic' which meant a bit of a mess, accurately summing up the way we came to terms with our new uniform ... or maybe our marching ... or our ironing.

I was into double figures: it was Thursday 14 January and my tenth day in service. The rig-of-the-day for mast climbing was white sports shirt, white shorts and white plimsolls with no socks, no doubt to match the colour of the mast. Someone jokingly told us that he was wearing his brown underpants.

No transport for us today: we were marched out of the Annexe and down the narrow roads towards *Ganges* proper. I could see the mast towering above the roofs of the surrounding buildings. The closer I got, the taller it got. I was OK on a high diving board above water but I couldn't remember being more that six feet above solid, hard ground in my life.

The impressive and ornate gates of *HMS Ganges* were opened for us 'Heyft ... Ryte ... Heyft ... Ryte ... Heyft ... Ryte ... Heyft!' We probably didn't impress anybody. Annexe marching was like no other: we were taught to swing our arms so that they were horizontal with the deck and this clearly identified us as Nozzers.

We were halted at the base of the mast, the Establishment's pride and joy, erected in 1907 for sail training purposes. A large, painted wooden figurehead glared down at us. A barrel chested PTI stood to attention in front of us: he adjusted his trousers and spoke in a strangely high-pitched squeak. 'My name is Petty Officer PTI Morgan and it is my job to get you all up and over the mast of *HMS Ganges.*'

What did he mean ... over?

'Squeaky' continued. 'The Mast Of *HMS Ganges* Is Exactly 143 Feet 10 Inches Tall. The Lower Part Belonged To *HMS Cordelia* And The Upper Section Is From The Mizzen Mast Of *HMS Agincourt.*'

Brilliant. So what?

A battalion of bouncing, star jumping PTIs appeared from nowhere. PTI Morgan waited for them to clamber up through the safety net and take up their positions on the mast. 'Your Task Today Is To Clamber Up To The Half-Moon.' He turned and pointed skywards. 'That Is The Structure Shaped Like A Semi-Circle Approximately Three Quarters Of The Way Up The Mast, Just Below The Top Yard.'

We craned our necks and looked up ... up ... up.

'Dinger' Bell, who was standing alongside me, suddenly turned all religious. 'Holy shit!' he whispered.

'When You Reach The Half-Moon You Will Swing To The Opposite Side Of The Mast And Climb Back Down,' said Squeaky. 'There Is One Major Obstacle On Your Way Up ... And On Your Way Down.'

Dinger said 'Holy shit!' again.

'And That Is The Devil's Elbow.' The PTI pointed to a complicated looking platform structure above the lower yard arm. 'In Order To Negotiate This Structure You Will Have To Climb A Part Of The Rigging That Angles Outwards At Approximately Forty-Five Degrees. Anybody Unable To Complete This Manoeuvre Successfully Will, After A Number Of Attempts, Be Allowed To Scramble Through An Escape Hole In The Platform Called The 'Lubbers Hole' Before Continuing Upwards Towards The 'Half-Moon'. However, An Inability To Correctly Negotiate The Devil's Elbow Will Constitute A Mast Climbing Failure.'

I knew that there would be a catch somewhere.

'Anybody Unable To Complete The Climb In The Correct Manner Will Be Required To Undertake Extra Mast Climbing Instruction Until They Can Successfully Complete The Task. Nobody Will Leave The Annexe Without Having Successfully Negotiated The Devil's Elbow And Climbed Up To The Half Moon.'

At the base of the mast was a large safety net, which should have allayed any fears about falling until Squeaky told us about the boy who fell from the mast, hit the safety net, bounced onto the Mail Office roof and died.

I looked up at the two PTIs who were positioned on either side of what I guessed was the Devil's Elbow and a couple higher up just below the Half-Moon. They looked small and a long, long way away.

We were divided into small groups and I waited my turn to take my first tentative steps onto what looked more terrifying the closer I got to it.

I surprised myself: clinging tenaciously to every convenient bit of rope, I climbed slowly through the safety net and upwards.

Dinger froze.

'You Lad ... Get A Wriggle On. You're Slowing Others Down!' another shrill PTI yelled from above.

'Don't look down Dinger,' I said.

'Too ferkin late,' he replied.

I managed to scramble over the dreaded Devil's Elbow: it was scary. Then up to the Half-Moon and back down again without any physical or verbal encouragement from anybody. The PTI who gave my backside an encouraging tap on the down side of the Half Moon was just being helpful I suppose. I'd discovered that I had no problem with heights providing I had something to hold on to. Dinger and Slattery didn't fair that well. Slattery had crawled through the Lubber's Hole and back down again without going any higher. Dinger had frozen midway between the Devil's Elbow and the safety net. A couple of Arry boys asked if they could climb higher: but they were refused.

Once back in the mess the names of those individuals who had to do extra marching practice, improve their kit or re-climb the mast, were posted on the mess noticeboard. 'Every Body On These Lists Will Achieve The Necessary Standard Before They Can Progress To Ganges Proper … the Big Boys' Camp!'

I wasn't on any of the lists.

We were all issued with two copies of the mess photograph taken the previous week. Thankfully I'm not the only one looking totally bewildered. My arms are folded in the prescribed naval fashion and my cap doesn't fit. In the mess I wrote the names of all the boys on the back. I surprised myself that I knew them all already.

It wasn't until somebody mentioned Bromide, and how and why it was administered, that I realised I hadn't thought about girls for ages: for ten and three quarter days to be accurate. The Annexe tea tasted different but I put that down to the difference in water and the Navy not using the same tea as Mum did.

I stared at my roof rafters, but not for long. It had been a tiring day and I was knackered. This Bromide stuff was troubling me: what if it prevented me from thinking of girls forever! The words and phrases that stuck in my mind today were 'Sparrowfart' which meant dawn and 'Fart In A Trance' which was normally attributed to anyone of us who were a bit dreamy.

It was 15 January. We noticed a few gaps in our ranks when we mustered on the Parade-Ground after breakfast. Later in the day we discovered that three more of the mess had been discharged from the Royal Navy as 'Unsuitable for Further Naval Training'. I don't know if I was jealous of them or not. Cliff Barker, who had been in the next bed to mine, was gone, as were a couple of others from the top end of the mess.

After dinner, Whacker arrived with the mail. He stood in the centre of the mess and called out the names of those who had a letter: not everybody did. I had two, one from home and a bright red envelope from Christina in Berne. The colour and the foreign stamp provided Whacker with all the ammunition he needed.

'Red Letter From Switzerland For Junior Seaman Second Class Broadbent!'

'Thank you sir.'

'Tell Us All About The Red Letter Then!'

'From a girl I know sir.'

'A Girlie From Where?'

'Switzerland.'

'Switzerland WHAT?'

'Pardon?'

Whacker looked exasperated. 'Switzerland ... Sir!'

'Switzerland sir. Sorry sir.'

'And The Name Of This Girl Who Lives In Switzerland Is?'

'Christina sir.'

'Nice Looking Girl Is She?'

'I think so sir ... yes.'

'What Colour Is Her Hair?'

'Blonde sir.'

'And Her Eyes: What Colour Are They?'

'Can't remember sir. Blue I think.'

'Blue You Think Lad ... Blue You Think! Haven't You Gazed Longingly Into Her Eyes Then?'

'Not really, no sir.'

'Christina Doesn't Get Your Juices Flowing Then?'

'Pardon sir?'

'Is She A Bit Of A Dog Then ... This Christina From Switzerland, Is She A Bit Doggo?'

'Pardon sir?'

'Is Christina A Bit Uggs ... A Bit On The Ugly Side?'

'No sir.'

'But You Haven't Gazed Longingly Into Her Eyes Yet?'

'Not really, no sir.'

'You'll Have To Learn To Do That, Lad. If You Are Interested In Furthering English-Swiss Relationships.'

'I'll remember to do that in the future sir.'

'When Your Royal Navy Ship Goes To Switzerland Perhaps?'

'Perhaps sir yes.'

'That Would Be A Bit Of A Problem, Even For Her Majesty's Royal Navy. Do You Know Why That Might Be, Junior Seaman Second Class Broadbent?'

'Switzerland is a land-locked country sir.'

'So It Is, Lad, So It Is.' He held my letter out for me. 'Take Your Letter Lad! Send Christina My Love When You Next Write.'

'Thank you sir, I will.' As if I would.

I slunk away, secure in the knowledge that I had identified myself as someone who had Europe-wide connections with the opposite sex.

'Junior Seaman Second Class Ray ... Letter From Dulwich!' Whacker turned the envelope over. 'No Crosses On The Back. Must Be From Mummy!'

Jimmy wandered over, hand outstretched to take his letter.

'What's Your First Name, Junior Seaman Ray?'

'James ... sir.'

Whacker wafts the letter from Dulwich. 'You've Got To Be Called Johnnie Haven't You?'

'My name is James.'

'PARDON!'

'I mean my name is James sir.'

'That's Better, Lad!' He waved the letter from Dulwich in front of his face. 'Henceforth You Will Be Known As Junior Seaman Second Class 'Johnnie' Ray ... Understand?'

'Yes sir.' He took his letter and wandered back to his bunk

space, shoulders slightly hunched.

'Can You Sing Junior Seaman Ray?'

'No sir.'

'Just As Well I Suppose.'

Other names were called. Comments made on postmarks. 'Where In God's Name Is Giggleswick? Must Be A Laugh A Minute Living There!'

Eventually Whacker came to a letter addressed to Kevin Knight. He couldn't read the postmark. 'Where Would This Letter Have Come From Then, Junior Seaman Knight?'

'Mi Mum probably.'

'Mi Mummy Probably ... SIR!' Whacker slapped the outside of his leg in frustration.

'Pardon?'

'Pardon WHAT?'

'Pardon ... sir.'

'Where Would This Letter Have Come From Then Junior Seaman Knight? Where Would It Have Been Posted?'

'Post box on t'end of t'street ... sir.'

'And In What Town Would That Post Box Be Situated, Junior Seaman Knight?'

'Er ... Bridlington sir.'

'Bridlington? ... Bracing Bridlington?'

'Yes sir.'

Whacker flicked his letter to him. Kev' caught it: later we learned that he had played cricket for Yorkshire boys.

'In This Man's Navy People Who Have The Surname Of Knight Are Called Bogey!'

'Thank you sir,' said Kev'.

A few of us sniggered. Those of us who knew that bogeys grew up your nose.

After a few more letters Whacker came across one with lots of crosses on the back. 'And What Do We Have Here? Do We Have A Junior Seaman Second Class Steven Nigel Harbour In The Mess?'

Steve, who slept in the bed directly opposite mine, raised his hand. 'That's me sir.'

'What's All This Stuff On The Back Then, Lad?'

'Don't know sir.'

'Is It A Code Of Some Description?'

'Don't know sir.'

'Couldn't Be A Code Of A Sexual Nature Could It Junior Seaman Second Class Harbour?'

'No sir.'

'From Mummy?'

'Pardon sir?'

'Is Mummy Sending You Kisses And 'Swalks' And 'Boltops' Then?'

'Wouldn't think so sir. Hope not sir.'

'So If It's Not From Mummy Who Is It From Then?'

'Diane sir. Probably.'

'Probably! ... Probably?'

'Yes sir.'

'How Many Girlfriends Have You Got Then Junior Seaman Harbour? How Many?'

'Just the one sir.'

'Is She A Looker Then This Diane?'

'Yes sir.'

'How Old Is Diane?'

'Fifteen sir.'

'Not Legal Yet Then?'

'Not yet sir, no.'

'But Old Enough To Write 'ITALY', 'SWALK' And 'BOLTOP' On The Back Of Her Letters. Words With Sexual Overtones.'

'Yes sir.'

'Do You Think That Her Mummy And Daddy Know That She's Writing Coded Messages Of A Sexual Nature To A Spotty Individual Who Finds It Difficult To Wash His Own Underpants Correctly?'

'Probably not sir ... no.'

Whacker handed him his letter. 'With A Name Like Yours, Lad, You've Got To Be Called After A Well-Known Harbour. But I've Never In My Life Heard Of A Port Called Steven ... Have You Junior Seaman Harbour?'

'No sir.'

'What Did They Call You At School, Junior Seaman Harbour?'

'Volcano face sir.'

'Because You Have Lots Of Spots?'

'Yes sir. Sorry sir.'

He looked around the mess. 'I Need The Name Of A Port That Will Suit Junior Seaman Second Class Steven Nigel Harbour.'

From the top of the mess someone shouted 'Lowestoft sir.'

'Don't Be Silly!' replied Whacker.

'Hull sir.'

'That's Rubbish!'

One of the Arry boys stuck his hand up. 'Sydney sir. Sydney Harbour: that's a port.'

'That, Junior Seaman Second Class Boyd ... Is Perfect! Give Yourself A Pat On The Back!'

'Thank you sir,' said Boydie.

Steve gulped as he started to open his letter carefully with a forefinger.

'Henceforth, Junior Seaman Second Class Steven Nigel Harbour, You Will Be Known As Sydney. Tell Mummy, Daddy, Diane And Anyone Else You Know That Can Write.'

'Yes sir. Thank you sir.'

The final letter was postmarked Ipswich. 'Junior Seaman Second Class Slattery, Why Would You Be Getting A Letter From Ipswich?'

'That's where my mother lives sir.'

'Grotty Ipswich?'

'Just Ipswich sir.'

'DON'T Bandy Words With Me, Lad!'

'No sir. Sorry sir.'

'So You Live In Ipswich?'

'No sir.'

'Explain!'

'I live in Surbiton with my father. My Mum lives in Ipswich: they're divorced.'

'Divorced Eh?'

'Yes sir.'

'Would That Have Anything To Do With You Being An Unattractive Individual Who Can't Climb Our Mast?'

'Don't think so sir.'

'So When We Eventually Let You Go Home On Leave, Where Will You Go, Posh Surbiton Or Grotty Ipswich?'

'Surbiton sir.'

'So Daddy's Place And Not Mummy's, Then?'

'Yes sir.'

'Everybody Fall-In Outside In Five Minutes! Those Of You Who Can Read, Can Read Your Letters Later. If You Can't Read, Ask Junior Seaman Slattery: His Daddy Lives In Surbiton, So He Can Probably Help You With Any Long Words!'

My letter from Mum confirmed that she had received my suitcase full of my civvies and asked me if I had forgotten to keep my electric razor. Christina's letter was in beautiful English, written with a fountain pen on bright red paper with just one polite kiss on the bottom. I made a note to ask for a photograph next time I wrote.

That evening we had to adjust our cap chin-stays and sew them in using some of our black cotton: it took a while to get the length right. The chin-stay material was designed to be irritatingly ticklish.

Maybe it was because we had received our first letters, but we were all in boisterous mood as we turned-in that night.

Whacker switched the mess lights on and ordered us out of our beds. We fell-in on the Parade-Ground, wearing our pyjamas, deck shoes and our cap with the chin-stay down: standing to attention facing the Annexe mast. Spotty stood in front of us glaring. Whacker marched up and around us, not too pleased. Specially for us, the sleet turned to snow and large Suffolk flakes settled upon us. Occasionally a freezing gust of wind blew the snow horizontal: snow drifting in through the front opening of pyjama trousers was not a pleasant experience. After half an hour or so of silent inactivity we were ordered back to our beds. Hushed and cold we shuffled back to the mess, dried ourselves off, changed into a dry set of pyjamas, curled up, cupped our frozen tackle and noiselessly tried to go to sleep.

Today's words were 'Doggo' which meant ugly or not good-looking, 'Tits Up' meant useless or broken and 'To Drop a Bollock' was to make a mistake.

On our second Naval Saturday, and our 12th day of service, we were further punished before breakfast by being made to double around the periphery of the Parade-Ground for half an hour wearing Number 8s, boots, gaiters and caps with the now familiar, irritating chin-stay down. When we eventually made it into the Dining Hall, late for breakfast, everything on offer was crispy and cold and even the tea was tepid.

Apparently, last Saturday wasn't a one off: mess inspections happened every Saturday. Once again we were all given a specific cleaning task. Dinger and Slattery, our two mast-climbing failures, were given the job of climbing the mess rafters to clean them. The less fortunate, or those who were not deemed to be pulling their weight, were given the heads or the showers to clean. The most muscular were made to scrub the linoleum deck; another team, on hands and knees, dried it and yet another group laid polish and shined it. Large circular objects (spitkids), that we had not yet found a use for, were polished with a noxious substance called Bluebell, as was a large oblong container with a handle, comically called a Fanny. I was a member of the team charged with polishing the mess dustbin inside and out: a large piece of mess equipment that was purely decorative. It's amazing what can be achieved when a bunch of unenthusiastic cleaning virgins are organised. Finally we tidied our blankets, sheets and pillows, and pulled our mattress cover tight before falling-in outside the mess to await our mess inspection.

Eventually an Officer with two gold rings on his cuffs was officially welcomed to the mess by a saluting Whacker, 'Hardy Mess Ready For Your Inspection Sir!'

We waited whilst Whacker and JI Hawthorne followed the Officer into the bowels of our gleaming mess. We didn't realise it at the time but it was the first time we, as a class, had been left completely alone since we arrived.

After all six of the messes had been inspected, a cake was awarded to the best: and it wasn't Hardy mess. Whacker told us that we had done a good job and that after dinner we could spend the afternoon on our kit. For me that meant sewing. Optimistically, I thought that I was about halfway through my sewing: there were no short cuts and I did wonder whether or not I would finish before the end of the month and our scheduled move to the Main Establishment.

My words this evening were 'Berseyquack': which meant half-crazy, 'Humming' which meant smelly and 'Skate' which was a workshy individual.

I had found a way of closing the window above my bed a little without it being noticed.

Ganges Sundays weren't real Sundays. We spent the day sewing, washing, ironing and polishing, interrupted by brief periods of eating. Once again, Sunday dinner was terrific: a traditional Sunday roast with lots of thick brown gravy from an urn situated next to the tea urn. The label said it was gravy, however it could have been soup, or loop, as sometimes the chefs moved the labels around for a laugh.

Day number 14 and the start of our second week. After breakfast we were mustered outside the mess and JI Hawthorne took charge while Whacker disappeared inside the mess. Unbeknown to us, part of his morning mess inspection was the towel test. We already knew that anybody who had a dry towel draped over their locker towel rail for more than a day would be in serious trouble. We were surprised to learn today that we had a serial dry-towel offender in our mess: Magnus Fleming-Wainwright's towel had been dry since last Friday. 'Maggie' had lived on a small-holding in the Midlands somewhere and apparently his idea of keeping himself clean was an occasional rinse in the waters of a conveniently placed trough. It was the second time that he had been caught and this time he was subjected to the traditional Naval punishment. We mustered outside the mess bathroom whilst the Arry boys, wielding stiff brooms, gave Maggie a scrub down with cold water and the foul smelling liquid soap we used to clean the heads. It wasn't a pretty sight. A wet, scratched and smashed, naked Maggie was left snivelling on the edge of his bed as the rest of us were ushered outside.

We never saw Maggie again. The next day his bed had been cleared and his locker emptied.

After breakfast the following morning, Whacker, with a smile on his face, told us that today we were going to be 'Gassed!' Even the Arry boys looked confused. We were marched over to a patch of Suffolk scrubland behind the Annexe and ordered to 'Stand Atta Heyse!' outside a building where a number of other Instructors were standing, each with a small khaki bag slung over their shoulder.

We were all ceremonially issued with a Respirator (gas mask) and shown how to test and adjust it so that it fitted around our faces with no gaps. Attached to each Respirator was a circular red tag on which was stamped our name, official number and our religion. How peculiar. Having marked all the rest of our kit with paint and red silk, this seemed an odd way of marking such an important piece of equipment.

With our gas-masks on we were ushered into a dark, dirt floored, windowless room and made to form a circle. It felt weird: the atmosphere was strangely intimidating ... and why were there lots of Instructors standing around? We were told that no matter what happened we were to stay inside the room until the door was opened and we were told to leave.

We all nodded. Speaking was difficult when you were wearing a ferkin gas-mask. Whacker stood in the centre of the circle and put his gas-mask on. There was a crack, which made me jump, and the room quickly filled with a billowing cloud of bright yellow smoke. A few of us coughed and spluttered. I couldn't see much, but I saw one individual being dragged out, followed shortly afterwards by a second. I tried not to breathe: this yellow cloud was obviously some kind of poisonous gas that had already killed a couple of my messmates and would kill me if I inhaled it. Something got into one of my eyes and made it sting. The eye-glasses of my gas-mask began to steam up and everything turned a misty yellow-brown. Around me boys were coughing and spluttering. I kicked the dirt floor in frustration. Eventually a door at each end of the building was opened; the through-draft quickly dispersed the yellow cloud and we were ushered outside. Once in the fresh air we were instructed to remove our masks and to inhale slowly and deeply. Never had Suffolk air tasted so good. Everybody's eyes were red-rimmed and streaming. We were told that we had been subjected to a very low-density irritant gas designed to demonstrate how important it was that we kept our gas-masks in good condition and well fitted. They now belonged to us, our only personal protection against any form of chemical attack that a potential enemy could waft our way. Thankfully, those who had been dragged out early were still very much alive and their gas-masks were readjusted before they were ushered back inside the windowless building to be retested. We waited, standing at ease, until they successfully completed the prescribed three minutes or so within the yellow cloud.

Once back in the mess, we were told to check that the correct information was shown on our circular red tags. In the event of a chemical attack, these tags would be removed and used to identify and bury casualties in accordance with an individual's religious beliefs. Casualties? Bury? Come on! I've joined the Navy to see the world, not to become a casualty ... I'm only fifteen!

After yesterday's traumatic experience we all woke the following morning wondering what painful experience the Navy would deem fit to inflict upon us today.

After breakfast we were marched over to a patch of spare ground at the back of the building where we had been gassed yesterday. We were brought to a halt facing a wall in front of which was a pile of rubbish and a large trough full of a smelly black liquid.

'This Is Your Chance To Play At Fire-Fighters!' bellowed Whacker.

Two individuals, dressed in long black inflexible coats and seaboots, busied themselves unrolling a couple of long khaki-coloured hoses and a large yellow-brown container in the space between us and the wall. I switched my concentration switch 'ON': this was important ... this was fire, real fire!

I hung on every word as Whacker told us about the three types of portable fire extinguishers we would find onboard a ship: the two-gallon water extinguisher painted red that was used to fight domestic fires, the two-gallon foam extinguisher coloured pale cream used to fight oil fires and a two-and-a-half pound carbon dioxide extinguisher for use exclusively on electrical fires.

A pile of waste and a trough full of an oily liquid were lit and allowed to burn for a while before a couple of Arry boys on the front rank were each given one of the hoses and shown how to extinguish the fire. The domestic waste was sprayed with water and was quickly extinguished. The oil fire required a touch more skill to put out: the foam mixture had to be bounced off an adjoining wall so that it flowed over the surface of the oil, cutting off the air supply.

'As You Progress In Your Naval Career, Your Fire Fighting Skills Will Be Developed Until You Yourselves, At Some Time In The Far, Far Distant Future, Could Find Yourselves In Charge Of A Fire-Fighting Team,' Whacker explained with a twinkle in his eye.

Fire-fighters eh? There were occasions when this Royal Naval thing became interesting.

In the afternoon we watched an American film about fighting fires onboard one of their Aircraft Carriers: very graphic and a little frightening. Whacker tried to impress on us the importance of efficient fire-fighting techniques onboard ship. 'Read Chapter Eleven Of Your Naval Ratings Handbook.'

And I did. Curled up in my bed, I scanned through the sections on Fire Prevention, learning all about the three elements of fire: fuel, oxygen and heat. The following bit about our new Respirators was an eye opener ...

> 'The service anti-gas respirator must not be worn for fire fighting, except as a means of escape in extreme emergency. Although it gives limited protection against most poisonous gases it does not provide the wearer with oxygen, of which there is often a lack in the fire area, particularly near a fire which intermittently gives off dense volumes of smoke.'

The phrase 'In extreme emergency' had me worried.

Thursday 21 January was our 17th day in the service of Her Majesty. Dressed in white sports clothes, with our swimming gear wrapped in our sparkly white towels, we were once again marched smartly out of the Annexe gates and down the road to *Ganges* proper. It was the first time we had marched while carrying something and this proved to be difficult for those who already had problems co-ordinating arms and legs. We were marched up and down the short road outside until we all mastered the marching and carrying combination. A civilian bloke who was washing his car outside his house stopped to watch us.

Our destination today was the swimming pool, where we were to be subjected to the Royal Navy Swimming Test. I was a good swimmer, breaststroke champion of my school, and the proud recipient of a Royal Lifesaving Society's Bronze Medallion. I had the Society's badge sewn prominently on the front of my swimming trunks.

The *Ganges* pool was impressive, a full 25 yards in length with high diving boards at the deep end and large spectator balconies high on three sides. The water was crystal clear and freezing cold. The first and most uncomfortable part of the Royal Naval Swimming Test was putting on a pair of cold and sopping-wet overalls: we obviously weren't the first group to be tested this morning. Once in the water, we had to swim a couple of lengths and then tread water in the deep end for five minutes. Anyone who attempted to grab hold of the side was pushed away by PTIs wielding long poles; ironically the same poles that were used as lifesaving aids. There were a number of reluctant swimmers and Lash was found to be a complete non-swimmer, never having been in the sea or a swimming pool in his life. I found it hard to understand that anybody would join the Navy without knowing how to swim, but Lash did.

The final part of the swimming test was a jump from the top diving board, still dressed in our dripping wet overalls. Inevitably, those same individuals who had found the mast climb difficult, needed a degree of sympathetic and psychologically inspired encouragement. 'Jump Junior Seaman Bell... Jump! If You Don't Jump Before I Get Up There, My Son, You Will Have My Size Twelve Boot Up Your Arse!'

The whole thing was finished in time for dinner. Lash was classified as a complete non-swimmer, and Dinger and Slattery were both designated as abandon-ship failures. There was a subtle difference apparently.

As we marched back through *Ganges* proper we saw more senior and experienced groups of sailors marching or doubling. They looked smart and relaxed and the Instructors had something to say to each other as they passed.

The list of those who had failed the swimming or jumping test was pinned to the mess noticeboard alongside the other lists. Whacker explained that when we were in *Ganges* proper, 'abandon ship failures' and 'non-swimmers' would be getting up an hour earlier than the rest of us for extra tuition.

In the afternoon, we were taught how to salute.

'Page 17 of your Naval Ratings Handbook explains when, why and who you salute,' explained Whacker. 'Page 18 shows you how to salute.'

Chapter 2, entitled Saluting, started ...

'The personal salute for Officers and Men of the Royal Navy in its present form is of comparatively recent origin, having been introduced in 1890 to conform with the Army.'

The Navy conforming with the Army? Surely that was the wrong way round.

We stood to attention at the end of our beds as Whacker showed us how to salute. 'Hands Palm Down, Bring The Tips Of The Fingers Of Your Right Hand Smartly To A Point Above Your Right Eye-Brow Whilst Keeping The Upper Arm Parallel To The Deck And In Line With Your Body. Longest Way Up ... One Two Three ... And Shortest Way Down. Class ... Class ... To The Front ... Salute!'

He adjusted us all and watched as we saluted him. There was a lot of arm and hand adjustment. 'Don't Bend You Head Sideways Lad! Head Straight And To The Front ... The Front LAD!'

The biggest surprise of the day was that we were going to be paid. The thought of being paid to be yelled at, mentally insulted, forced to walk outside in the freezing cold to have a shower, and to sew my name in unfashionable articles of clothing, just hadn't occurred to me.

Whacker called us to attention as a man in a peaked cap with a single gold ring on his cuff marched up the centre of the mess and waited until the sailor, who followed him at a respectful distance, unfolded a small table and placed a chair behind it at the top of the mess. Another sailor placed a wooden tray centrally on the table as the bloke with the gold ring sat down unsmiling.

Whacker strutted up and down the mess slapping his stick on his thigh. 'You Will Be Paid In Ships Book Number Order.' He stood and glared at us all. 'As Your Name Is Called, You Will March Smartly Up To The Pay Officers Table, Come Smartly To Attention, State In A Clear Voice Your Rank And Name, Salute And Hold Your Left Hand Out, Palm Uppermost.' He stopped in front of Blacky. 'Her Majesty Will Then Present You With A Small Buff Envelope Which The Paying Officer Will Place In Your Outstretched Left Hand. You Will Then Drop Your Salute, Turn Smartly To Your Right And March Smartly Back To Your Bed Space And Stand Quietly To Attention Until Everyone Has Been Paid. Understand?'

It was another of those questions that didn't require an answer. Whacker marched to the top of the mess and took up position alongside the table. 'In Your Envelope Will Be The Princely Sum Of One Pound and Five Shillings That Is Your Pocket Money For Two Weeks. Is That Clear?' He swiped his legs with his stick: I noticed a momentary wince.

Stunned silence.

'Good!' He turned smartly towards the Officer sitting behind his table and saluted. 'Hardy mess mustered for pay parade sir!'

The officer nodded. 'Carry on, Petty Officer.'

Whacker whipped his saluting arm to his side. 'Aye aye sir!' With a click of his heels he turned to his right and took up position to the right of the small table.

That had been a lot of information to take in at one go and inevitably there were a few mistakes as we each marched up to the table to collect our twenty five bob.

'When I Said Turn Smartly To Your Right ... I Meant Your Other Right, Lad!' Whacker yelled at one disoriented individual: I think it was Sydney who got it wrong this time.

Eventually the ritual of payment was complete, the man with the one gold ring departed and we stood there clutching our small buff envelopes.

'Put Your Envelopes In Your Pocket ... Trouser Pocket! And Fall-In Outside!'

Needless to say it was overcast and cold as we fell-in on the Parade-Ground outside the mess.

'Hardy Mess ... Hardy Mess ... Harrh ... Ten ... Shun!'

Our heels clicked together, reasonably well co-ordinated. We were getting better at this coming-to-attention business.

'Hardy Mess ... Stand ... Ahrt ... Ease! Let's Try That Again Shall We?'

We hadn't been that good after all.

'Hardy Mess ... Hardy Mess ... Harrh ... Ten ... Shun!'

We clicked.

'That's Better! Now Pay Attention. The More Intelligent Amongst You Will Have Realised That Her Majesty Has Not Given You All Your Money Today. As A Junior Seaman Second Class Her Majesty Will Pay You Forty Two Shillings And Three Pence Each And Every Week Before Standard Deductions. Goodness Know Why!' He almost smiled. 'However, As Junior Seamen Second Class Under Training At HMS Ganges You Will Only Receive Twelve Shillings And Six Pence Per Week In The Form Of Pocket Money.' He glared at us defiantly. 'This Will Be Sufficient For You To Purchase Those Luxury Items That Her Majesty Does Not Give You Free, Gratis And For Nothing ... Understand?'

Shocked and baffled silence.

'The Balance Of Your Pay Is Retained By Her Majesty. A Proportion Will Be Given To You So That You Can Enjoy Yourselves Whilst On Leave And Impress The Girls With Your Bulging Wallet ...'

Sniggers.

'The Balance Will Be Credited To Your Individual Pay Account When You Leave HMS Ganges.' Whacker took a deep breath and called himself to attention. 'In Appreciation Of Your First Pay Day We Will Double Around The Parade-Ground A Few Times To Say Thank You To Her Majesty! ... Hardy Mess ... Hardy Mess ... Tin To The Right In Threes ... Ryhta Tin! By The Ryhta Double March!'

So we did as instructed: we doubled around the Parade-Ground six times. Each time we came to the mast flying the white ensign, we were halted, stood to attention facing the mast and ordered to say, in a loud clear voice, 'Thank you for our money your Majesty!' Then we would go round again ... and again ... and again ... six times.

In the Annexe there is nowhere to spend money: no shops, no coffee bar, no nothing. That evening Whacker offered to look after any buff envelopes full of money until we were over in *Ganges* proper where there were places to spend our hard-earned cash. Some trusting individuals handed over their earnings but most of us, mainly those of us from the north of England, didn't. On the advice of one of the Arry boys, I kept hold of my money and put it into the money pocket of my belt and wore it to bed over my pyjamas. It was a sensible precaution, as I had no means of locking either my locker or my Little Brown Case.

Now is perhaps a good time to explain what my financial position was in January 1960. Currently the average house price was about £2,500 and the average family car cost about £1,000. Most people rented televisions, which on average cost about 9 shillings and 6 pence a week. A pint of good beer cost 1/3d, a packet of twenty cigarettes 3/4d. A gallon of petrol was 2/6d, a sliced white loaf was 5d and a Cadbury's Flake or a Mars Bar would set you back 6d.

In the information pack sent to my mother was a sheet headed 'NOTES ON THE PAY OF A JUNIOR IN *HMS GANGES*'. After stating that as a Second Class Junior, I would be earning six shillings a day it explained ...

> 'The Navy is bearing a heavy cost in keeping and training him, and it cannot therefore be expected that he should be much of a wage earner at this stage.'

It went on to explain my financial standing in some detail. As I was paid for seven days a week, 52 weeks of the year, my weekly wage was 42 shillings and three pence. Out of this were deductions: As a Junior under training, I paid 3/5d in National Health Insurance and was deducted 2/3d to cover the cost of sports, cinema and laundry (what laundry? I did my own laundry). So, after all deductions and my pocket money was taken into account, I had a weekly credit balance of one pound four shillings and a penny that I didn't get ... yet.

Normally we received in total silence whatever the serving chefs plonked on our plate. This evening, however, was the day that Tug plucked up courage to talk to one of them.

'What's this then sir?' Tug said, pointing to a large tray of something yellow and floppy.

'Don't call me sir,' replied the tall, sweaty chef as he waved a food-encrusted spatula in front of Tug's face.

'Sorry.'

The chef wiped a hand on his grubby white jacket. 'Call me chef.'

Tug swallowed, 'What's this then, chef?' He pointed again at the tray of yellow floppy stuff.

'Cheese and Stuff.'

From behind us Muddy explained. 'It's called 'Cheese Ush'. It's great, try some.'

The chef scooped up as much as the spatula could support in one sweep and held it over Tug's plate; slimy cheese and grease dripped over Tug's fingers. Before Tug could say anything a wodge of the yellow floppy stuff landed with a resounding thud on his plate. Globules of exploding grease splashed both of us. I reckoned the Cheese Ush 'sauce' would be difficult to wash out of our shirts if it had caught us.

'Next!' ordered the chef.

Despite its appearance, Royal Naval Cheese Ush proved to be delicious. Tug and I always had it throughout our time at *Ganges* whenever it was on offer.

Today's word was definitely either 'Spondoolicks' or 'Spendoolicks' both of which meant money. I also learned 'Yaffle', which meant to eat quickly and the memorable phrase of the day was 'Wind Your Ferkin Neck In!' that was yet another way of telling somebody to shut up.

Judging from the night-time sniffles, coughs and splutters it was inevitable that some of the mess members would fall ill. It was already becoming routine for Harry from Holbrook to contract a different ailment almost every other day. In particular Harry had problems with his feet and lower legs, which materialised whenever we had Parade Instruction. Within minutes of the start of a manoeuvre, he would stumble before grasping a foot or an ankle and collapsing onto the deck.

'And What Is The Matter With You Today, Junior Seaman Gregg?' Whacker asked one surprisingly sunny morning.

'Feels like a serious bout of cramp again sir.'

'Similar In Any Way To The Cramp You Suffered Last Time We Were On Parade ... And The Cramp You Suffered The Time Before ... And The Time Before That?'

'Worse this time sir,' Harry responded, grimacing.

Whacker detailed-off a few of the class to help a limping Harry to his feet and take him over to a spot alongside the Dining Hall door where they slumped him onto the deck. Whacker told JI Hawthorne to march the remainder of us to the opposite end of the Parade-Ground while he dealt with Harry.

Later that evening, as we were getting ready for bed and most of us were dressed in our pyjamas and deck shoes, Whacker burst in and took up a barrel-chested position at the bottom of Harry's bed. 'Junior Seaman Gregg, Put Your Boots On!'

'What sir?' said Harry, as he was putting the final touches to his top blanket.

'Don't You 'What' Me, Lad. Deaf As Well As Cramp-Prone Are We?'

'No sir.'

'Put Your Boots On, Lad!'

I watched, wondering what was about to happen.

Whacker waited. 'You Finished, Lad?'

'Yes sir.'

'Comfortable Are They, Lad ... The Boots?'

'Yes sir. I think so.'

'Don't Think So, Lad. Are They Comfortable Or Not?'

'Yes sir. Comfortable. Thank you sir.'

'Don't Thank Me, Lad. Thank Her Majesty For Giving You Such A Comfortable Pair Of Free Boots ... Gratis And For Nothing!'

'Yes sir.'

'Stand Correctly To Attention, Lad!'

Harry stood to attention at the bottom of his bed facing a palpitating Whacker.

'Now, Lad ... At The Order Quick March You Will March Smartly Up To The Top Of The Mess, Arms Swinging Exactly As You Have Been Taught ... Do You Understand Me So Far?'

'Yes sir.'

'When You Reach The Top Of The Mess You Will Instruct Yourself To 'Hay-bart-Tin' In The Correct Naval Manner ... And You Will March Back Down To The Bottom Of The Mess Where You Will Repeat The Process ... Understand, Junior Seaman Gregg?'

'Yes sir.'

'And You Will Continue To Do This Until I Tell You To Stop ... Is That Crystal Clear, Junior Seaman Gregg?'

'Yes sir.'

'Off You Go Then. Junior Seaman Gregg Right Turn! ... Quick Arghh March!'

Harry clattered up the mess while we all watched. At the end he turned about.

'I Didn't Hear You Tell Yourself To 'Hay-bart-Tin', Junior Seaman Gregg!'

'I did sir.'

'But I Didn't Hear You!' Harry marched passed a straight-backed Whacker 'Swing Your Arms, Young Man, Horizontal To The Deck ... Swing Those Arms!'

'At the bottom of the mess Harry mumbled 'About turn.'

'You!' Whacker pointed at Boydie. 'Go To The Top Of The Mess And Issue Junior Seaman Gregg With The Order To Hay-bart Turn When He Reaches You!' He swung around and told Spotty to do the same at the bottom of the mess. 'The Rest Of You ... Turn-In! You Will Continue With This Exercise Until I Return. Capiche, Junior Seaman Gregg?' He didn't wait for a reply and shouldered his way through the swing doors.

Within ten minutes, Harry started to grimace and drag one of his feet. Boydie and Spotty tried to encourage Harry in their different ways, but it didn't make any difference.

Some 20 minutes later Whacker rattled the doors and stood rigidly to attention at the bottom of the mess watching Harry limp up towards the top of the mess and back down towards him. 'Halt! Junior Seaman Gregg .... HALT!'

Harry stopped approximately opposite his bed space. He was leaning to one side.

'What's The Problem, Lad?'

'Cramp sir ... I think.'

'Socks And Boots Off Then, Lad, Let's Examine Your Plates Of Meat!'

With a pained expression on his face Harry sat on the edge of his bed, slowly removed his boots and peeled off his socks. There were some serious looking red markings on his feet but no more than the rest of us had, courtesy of Her Majesty's free footwear.

Whacker remained at a distance and pointed his stick at one of Harry's feet, 'That Looks Sore, Lad!'

'It is sir.'

'So, As Well As Cramp, Your Feet Are Also Damaged?'

'Yes sir.'

'Go And Wash Your Feet In Cold Fresh Water!' He swirled and pointed his stick at Spotty, 'JI Hawthorne Go With Him, Make Sure That He Washes Both Of His Feet Thoroughly With Cream Of Pussers 'Ard!'

Harry gently put a pair of plimsolls on and paddled away down the mess with a starboard limp. Spotty grabbed a block of Pusser's Hard from the cleaning locker and followed him out of the mess door towards the bathroom.

The phrase I liked today was 'Virgins On The Verge' which was used to describe anybody who couldn't immediately make a decision. It wasn't used regularly because we weren't allowed to make decisions ... as Junior Seamen Second Class.

Saturday was the same as the previous Saturday except Harry was missing. We later learned that Whacker had made Harry stand outside the bathroom in his bare feet while he waited for the duty Sick Berth Attendant to arrive. Harry was then whisked-away to the main Sick Bay for a full examination.

On Monday, Harry re-appeared smiling and told us that he was excused boots and Parade instruction for the foreseeable future. He had pulled off what was considered to be the most brilliant excuse; even the Arry boys were impressed. While the rest of us drilled, Harry was to do his sewing. As he could possibly finish all his kit well before everybody else, Whacker took a couple of my white fronts, one of my towels and a couple of items from someone else with a lengthy name and gave them to Harry with instructions to 'Sew Them In Before Doing Any More Of Yours!'

Day number 22 in the service of Queen and Country was 26 January. We thought we were getting on top of the Annexe routine when we were thrown sideways with the announcement that we were all to take part – no exceptions – in a boxing tournament. Whacker was smiling: this was obviously something that gave him particular pleasure. 'Fisticuffs ... Make Men Of You!' he told us. Based on our vital statistics taken at the Sick Bay, we were paired off according to a complicated height/weight *Ganges* formula. The fight programme was posted on the noticeboard and, after tea, we changed into our combat equipment: blue shirts, shorts and black plimsolls with no socks, and were marched the short distance to the Dining Hall. Where earlier there had been tables and chairs, there was now a full-sized boxing ring surrounded on all four sides by long wooden benches. A battalion of bent-nosed, cauliflower-eared PTIs flapped around punching the air and pretending to spar with each other. Away from everything, lounging against the Dining Hall walls, were the expectant faces of the Annexe galley staff and others who had obviously been invited to watch the latest batch of Nozzers knock ten-bells-of-shit out of each other.

We seated ourselves in mess groups and patiently waited to be told what to do. Once we were all correctly assembled, an enormous PTI with a chiselled chin took up position in the centre of the ring and took a deep, chest-expanding breath. 'My Name Is Chief Petty Officer PTI Ruffles. Welcome to 28 Recruitment's New Entry Boxing Tournament, The First Of The 1960 Spring Term.' He looked around. 'When Your Name Is Called You Will March Smartly To The Ring And Sit Yourself On The Corner Stool As Indicated By The Fight Referee. When The Order 'Box' Is Given You Will Try And Knock The Head Off Your Opponent Who Will Appear From The Opposite Corner. Each Fight Will Consist Of Three Rounds Of Two Minutes Duration ... Do You Understand?'

Murmurs and mumbles.

'As Spectators You Are Encouraged To Make As Much Noise As You Like During The Rounds. But You Are To Keep Silent ... Totally Silent Between Rounds.'

Each mess, orchestrated and conducted by their respective Instructors, chanted, yelled, whooped and stamped their feet. The atmosphere quickly became ultra-competitive, charged with choreographed hostility.

I was feeling more than a little apprehensive as I climbed under the ropes for my very first boxing bout. Seated in the opposite corner was a ginger-haired lad with white freckled arms who looked even more nervous than I was. Although I had never boxed before, thanks to my Granddad Ernest I had at least watched some boxing. My opponent obviously hadn't and after a first round during which I caught him with a couple of swinging right-handers he looked as though he was losing the will to fight. At the end of the round, Whacker offered words of encouragement as I sat slumped on my stool. 'Keep At It, Lad. Remember You're Fighting For The Glory Of Hardy Mess: The Glory Of Hardy Mess!' I came out for the second round with a different stance: it was an experiment, and I felt more comfortable leading with my left. Ginge was confused and I caught him with an opening combination that put him on the canvas. He stumbled to his feet on the count of eight. As he was cleaning his gloves I caught him with a good right hand and he went down again, banging his head hard on the canvas. The fight referee knelt down alongside my opponent, opened each of his eyes and decided that he was incapable of continuing. My right arm was raised and I was declared the winner. It was the first knock-out of the evening and there wasn't a scratch or a bruise on me.

As I left the ring, I removed my gloves and handed them over to Whacker who gave them to Harry, the next one from Keppel 9 mess on the fight list. I took my seat among my messmates, who patted me dutifully on my sweaty back. Harry suddenly contracted a severe bout of nervous stomach combined with a cramped ankle and a sympathetic PTI almost withdrew him before Whacker stepped in. After a brief exchange between them, Harry was escorted into the ring. He looked over at his opponent and gulped: his opponent slapped his gloves together, looking as though he had done this kind of thing before. As the bell rang Harry did nothing to defend himself and just stood in the centre of the ring while his opponent pummelled Harry to the canvas before Whacker had time to remove Harry's stool from the corner. The referee raised the victor's hand as a couple of PTIs dragged a comatose Harry out and onto an unoccupied bench at the back.

My second fight of the evening proved to be a much more difficult affair. I found myself pitted against a lad who had obviously boxed before. However, his first opponent had also done some boxing and he was helped into the ring sporting a partially closed eye. Being a 'Yorkshire gent' I clipped him around the head a few times, avoiding his injured eye. He in turn caught me with a couple of good punches and there was a point mid-way through the second round when he had me pinned on the ropes for half a minute or so. I changed my position for the third round and caught him with a couple of really good right-handers. All of a sudden he tired and I was eventually declared the points winner at the end of the bout.

As we shook hands he said 'Thanks, mate.'

'Any time.' I replied. What a strange exchange.

My third and final fight of the evening was against a boy who was spitting blood because he had, in the last half an hour, said farewell to some of his teeth. He could box, however, and I spent the first round avoiding everything he flung at me: he caught me with a couple of good ones but I managed to ride them reasonably well. Halfway through the second round he ran out of steam and I caught him with a perfect straight-arm jab that dumped him against the ropes. His mess Instructor quickly 'threw in the towel'.

I was at last able to sit back, relax and watch all the others display their pugilistic skills. By the end of the evening there had probably been 40 bouts, most of which lasted only a few minutes. There was a lot of teenage blood scattered about the place, not only on the participants but on the canvas of the ring, the ropes, the Dining Hall floor and the gloves. There was a good number of puffy lips and half-closed eyes. I had someone else's blood on my sports shirt and I wondered how I was going to wash it off successfully, such was my concern with my final Annexe kit muster that was only a few days away. As we made our way out, Whacker checked that Harry was breathing and instructed us to 'Leave Him Exactly Where He Is!'

After lights out Harry came shuffling in and quietly got into his bed. Nobody said anything.

My rafter word of the day was 'Fisticuffs!' which meant boxing. The phrase was 'Stroll On' which meant 'Well I never!'

A number of us were a bit delicate the following morning. Consequently, we weren't as quick getting out of bed as instructed and our tardiness earned us a short, but relatively static, period of early morning Parade Instruction. Whacker stood us to attention on the Parade-Ground outside the mess to watch all the other classes march over to the Galley for their breakfast. We were denied it.

We had a relaxing hour in the cinema before Stand-Easy. One of the films was about the Fleet Review held at the end of the Second World War in the Mediterranean. Apart from the long lines of ships it showed suntanned sailors wearing white uniforms, smiling and enjoying themselves. One day that will be me! There followed a couple of films on the benefits of physical exercise and a wholesome diet ... boring stuff. It did, however, emphasise the importance of a good breakfast.

Before dinner we enjoyed another hour of drill during which time we learned the complicated manoeuvre known as 'Eysah Right!' followed by 'Eysah ... Frint!' All done as the left foot hit the deck.

Then we had a period of sewing. I had been avoiding sewing my name on my belt as it was a piece of reinforced kit, manufactured from some kind of full-bodied material designed to resist a sharpened needle. However with the help of a thimble and something heavy to give it a good thwack I managed to red-silk my initials on the belt before dinner.

A couple of new phrases for today: 'Fill Yer Boots!' meaning help yourself and 'Thumb Up Bum, Mind In Neutral' which meant dreaming and was directed at me ... once.

Once again, the Dining Hall was transformed into Suffolk's equivalent of Madison Square Garden on Thursday evening. I had managed, by a liberal application of elbow-grease, to remove most of Tuesday's blood splatters from my sports shirt and was suitably attired and pumped-up for my semi-final bout. The lad in the opposite corner looked confident, bouncing up and down in fighter-like fashion, but I noticed that he had relatively short arms. I was in Rocky Marciano mode, confident that I could beat anybody. My opponent proved to be all show and little real substance: he had got a bye into this round because his previous opponent had been withdrawn. Early in the first round he caught me with a swinging right hand that blurred my vision for a few seconds. I retaliated with a manic, arm-flinging few minutes during which I caught him with a flukey haymaker that dumped him on his backside. My opponent waited until the Ref counted to ten, then slowly got to his feet, waved a dismissive hand at me, called me 'a jammy something or other' and retired to his corner, shoulders hunched.

I was in the finals of one of the four height/weight categories, one of the last eight in the entire Annexe. Because I was in the tallest height/weight group my fight was last on the schedule. My opponent was a lad who knew how to fight and over the course of six excruciating minutes gave me a real good pasting. I was grateful that we had professionals looking after us in our corners. At the end, after I had been declared the loser, the PTI who was acting as my second sat me down on my stool, splashed me with freezing cold water, slapped me around my bruised face, shone a torch in my eyes and told me to go and sit down with my messmates. Thanks a bunch! I found a chair in the corner and sat for a while, deep breathing and clutching a wodge of shiny toilet paper to my bleeding temple. I wanted my Mum and a warm, comforting bed.

I had a restorative, lukewarm shower ... and got myself ready for bed. As we all turned in, a smirking Whacker stood at the end of the mess holding a dark brown slab of something. He placed the slab on the mess table before strutted up and down the centre of the mess. With obvious pride, he informed us that Hardy mess had accumulated more boxing points than any of the others and had been awarded the New Entry Boxing Competition Cake, the most coveted cake in the Annexe. He made a ceremony of cutting the brown slab into slices. Lash, Taff and myself, who had reached the final or semi-final stage of the competition, were given first choice of pieces: I chose a crusty corner piece ... but it was disappointing. It was just rigid brown stuff: no jam or cream or anything. Not much of a trophy!

I crawled into bed that night with aches and pains all over. I had a large piece of Her Majesty's sticking plaster over a cut on my left temple and a piece of undigested *Ganges* cake lying in my stomach. There was no time for staring at the rafters tonight. Zonk! ... I was asleep.

H.M.S. GANGES

This is to certify that Junior 2 :- *P. N. Broadbent*

was a member of the *Hardy Mess* Boxing Team and

was Runner Up in The New Entry Boxing Competition of No. *28*

Recruitment during the *Spring* Term 19*60*.

H. Hacke
CAPTAIN, ROYAL NAVY.

My first certificate

On Friday morning Harry was sent home, classified as 'Unsuitable for Further Training'. Whacker referred to him as 'A Potential Sick-Bay-Ranger That The Navy Could Well Do Without!'

In a way I was sorry to see Harry go: I had hoped he would finish sewing my name on my belt for me while we were next on the Parade-Ground.

During Stand-Easy Whacker presented Lash, Taff and me with a certificate in front of the mustered mess members. It was a stiff card with a *Ganges* logo at the centre top and certified, in red ink script, that we had been Runners Up or Semi Finalists in the recruitments boxing competition. It was the first certificate of any kind I had ever been given.

Today was the day of our final Kit Muster that was to be inspected by the Commanding Officer of the Annexe. I was scared shitless. Before we laid our kit out we made our final visit to the slop room, the place where our kit was issued, where we were given a raincoat, complete with detachable lining, and a large khaki kit-bag. Once more we had to use our type to carefully mark the lining and our raincoat, which was inexplicably referred to as a Burberry. A series of larger block letters and numbers were placed on the mess table alongside a tray of black paint so that we could mark the bottom of our kit bags with our name and official number.

As I stood awaiting my inspection I wondered what the final decision on my sewing would be. Rumour had it that if anyone failed this kit muster, they would go through the Annexe routine again with the next batch of New Entries. Whacker didn't have to say anything else to justify the importance of this inspection.

We had all rehearsed what we had to say when the Commanding Officer confronted us.

My turn came. 'Junior Seamen Second Class Broadbent's kit ready for inspection sir.'

'What is your official number Junior Seaman Broadbent?' asked the Commanding Officer looking up at me.

'P-053653 ... sir.'

'Do you know what the 'P' stands for?' he asked as he picked up my blue sports shirt.

'Er, no sir.'

'Portsmouth,' he said.

'Thank you sir.'

Whacker glared at me.

'You have a long name I see. How is the sewing coming along?'

'Not yet finished sir ... completely.'

'Is that a blood stain on this sports shirt?'

'Yes sir.'

'Why is it not in the dirty pile?'

'Don't know sir.'

'Junior Seaman Broadbent was a finalist in the boxing tournament,' explained Whacker pointing to the certificate that he had insisted I lay out with my sports gear. 'His last fight was yesterday evening and was a bloody affair sir.'

'Whose blood is it?'

'Not sure sir.' I lied: it was probably mine.

'Well done.' The Commanding Officer used a stick to flick open some of my folded kit and paid particular attention to the marking of my name inside my newly acquired raincoat. 'Have you enjoyed your time in the Annexe?'

'Yes sir,' I lied again. Whacker had warned us about this question and told us how to answer it.

'Are you looking forward to moving to the Main Establishment?'

'Yes sir,' I lied for the third time.

'Good,' he turned to Whacker. 'Pass this Junior Seaman, but keep an eye on his sewing progress.'

'Stow Your Kit Away, Lad!' said Whacker before he moved on to the kit directly opposite mine. Bungy, who had the bed opposite, made a mess of his report and had to think long and hard to remember his official number. Bungy was always flustered when asked a direct question and he was border-line when it came to kit. His dirty pile was always one of the largest in the mess. When asked why it was so large he replied, as he always did. 'Dunno sir.'

That afternoon a list of kit muster failures was posted on the noticeboard. Bungy hadn't passed and, along with the two others, was told to lay his kit out again on the outside colonnade on Sunday. No matter how hard Bungy tried, he couldn't master the skills required to present an acceptable kit. To wash, dry, iron, fold and display everything were steps too far, despite the ultimate threat of having to lay his kit out on the centre of the Parade-Ground.

Mess allocations and specialisations for the Main Establishment were posted on the mess noticeboard that evening. I was to be in one of the two Seamanship classes in Keppel 9 mess. Others were to be trained as Communicators or Mechanical Engineers and accommodated in different messes. Since that first day in the Leeds Recruitment Office, I was determined to be a Seaman. I had ambition, although to be perfectly honest I didn't know exactly what I was letting myself in for. I certainly didn't realise that Her Majesty's Royal Navy was desperately short of Seamen in 1960.

We learned today that although we had all signed on for nine years, those nine years didn't start until our 18th birthday. That particular clause must have been tucked away in the small print of the contract signed by Mum. I would have to do more than 11 years ... by the time I was finished I would be 27 years old ... 27 years old. The sneaky bastards!

Shortly after lights out, Dinger Bell, in his strange Brummie accent, informed us all that it was only 84 days until Easter leave. That made us all reflect ... silently of course. Those 84 days were more than ten weeks ... 12 weeks actually.

Today's new word was 'Skirmishing'. Earlier in the day I, and a number of my messmates, had spent an hour picking up rubbish from the Parade-Ground as we had been caught having a nifty smoke in a designated no-smoking area. 'Skirmishing' meant picking up rubbish ... with your hands!

Later, staring at my rafter, I imagined all sorts of things seamanlike. Hoisting the anchor on the capstan, pulling in sails, peering out over blue horizons and having a smoke whilst watching a tropical sunset. I decided that it was time I got stuck into my copy of B.R. 67(1/51) Manual of Seamanship Vol 1 1951 which would no doubt tell me all I wanted to know about this Seamanship business.

At our third attempt, we won the cake for the best mess the following Saturday. I realised that all the messes had won a Saturday cake once: it was obviously planned that way. This yellowish cake was slightly better than the brown boxing cake; there was a thin layer of icing on top, but it sat heavily in the stomach nevertheless.

A number of us surreptitiously helped Bungy and a couple of others with their kit in preparation for tomorrow's re-inspection. One of the Arry boys even offered to spit and polish his boots. We kept an eye on them as they ironed and taped their final pieces. They didn't have time to reduce the dirty pile, so a few items were temporarily spirited away to make the pile look smaller. It only took a few hours before all three re-musters were able to stow a reasonably acceptable kit in their lockers ready for tomorrow.

Whacker was not in the best of moods that evening and when he said 'Pipe Down!' he meant it. Later, as I was musing over the events of the day and recalling my clutch of new Naval words and expressions, there was some raucous banter between a couple of lads at the top end of the mess. JI Hawthorne told them to 'Pipe down!' a couple of times but it only quietened things down temporarily.

The doors swung open and the lights were switched on. Whacker adopted an aggressive pose alongside Spotty's bed. 'All Of You Get Dressed, No 8s, Boots, Cap And Gaiters. Fall-in Outside The Mess ... Now! Chin-stays DARN!'

That was straightforward enough. He strolled to the top of the mess making sure that we were all out of bed and stopped opposite the beds of those that he had identified as the main noisemakers. 'You Two, Grab A Messmate Each And All Four Of You Carry Junior Seaman Gregg's Empty Bed And Its Mattress Out Onto The Parade-Ground.' He looked at his wristwatch. 'You Have Three Minutes And Twenty Seconds EXACTLY!'

It was cold outside and the wind was whipping around the colonnade. Whacker brought us to attention as the bed, carried by four bemused and sorrowful looking individuals, was placed on the Parade-Ground in front of us.

'The Rules Of This Night Time Exercise Are Simple.' Whacker was puffed-up and strutting, which we had learned was the sign of something seriously unpleasant. 'A Team Of Four ... One On Each Corner ... Will Carry The Bed Around The Perimeter Of The Parade-Ground ... At The Double!' He looked directly at Chinless. 'For Those Of You Who Don't Know What Perimeter Means, It Means Round The Edges. If The Mattress Falls Off The Bed, Or If The Bed Touches The Parade-ground, The Team Will Do An Extra Circuit. After Each Successful Circuit The Bed Will Be Handed Over To The Next Four ... And Then The Next Four Until You Have All Contributed To The Exercise. The Longer You Take ... The Longer You Will Be Outside. Understand?'

We all nodded. The four, who were still standing by the bed, were the first to go. It obviously wasn't easy judging by their pained expressions and stumbling gate.

'Remember, If The Bed Touches The Ground Or If The Mattress Falls Off, You'll Do An Extra Circuit!' yelled Whacker.

Spotty stood to one side staring at the top of the building opposite. I was part of the final team. By the time I grabbed my corner the remainder of the mess were a coughing, wheezing, spluttering heap. I never realised how heavy HM Government beds were. or how awkward it was to run while carrying one. We each had to hold a corner with one hand to avoid banging our shins against the iron legs. As a team we had a few problems to overcome. The mattress almost blew off on the Dining Hall straight and Lugs, on the port forward corner, smashed his starboard heel badly and almost stumbled as we approached the finishing line. We came to a breathless halt and lowered the bed.

'You Four.' That was us. 'Return Junior Seaman Gregg's Ex-Bed To Its Rightful Place In The Mess! Then Everybody Turn In ... AND BE QUIET!'

No rafter dreaming tonight.

Sunday 31 January was hopefully our last Sunday in the Annexe and our 27th day in service.

'If You Think That Last Night Was Bad, Then Imagine How More Difficult It Will Be Over In The Main Establishment Where The Parade-Ground Is Ten Times Bigger!' said Whacker. 'You May Not Fully Appreciate It Now, My Little Sparrows ... But I Have Taught You All An Important Lesson!'

Along with others, I nodded: although I didn't fully understand what the favour was. I had this huge bruise developing on the outside of my right calf, the bridge of my nose ached and the cut on my temple still throbbed. After breakfast we put on our best uniform. Naval blue serge had peculiar qualities; it attracted debris from the Admiralty fluff-cloud that permanently hovers somewhere above the Shotley Peninsular.

No matter how hard we tried it was impossible to rid our suits of contrasting fluff completely. One of the Arry boys showed us a trick with sticky tape, but there wasn't enough tape for us all.

Along with those from the other messes, we mustered on the Parade-Ground. Yesterday's rain puddles had frozen overnight. Whacker explained that what we were about to experience was called Divisions and was something that would take place, on a much larger scale, every morning in the Main Establishment. Today we would be inspected by the Senior Training Officer of the Annexe, following which we would march past the ceremonial podium 'As You 'Ave Already Been Taught!'

The Inspection by the Senior Training Officer of the Annexe was more prolonged and more critical than I expected. He actually passed judgment on the way we dressed, the cleanliness of our footwear, the amount of fluff on our blue serge uniforms, and the way we stood. Only the Arry boys went un-criticised. Me? I hadn't achieved a sufficiently reflective shine to my boots, my lanyard wasn't tucked in correctly and the bow on my cap tally 'Wasn't Up To The Required Ganges Standard!' Whacker had three notes to write alongside my name. The poor sod standing alongside me got 'picked up' for almost everything: the Senior Training Officer of the Annexe found something in one of his ears and instructed Whacker to remove it: which he did with the point of his pencil.

After prayers, conducted by a bloke wearing a grey and green cassock, the Senior Training Officer of the Annexe took to his podium and slowly scanned us. 'Now That You Have Almost Completed The First Part Of Your Royal Naval Training ...'

My inability to concentrate for any significant length of time kicked in and I immediately lost interest: I could see his mouth opening and closing but the message whizzed right over my head, north west towards somewhere distant.

The march-past was a torrid and uncoordinated affair. As we marched, we had to maintain a straight line as we passed the mast where the Senior Training Officer of the Annexe stood on a small polished wood podium ... and we had only practised this once before. Consequently our lines were 'Like A Dog's Hind Leg!'

and, along with all the other messes we had to 'Do That March Past AGAIN!' We were more ragged with each passing attempt. Eventually our first Divisions experience was terminated. A jaw-clenching Whacker was unimpressed.

After dinner Bungy and two others laid out their kits under the colonnade by the mess doors. We noticed with some satisfaction that there were a similar number of kit re-musters outside all the other messes.

We spent the afternoon packing our kit into our kit-bags. Our Number 8s were packed but not our best suit and associated equipment, because we were to enter the Main Establishment tomorrow morning wearing our blue serge uniform ... and marching.

Arry boys apart, nobody in Hardy mess had experienced living with 20 other boys for 24 hours a day, every day. I came from a small family that rarely gathered, so I had to rely on pure instinct to learn how to socialise and establish my position within a group. Initially those of us from Yorkshire had bonded, but that didn't last: Ganges friendships were built on firmer foundations than geography ... or which football team you supported.

Over in the Main Establishment, the entire recruitment would be rearranged; only a small percentage of Hardy mess would remain together and the whole process of establishing my position within a mess or class group would have to start all over again. At least Tug, Sydney, Bogey, Lash, Lugs, Johnnie, Muddy and Bungy were to be in Keppel 9 mess with me. Unfortunately so was Blacky.

5

THE REAL *GANGES*

Monday 1 February was the big transfer day. I'd been in the Royal Navy for exactly four weeks now; my boots no longer looked brand new. I checked that I'd left nothing behind in my locker or the drying room, secured my kit bag and left it on the colonnade with the others destined for Keppel 9 mess ... the real *Ganges*!

After breakfast we fell-in on the Parade-Ground and were reorganised into our new mess and class groups. About 40 of us were in Keppel 9: divided equally into two separate classes. We were marched around the Annexe Parade-Ground to co-ordinate ourselves, to get our arms swinging like proper Nozzers and to say a ceremonial farewell to the mast and its wind-swept white ensign. Then we marched smartly out of the corrugated green gates for the final time, down the road past the Shotley Gate Post Office and in through the open and welcoming gates of *HMS Ganges*. This was a significant step in my chosen career

path: from a closed community of about 100, I was now joining about 2,000 other Juniors under training.

We passed the mast on our left and as we wheeled right on to the Quarterdeck, an area with a large brass bell on a stand in the centre, we were doubled the short distance to the top of the Long Covered Way. We later learned that this part of *Ganges* was hallowed ground: officially only Officers and visitors were allowed to walk across the Quarterdeck. As we marched under the pitched entrance of the Long Covered Way I noticed the spanning legend 'FEAR GOD, HONOUR THE KING' in large white letters. Had I missed something? I distinctly remember going to the cinema to watch the Queen's Coronation ... and that was only seven years ago: don't tell me she'd kicked the bucket already. It was only days ago that we had given her three hearty cheers!

We were halted outside the fifth mess on the north side where a pair of Petty Officers stood ramrod straight, chests out, shoulders back and sharp eyed.

Whacker gave us his last series of orders 'Keppel Nine Mess Halt! ... Keppel Nine Mess Turn To The Left In Threes, Lefta Tin! Keppel Nine Mess ... Stand At Ease!' He then took a step to the rear that effectively handed control of us over to our new Petty Officers. The taller of the two, the one with the chiselled face and square jawline had a badge of crossed gun barrels on his arm and a double row of medal ribbons on his chest. His companion was smaller, rounder of face and a little younger. He had a badge like a spider's web on his arm and half a row of medal ribbons. The one with the most medal ribbons called us to attention, introduced himself and explained that he and his colleague would be responsible for our training during the rest of our time at *HMS Ganges*. Our training was going to be hard, necessarily so, because life at sea was hard. He ended by saying 'A Ganges Boy Is A Well-Trained Boy – Or Else!'

The younger, round-faced Petty Officer coughed and in a slightly less gravelly voice, explained to us that virtually all the *Ganges* Instructors were experienced men, who had many years of Naval experience behind them, in both peacetime and wartime. 'All Members Of The Instructional Staff At HMS Ganges

Are Experienced Men And Their Job Is To Mould You Into Fit, Professional Members Of The World's Finest Fighting Force: Her Majesty's Royal Navy. You Have A Lot To Learn In The Forthcoming Year. The Instructional Staff Will Work Tirelessly To Ensure That You Receive The Highest Standard Of Training And In Return, Will Expect The Same Standard Of Commitment From Each Of You.' He gave us the evil eye. 'You Joined HMS Ganges As Boys ... But You Will Leave HMS Ganges As Men ... Well Trained Young Men ... Ready To Join The Finest Navy In The World!'

The truck with our kit bags pulled up alongside the rubbish bins and the driver pipped his horn.

Once in the mess, with our kit bags on our chosen bed, our new Instructors told us to 'Stand At Ease!' at the foot of our beds. Apparently our new Divisional Officer had something to say to us.

'Keppel Nine Mess ... Atten ... Shun!' We all clapped our boot heels together at about the same time.

'Keppel Mine Mess Stand At Ease! Let's Try That Again Shall We?'

We hadn't been as good as I thought.

The Divisional Officer was a tall, refined-looking gentleman with two thick and one thin gold rings on the cuffs of his jacket. He didn't stand us at ease: instead he walked slowly up and down the centre of the mess eying us all up. At the bottom of the mess he turned. 'Welcome To Keppel Division.' He paced slowly up to the centre of the mess. 'Keppel Nine Mess Is Now Your Home. The Year Ahead Of You Is Going To Be The Toughest And Most Demanding Of Your Young Lives.' He paused for emphasis and smiled. 'Your Training Has To Be Tough ... If We Are To Continue To Produce The Best ... The Best Disciplined And Most Professional Sailors In The World!'

My concentration level was improving, I began to look around at Keppel 9 mess. I was a little irritated to see that Blacky had chosen a bed almost directly opposite mine. I re-focused.

'Those Of You Who Will Successfully Complete Your Training Will Join The Fleet As A Ganges-Trained Junior Seaman, And Be Justly Proud Of That Fact.' He removed his cap, rubbed the peak and replaced it. 'The Training Given To You At Ganges Will

Be Hard And Unrelenting.' He rubbed his hands together and nodded at the polished wooden deck. 'There May Be Times When You Will Feel That The Ganges Regime Is Too Hard For You To Continue. It Is At Those Times That You Will Draw On Your Colleagues' Resolve, Your Own Mental And Physical Reserves And Battle On.' He stood by the main doors and inhaled deeply. 'In Short: Keppel Nine Mess: Do As You Are Instructed, Keep Yourselves Out Of Trouble, Play Hard And Work Hard And You Will Benefit From All That HMS Ganges Has To Offer You. Carry On Petty Officer!'

Both Petty Officers saluted at slightly different times: our Divisional Officer turned smartly and left us.

Unofficially, we had already named the older Instructor 'Guns' and the younger one 'Spider', because of their badges.

Keppel Division had the top five messes on the north side of the Long Covered Way. The Divisional messes were numbered 1,3,5,7 & 9 and ours was number 9, the bottom one of the block and the one nearest to the rubbish compound. It was similar in layout to Hardy mess, but on a slightly larger scale. There was a washroom and night heads (with half doors) and a drying-room. The mess itself was freshly painted in Ministry cream and green paint and large enough to accommodate 40 of us, half on each side. Our main door opened onto the Long Covered Way, a long colonnade that covered the entrances to 20 or so messes on each side and sloped down from the Quarterdeck to the foreshore.

Our new Instructors checked us off on a list and asked us all how much more sewing we each had to do. Once the older of our Instructors had taken all the necessary notes, he smiled and offered an unexpected and surprising piece of advice to those of us with lengthy names. 'To Those Of You Who Have The Misfortune To Have Lengthy Family Names And Have Sewing Yet To Do ... Pull Your Fingers Out And Get On With It! I Don't Want To See Any Of You Wandering Aimlessly Around Camp Until You Have Sewn All Your Kit In ... Understand?'

'Yes sir,' we with lengthy surnames said.

The younger of the two Instructors then explained some basic kit rules. Now that we had marked every item of kit there was no excuse for losing or misplacing anything. It was a serious offence to be found in possession of any item of kit marked with anyone else's name. Punishable by six 'cuts' for the first offence.

From the top of the mess someone asked, 'What if we were collecting a friend's kit from the drying room or somewhere sir ... as a favour like?'

'Name?' Spider marched up the centre of the mess and came to a clicking halt at the foot of a bed. 'What Is Your Name, Lad?'

'Junior Seaman Second Class Borrowdale sir. Official num ...'

'What Was Your Question Again?'

'If I was collecting a friend's kit from the drying room or somewhere sir? ... as a favour like ...'

'If You Are Found In Possession Of Anyone's Kit Other Than Your Own You Will Be On A Charge! Is That Clear, Lad?'

'Yes sir. Thank you sir.'

'Can I Continue?'

'Yes sir.'

Spider then explained to us that all of our kit was to be stowed away in our lockers apart from our Little Brown Case and our caps which were to be stowed on the top of our lockers or on the bulkhead shelf closest to our bed. Our Burberry was to be rolled and taped correctly and hung on the pegs at the top end of the mess Any item of kit not stowed away correctly with name showing, left loafing or not removed from the drying room when dry would be placed in something called The Mess Scran Bag. Scran meant food in Yorkshire. In the Royal Navy, however, it was a place where sculled items of kit were placed and only recovered on payment of a fee. The Instructors of Keppel 9 mess had established an extortionate release fee of a tanner per article.

That first night I stared at the Keppel 9 rafters; they were different but served the same purpose. The mess smelled of paint and my bed was directly under an open window: big mistake. Tug and I once again had taken beds next to each other; I suppose subconsciously it made the change of mess a little less different.

The following day, while the rest of *Ganges* were at morning Divisions we were ordered to dress in blue PT gear in preparation for a tour of the camp.

Waiting for us outside the mess were a couple of chest-puffing PTIs. It looked as though our introductory *Ganges* tour was to involve something sporting.

Ganges was a huge place and we covered it all at a good 'double'. The main accommodation and administration blocks, gymnasium, swimming pool, shooting ranges, galley, dining hall and places of worship were all located on high ground surrounded by sports fields. All the specialist training blocks were situated down by the foreshore, as was the assault-course, running track, sick bay, a jetty and a variety of smaller buildings. The establishment comprised 12 divisions: apart from Keppel, the other 11 were Anson, Benbow, Blake, Collingwood, Drake, Duncan, Exmouth, Frobisher, Grenville, Hawke and Rodney. Surprisingly, Lord Nelson didn't have a division named after him ... but he had the large hall next to the Parade-Ground, so maybe that was good enough.

At the end of our tour, heavy legged, we shuffled back up the Long Covered Way to our bathroom: we had our bearings, we were caked in *Ganges* mud and knackered. Thankfully, our first lesson of the afternoon was school, which hopefully would be a sitting down job.

School, housed in an attractive Georgian brick building, was brilliant. Classrooms were different: we didn't have individual desks but sat behind rows of long continuous worktops. Our school Instructors treated us in a less aggressive, more academic manner. We had to sit to attention with our arms folded whenever an Officer entered the classroom and we had to remain like that until we were told to 'Carry On!' On the plus side we were allowed to smoke in the classroom. Ashtrays in a classroom, how agreeable was that? It was explained to us that during our time at *Ganges* we would all be taught mathematics, English and Naval History to a standard that would qualify us for promotion in future years. Lounging over my bench, enjoying my very first classroom smoke, this sounded OK. Those who couldn't reach the required level in Mathematics and written English would be placed into special 'cramming' classes. I looked forward to school: cigarettes certainly improved my concentration levels.

That evening, 'Guns' strolled the centre of the mess while issuing us with the latest in a long series of instructions. 'HMS Ganges Controls Two Thousand Teenage Boys By Ensuring That The Rules And Regulations Are Followed. My Job, And The Job Of All The Other Instructors, Is To Ensure That You Do Exactly As You Are Told! ... Exactly ... Any Questions?'

Deathly silence.

As more than half of us in the mess smoked, we weren't surprised that the first *Ganges* rule was smoking-related. We weren't allowed to smoke in the mess, while walking around the camp, in any of the instructional blocks, the gymnasium, the swimming pool, on, or near, any of the many sports pitches or the galley.

Dinger and Slattery, the Hardy mess mast and swimming failures, were not in Keppel 9. We did however have a couple of Mast Climbing failures: Conkers and Stumpy Borrowdale. Along with Lash we had another backward swimmer: a lad nicknamed Mucker. They each had a board to hang on the bottom of their beds and were all dragged out each morning an hour before the rest of us by a chest-puffing PTI and doubled away to the pool or the mast. I learned that the lad who occupied the bunk on my starboard side was Stuart Melrose: otherwise known as Misty.

I quickly got to grips with the routine. 'Charlie' sounded over the Tannoy at exactly 06:00. Once washed and dressed there was usually a mad scramble to do any last minute ironing, boot-polishing or gaiter-cleaning in readiness for Morning Divisions. At 06:45 we mustered outside the mess and were checked before being marched to the Central Mess Galley (CMG) for breakfast. With about 2,000 hungry Juniors converging simultaneously, the breakfast queues were always lengthy. *Ganges* had its own queue etiquette: whoever had been at *Ganges* the longest had priority, and could jump ahead of those with less seniority whenever the Duty Dining Hall Instructor's back was turned. During our first month everybody, including a good number of the Establishment's cockroaches, were senior to us, and we silently accepted the fact that everybody else was fed before us. Later, we ourselves would jump the queue at the expense of others, so over a year the 'queue rule' eventually evened itself out. Deep-fried bread, crispy bacon, crispy black sausages, tinned tomatoes, musical beans and bright yellow scrambled cackleberries were always available, as were cereals, pre-buttered slices of white bread, marmalade and excessively Bromided tea. Never coffee. We burned calories quickly at our age and, unconstrained by any healthy eating mumbo-jumbo, we all piled our plates as high as possible with just about everything that was warm and fried. What a wonderful word 'cackleberries' was.

We had mastered the business of saluting some weeks ago, but knowing exactly who to salute, and when, was more of a problem. 'Saluting Is A Mark Of Respect Shown To Military Commissioned Officers Of All Ranks. In The Royal Navy Officers Have Gold Rings On The Cuffs Of Their Uniform Jacket Or If They Are Wearing A Coat, Gold Stripes On Their Shoulder Tabs!' Spider explained.

Up until now we had not encountered Officers while on our own. When we had our kit inspected or when we were on Parade, we were well-schooled in exactly what to do and say. Decision-making was not yet one my skills, so when I was walking back to the mess on my own and our Divisional Officer was approaching me, I panicked. He was approaching on my left side ... so I saluted smartly with my left hand as he passed. He replied with a salute, took a few paces beyond me and turned. His medal-beribboned chest heaved as he explained, in simple, clipped English, that you saluted with the right hand, no matter what side the Officer was on.

During our first week in Keppel 9 the first class promotion occurred. It was impossible for our Class Instructors to control us for 24 hours a day. It was necessary therefore, for them to have some help, and this was provided by Juniors who were identified as having Leadership Potential. At this stage of our training it came as no surprise when Johnnie Ray, who excelled at absolutely everything, who had a wonderful kit, volunteered for everything and was a bit of a sniveller, was promoted. It was made clear to us that our first Leading Junior had absolute authority over us in the absence of the Class Instructors. To disobey an order given by a Leading Junior would be a punishable offence. Occasionally he would be responsible for marching the class to and from instruction. Johnnie was given a chevron stripe to sew onto his uniform sleeve and his khaki gaiters were replaced with white ones: identical to those worn by our Class Instructors. He could also go to the front of the CMG queue. This was a clever *Ganges* move, as queuing for food was one of the more irritating things we had to do ... three times a day.

Pay Parade took place after morning Divisions on alternate Thursdays. We queued in classes and arranged ourselves in Ships Book Number order. With 2,000 individuals lined up to be paid, all hell would break loose if anybody was out of sequence. Instructors patrolled the lines ensuring that we were in the correct order. Despite having just been subjected to an inspection during morning Divisions, this was another opportunity for Instructors to achieve their 'pick-up' quotas by finding fault with our standard of dress, length of hair, shininess of footwear and anything else they could invent. It wasn't easy to survive a Pay Parade without being noted in someone's book. Once at the front of the queue we would salute smartly (up ... two ... three ... down!) and state our name and ships book number while holding our left hand out. Someone would check the name above our left breast pocket before placing a small buff envelope onto our outstretched hand. We would then turn smartly to our right (click of the heels) and march smartly over to an adjacent dustbin where we removed our money from our envelope and checked that it was empty before dropping it in the bin. The pocket-money was just about worth the hassle. Out of our meagre payment we had to purchase soap, soap powder, writing paper, envelopes, writing implements, stamps etc. It left us with just barely enough spare to buy the occasional bar of chocolate and maybe a packet of fags. Apparently the toothpaste, razor blades and shoe polish we had been issued with when we joined, was a one-off: now we had to buy those as well.

Cleanliness is next to Godliness: we were told. The Laundry system in the Main Establishment was slightly better than that in the Annexe: we now had access to the NAAFI shop and a few washday luxuries. For the first time in or young lives we could wash our kit using the magic silver granules sold as washing powder but now officially known to us as dhoby-dust. Our washing skills were slightly improved thanks to 'Daz', or the slightly less expensive 'Omo' or 'Tide'. While we were allowed to wash our underwear, socks and handkerchiefs in the mess sinks, large-scale kit-washing was done at a prescribed time in the *Ganges* laundry. When instructed to do so, we removed the dirtiest of our two bed sheets ... always the bottom one ... and piled all our dirty kit onto it. Then we fell-in outside with our scrunched up sheet full of washing slung over our shoulders, to be marched to the Laundry. The scrubby Victorian vastness of the *Ganges* main laundry took my breath away: literally. It was a vast, damp vault, with a permanent, breath-catchingly clammy atmosphere. We would strip down to our shorts, remove our plimsolls and select a large butler sink alongside a mate. As in the Annexe, our Instructors strutted around in their Wellington boots, fine-tuning our washing technique; showing us how to identify those parts that required a special concentration of effort.

All washed items were inspected and approved before being hung in the large drying racks. The punishment for failing an inspection more than once was immersion in the huge *Ganges* cold-water bath. Sometimes the opportunity to bypass the inspection process presented itself and we would go straight to the drying racks, large eight-foot-high frameworks on rollers that were pulled out of a heated cabinet by an elderly Shotley civilian known to us as 'Rack Man'. If we were caught, we were subjected to the cold-water punishment with knobs on.

I remember a short exchanger of information with 'Rack Man'.

'What made you join the Navy then, son?'

'Wanted to see the world ... sir.'

'You're doing that then.'

What a job ... and what an observant arsehole!

Later that same evening we were required to collect our dried kit from the laundry. They were never fully dry: there was always a clammy feel about everything when removed from the drying racks. Any items not collected were placed in the main *Ganges* scran-bag. Consequently, we only forgot to collect our drying once! We were allowed to place items that were not completely dry, in the small mess drying room until the following morning when they had to be removed before breakfast. Any item left beyond this time was removed and placed in the mess scran-bag. Every week or so the mess scran-bag would be dumped on the mess table and items sold back to us for sixpence. All the money raised was apparently given to a Naval charity, the one specifically for the gratification and enjoyment of Petty Officer Instructors probably.

Although we had a single shower in the mess bathroom, our main bathroom was some distance away and shared with the top ten messes on our side of the Long Covered Way. It was always crowded at peak times and in the early months we would visit the bathroom as a protective group, because other classes, who had been in *Ganges* much longer than us, also used it. It had a large communal shower area with shower nozzles at close, almost intimate intervals around the walls. Generally we showered facing the wall.

Morning Divisions was something we hadn't suffered in the Annexe. Here, we had to gather each morning to witness the ceremonial of 'Colours' which signalled the official start of the real Naval day. At exactly 07:40 we would fall-in outside the mess in the dress of the day, which was No 8s, cap, boots and gaiters. Two unfortunate individuals, probably those who had last upset one of the Mess Instructors, were detailed as class markers and they doubled away early to report to the Parade GI.

We were marched to the edge of the Parade-Ground where we would be stood 'At Ease!' until the Parade GI (a man of upright posture with a stentorian voice that emanated from the very bowels of the earth) invited us to 'Fall-In On Your Class Markers!'

He would then call the parade to attention as the Bugle Band marched on to take up position in the centre, opposite the saluting dais.

'PARADE AH! ... Parade ah ... Turn To the Left in Threes ... Left ah Tin!'

A small team of individuals unfolded the large white ensign and organised its hoisting up to its position on the *Ganges* mast. This was 'Colours' and the sole reason we were here. As the ensign rose, I watched as it shook itself out, interested to see whether it would reach the top of the yardarm before or after the band had come to the end of the anthem. Instructors and Officers saluted: we didn't. We just stood silently to attention ... and watched. Then we were subjected to our first inspection of the day. The Divisional Officer, or his Assistant, would stand in front of each of us in turn and look us up and down. Our Instructor stood slightly to one side, book and pencil at the ready. Apart from the length of our hair, which was an obvious favourite, we could be picked up for how badly we had shaved, washed our neck, our ears or our cap. We were criticised for not polishing our boots or ironing our shirt well enough, or not pulling our shoulders back far enough. The Instructor's pencil flew over the flicked pages of his little book. Getting away without a comment of any kind rarely happened. The Church of England Padre would then mount the dais, the Parade GI would bellow 'Roman Catholics Fall Out!' and the RCs would double away to where the Catholic Priest waited around the side of Nelson Hall. Whilst the Church of England Padre said a short prayer, the RCs got stuck in to some seriously lengthy stuff and it was normal for the Catholics to rejoin the Parade long after the C of E bloke had departed his dais and was probably back in the Wardroom enjoying his breakfast. Each class would then march past the saluting dais in seniority, junior classes bringing up the rear of course. Accompanied by the strident noise of the Bugle Band each march-past was strictly observed. As each class approached the dais, the order 'Eyes ah Rayt!' was given, shortly followed by 'Eyes ah Frint!' The Parade GI would draw a circle in the air if a class failed to reach the prescribed standard and they would have to go round again. If a class didn't have to 'Go Round Again!' they would then march away to the first activity of the working day.

During February 1960, *Ganges* was hit by a serious flu epidemic. Wards in the sick quarters that had been shut since the second World War were opened. At the height of the epidemic, six of Keppel 9 mess were in sick bay. Fortunately I didn't catch it: I remember having had some strain of flu from Spain in my final year at school and maybe I was immune.

Sydney Harbour was the only one in the mess who received a daily letter from his girlfriend. As in the Annexe there were a couple of drawbacks to receiving mail ... Spider and Guns.

Today Spider was dishing out the mail. 'Junior Seaman Second Class Harbour: You Have Your Daily Letter From Diane!'

Sheepishly Sydney walked to the front with his hand partially outstretched. 'Yes sir. Thank you sir.'

'What Exactly Does This Boltop Nonsense Mean Then, Junior Seaman Harbour?' asked Spider

'Not sure exactly sir.'

'Not Sure? You Receive A Letter Every Day For The Past Two Weeks With 'BOLTOP' On The Back Accompanied By Loads And Loads Of Kissy-Kissy Crosses ... And You Don't Know What It Means. You Are Not Keeping Something From Me Are You, Junior Seaman Harbour?'

'No sir.'

'I'm Glad About That, Junior Seaman Harbour?'

'Yes sir.'

Blacky stuck his hand high in the air. 'I know sir. I know what BOLTOP means.'

'Tell Us All Then, Junior Seaman Yardley!'

'Better On Lips Than On Paper ... sir.'

'Better On Lips Than On Paper ... Goodness Junior Seaman Harbour ... That Sounds Like Serious Stuff To Me!'

'It's just ...'

'Don't You 'Just' Me, Young Man!'

'Sorry sir.'

Spider's eyes suddenly opened wide and he sniffed the air. 'Do I Also Detect A Whiff Of Feminine Perfume?' He sniffed the air again. 'Do I?' He glared at Sydney.

'Don't know sir,' said Sydney who by this time was standing to attention in front of Spider with his arms down by his sides and his thumbs in line with the seams of his trousers.

Spider sniffed the envelope. 'That, Junior Seaman Second Class Harbour,' he waved the envelope. 'Is Seriously Good Perfume. It's The Sort Of Perfume That A Real Woman Would Wear.'

Up until now my Manual of Seamanship had been sitting more or less undisturbed in my Little Brown Case. Apart from the Naval Ratings Handbook, it was the only book I had, and as an avid reader who had finished sewing-in his names, I now thumbed through its 290 pages. It revealed to me that this Seamanship lark was going to be a much more complicated affair than I originally thought. The text was dotted with phrases and terms that I hadn't come across before. The illustrations were interesting, particularly Fig 235 that illustrated the types of buoys and 'buoyage of Port Liberty'. Apparently the height of a lighthouse light above something called M.H.W.S was 60 feet. I was never going to become Captain of my own ship if I had to remember all this.

Before we got down to the real detailed Seamanship training we were issued with a Seaman's clasp knife which incorporated a spike and which we had to wear on a clean lanyard around our waist when we were doing anything vaguely seaman-like. Surprisingly it had already been stamped with our name. It was a punishable offence to wear it at any other time, or to have it on a dirty lanyard. We were also issued with our own personalised pair of scissors, our names having been engraved on the inside of one of the blades. Why we had not been issued with these earlier was a mystery and was never explained, because we never asked. Maybe it was for the same reason that the doors on the Annexe heads had been removed. The scissors weren't very sharp and if you got them wet they went rusty: or maybe it was just my pair.

The waters of the River Stour and Orwell looked particularly uninviting for our first boatwork lesson; storm-grey, windswept and disturbed. It was mid February, freezing cold, and the saturated Suffolk rain was coming at us from all directions. We were mustered outside the oilskin Cabooch where piles of the sticky, damp, smelly monstrosities were stored. Dressed in sports gear that was already rain-soaked, I encapsulated myself within the inflexible folds of my first Royal Naval oilskin. It was reluctant to move with me ... it moved after me; some considerable time after me. The hem of it rubbed painfully against my exposed pink legs. Although the rain ran off the main body of the oilskin well enough, it gushed in the neck and the sleeves, neither of which were designed to be watertight.

We were then issued with an oar each; weighty lengths of sun-bleached wood. Alongside the small jetty were a number of Whalers and Cutters and at the very end, a large vessel called an MFV (Motor Fishing Vessel). I hoped that we weren't going to have row that. The Arry boys knew what this boatwork stuff was all about and during our short trudge down the jetty, our oar bouncing on our shoulders, they explained to the rest of us the differences between the Whaler and the Cutter. Apparently the Whaler was much lighter than the Cutter and more streamlined but had fewer crew. It had something to do with the shape and the width of the thing. We were split into teams of five, a team for each Whaler, and set about learning all about the rudiments of 'pulling' Navy style.

A well-wrapped-up Guns explained. 'The Navy Do Not Row They PULL!'

What was difficult was understanding and remembering the various orders. 'Ship Your Oars!' was the first order, followed by 'Give Way Together!' which got us away from the jetty and out into open water. The oars were heavy and well used, but it was surprising how quickly we got our whaler moving across the disturbed grey waters, despite the oilskins. Royal Navy Pulling wasn't that difficult to master; it was just a matter of positioning yourself right, bracing your lower body correctly and applying as much force as was required. We 'Backed Together!', 'Held Water!' and 'Stroked Together!' over and over again until we all understood what the heck Guns was on about. There were a number of other classes undergoing instruction at the same time and our first hour-long pulling session ended with one of the other Instructors challenging Guns and Spider to a race.

Guns accepted the challenge enthusiastically and steered us towards the official start line. I noticed Tug was in Spider's crew: at the front. Over a course, which felt much longer than it actually was, we put as much of our backs into it as we could and came a very poor third, three boat-lengths behind Spider's boat and way behind our original challenger. A hoarse Guns steered us back to the jetty and the croaked order 'Boat Your Oars!' signalled the end of our first boatwork session. After a solid hour's pulling, muscles that I didn't know existed were saying something unpleasant to me. Guns explained to Spider, so that we could hear, that we had caught an unexpected number of 'crabs' otherwise we would have fared better. Personally I never saw any crabs: I liked crab, mashed up with vinegar and sugar with toasted brown bread. Muddy explained to me that a Naval crab was a badly applied oar blade.

Despite being cold, wet and miserable I now knew what thwarts, rowlocks, duck-boards, poppets and stretchers were.

Later the same day we were given our first tour of the Seamanship Block located down by the foreshore. It consisted of a number of classrooms each dedicated to a different Seamanship speciality. One contained a model of a ship's forecastle with all its anchoring equipment. Another had a model of Replenishment at Sea equipment; a mind-bogglingly complicated arrangement of ropes, pipes and pulleys that were used to bring an oil tanker alongside so that fuel could be transferred from one ship to another. There was another room dedicated to boats and their davits, and more rooms dedicated to knot-tying, scuttle management, splicing, shackling, lifting, sailing, pulling and a whole lot of other Seamanship-related activities. The rope-work room was to become one of my favourite places. As an ex-Cub, I already knew how to tie some knots and it was something I was good at.

Behind the Seamanship block was an area known as the heaving-line ground where we were taught how to throw a weighted rope. A heaving-line was a length of hairy rope with a weighted monkey's-fist on one end and according to Guns, the ability to throw a good one would be a much valued skill once we were at sea. It would guarantee an individual a prominent position when coming alongside a jetty or another ship. When handled correctly and swung in the prescribed Royal Naval manner, with a following wind, it could be thrown a significant distance. Of course, *Ganges* held regular 'heaving-line' competitions: there was even a trophy in the shape of a Monkey's Fist that was presented to the winning Division. As a cricketer I had a good arm and once I had learned to distribute the coils correctly I became quite good at throwing a heaving line. Unfortunately, none of 173 class ever got close to the 70-foot-plus distance achieved by other *Ganges* boys that were noted on an adjacent board and marked on the heaving-line ground with painted spikes.

The Seamanship block was within spitting distance of three flights of concrete steps known as Faith, Hope and Charity. They were the quickest way of getting from the foreshore back to the accommodation and the establishment's favourite punishment venue. Already we had seen many a class doubling up and down them.

Guns decided that it was time that 173 class had a trial run, to acquaint ourselves with the only females in *HMS Ganges*. There was a smile on his face as he marched us along the foreshore towards the jetty and stopped us at the bottom of Faith. 'Let Me Introduce You To The Three Ganges Ladies Known As Faith, Hope And Charity.' He waved an introductory arm. 'They Love To Acquaint Themselves With Young, Energetic Boys!'

I looked up towards the top of Charity. She looked to be a long way away to me.

Guns looked at his watch. 'As We Have A Spare Five Minutes I Have Decided That You Should Become Better Acquainted With Our Three Attractive Ladies. Claaasss ... Claaasss .... Rayta Wheel ... Double March!'

We then doubled up the three flights of concrete steps. It was unexpectedly difficult: by the time we'd reached the top of Charity we were all breathing heavily. Coming back down wasn't as easy as it may sound as some of the steps were relatively short and we had to adopt a rather unnatural foot position in order to avoid stumbling arse-over-tit. The inflexibility of our relatively new boots didn't help. We did three 'ascents' and two 'descents' whilst a heavy-breathing Guns strolled his way to the top. He halted us at the top of Charity. It was a lung-searing warning: in the forthcoming weeks even the mention of Faith, Hope or ferkin Charity would be enough to quieten us down, but as boisterous teenagers we had short memories and it wouldn't be that long before we lost our virginity to the three ladies for real.

We were a bit chatty on the night after our first Boatwork lesson. Normally, after lights out, we'd wrap ourselves silently up in our blankets, isolated within our own private world: a pre-*Ganges* world where life was less hectic and much simpler. But tonight was different and it was almost midnight before we all began to doze off.

Then all hell broke loose. The mess lights were switched on and an unknown Petty Officer marched up and down the mess. 'Want To Make Some Noise, Do We? Lots Of Excess Energy, Have We? Get Out Of Your Stinking Pits, Fall-In Outside In Pyjamas, Socks, Boots And Cap! Chop Bloody Chop. Get Your Arses In Gear! Fall-In Outside In Two Minutes ... Two Minutes ... Don't Worry About Gaiters!'

I struggled into yesterday's socks and my boots, placed a cap on my head and fell-in outside the mess. It was a typically cold February Suffolk night and the combined mess breath hung above us all like a white shroud in the still, ice-cold air of the Long Covered Way.

'Chin-Stays Down!'

I removed my cap, tucked the irritating chin-stay under my quivering chin and waited. Lash hadn't sewn his chin-stay in correctly and in his panic it had come undone.

'Leave It, Lad, Leave It. Name?'

'Junior Seaman Second Class Trainer sir.'

'A Trainer Under Training Eh?'

'Yes sir. Suppose so.'

'Don't You Suppose Me, Young Man!'

'Aye aye sir.'

When our unknown Petty Officer turned his back, Lash gave him a two-finger salute and stuck his tongue out.

We were marched up to the Quarterdeck where we were stood to attention while our unknown Petty Officer disappeared into the Officer of the Day's Office. We christened him Pig-Face because he looked like one. The cold was starting to bite. Fortunately I was wearing my Pussers underpants beneath my pyjamas, but not everybody had put them on. Johnnie didn't: he stood buttocks clenched with the front of his pyjama trousers gaping and un-gaping in the wind.

Eventually Pig-Face, accompanied by an Officer, resplendent in a comfortably warm-looking double-breasted overcoat, appeared and exchanged a few private words.

Pig-Face coughed. 'Leading Junior, March Them Back To The Mess. You Will All Collect Your Own Burberry ... And Fall-In Outside Again! You 'Ave Two Minutes ... Two Minutes Only!'

Our Burberrys were hung up at the back of the mess, rolled and taped as for Saturday rounds. It was a mad scramble for us each to find our own as our names were hidden in the folds. The constant torrent of abuse from Pig-Face accompanied by high-pitched shrieks from Johnnie kept us on the move. Now cocooned within our raincoats, we were marched up to the Quarterdeck, this time doubled across it and brought to a halt by the mast. Conker's face fell: our first reaction was that we were going to climb the ferkin mast dressed in our raincoat, pyjamas, caps with chin-stay down and boots ... but thankfully we were wrong.

'Class Ah ... Class ... Tin To The Right In Threes ... Right Tin! Class ... Class ... Double March!'

We doubled around the two-acre Parade-Ground twice. By the time we were halfway round our first circuit I discovered yet another design fault with Pussers underpants: they required a substantial covering to prevent them from total collapse ... and pyjama bottoms weren't up to the job. I had a mental image of the rest of *Ganges*, snuggled up and asleep. After our second, and thankfully final circuit, we were doubled back to the Long Covered Way. Standing to attention outside our mess, shrouded once again in a youthful white swirling cloud of exhaled, spluttered air, we were told how lucky we were that the Officer of the Day had insisted that we doubled around the Parade-Ground in our raincoats.

'If It Had Been Up To Me,' spluttered Pig-Face. 'You Would Have Done It In Your Sperm-Encrusted Pyjamas And Nothing Else!'

We looked longingly at the interior of our cosy, warm mess and didn't pay too much attention when Pig-Face told us that he would be in communication with our class Petty Officers who would no doubt dish out further punishment the following day.

Never had a bed seemed so wonderful.

Guns woke us well before Charlie the following morning by enthusiastically clattering the mess dustbin with his stick. 'Fall-In Outside In White Sports Gear, White Plimsolls ... Two Minutes ... Two Minutes! ... I Don't Like Being Prised Out Of My Nice Warm Hammock At This Time In The Morning!'

'Doesn't sleep in a hammock does he?' I asked the Arry boy in the bed opposite as I wriggled into my white sports shirt.

'He's probably having us on.'

We stood outside the mess in three straight ranks, once again shrouded in plumes of white exhaled mist in the early morning dark. If anything, it was much colder than earlier: my exposed legs were the first part of me to go numb.

'I'll Teach You To Get Me Out Of My Hammock At This Time In The Morning. Leading Junior Ray, March Them Up To The Mast And Wait For Me There!'

Not the ferkin mast again! As we doubled across the Quarterdeck we could see that the lights at the bottom of the mast had been switched on. In the shadow of the figurehead were a pair of star-jumping PTIs, no doubt overjoyed to be bouncing up and down at this time in the morning. The upper reaches of the mast looked spooky and threatening in the crisp-cold morning light. There was a sparkling film of frost on the upper yards and the rigging.

Guns arrived. He took a deep breath. 'If I Had My Way You Would All Be Up And Over The Half-Moon, But Much Against My Better Judgement We Have To Abandon That Idea. Instead We Will Introduce You To The Joys Of One Of My Favourite Places ... A Place Known As Laundry Hill.'

Stumpy and Conkers, our mast-climbing failures, looked relieved. 'Tin To The Right In Threes ... Right Tin! ... Doouble March!'

And off we went, back across the Quarterdeck, down a section of the Long Covered Way and 'Righta Wheeeeled!' towards the laundry, accompanied by our pair of bouncing, bellowing, un-breakfasted PTIs.

Although Laundry Hill had a reputation, at first glance it didn't look that bad. It took time, and a few ascents and descents, before I began to appreciate its reputation as a punishing gradient. Our PTIs stationed themselves at strategic points along the length of the hill and by a combination of profanity, slapping and kicking, kept us moving up and down until a milky, pale yellow Suffolk glow, from somewhere in the north-east, slowly appeared. My starboard plimsoll rubbed painfully on my right heel.

Back in the mess all our lockers had been emptied. Our kit was strewn everywhere.

'I Want Everything Stowed Neatly In Your Lockers Before You Go To Breakfast!' bellowed Guns as he kicked items of kit within reach of his foot. 'Wash, Dress And Fall-In Outside In Quarter Of An Hour!'

It was Tuesday 16 February in the year of our Lord 1960: my 16th birthday. I decided to keep that piece of information to myself. On top of everything else, I didn't fancy 'bumps' or whatever the Naval equivalent was.

A few days later I received a birthday card from Mum: inside she had written that she wished me, among other things, 'A wonderful time on my special day'. If only she knew!

Our 15-minute mid-morning Stand-Easy break was taken outside the mess and followed a now set routine. When practical, a couple of class members were dispatched to the CMG ten minutes early to collect Kye and Stickies (currant buns) which were ready outside the mess by the time the rest of us arrived. This was the time when I enjoyed my first legal smoke of the day. We were allowed to smoke during our free time later in the day, but I never knew exactly where I could do it without getting into trouble; so, along with others, I became adept at cupping a lit cigarette in my hands so that it wasn't seen. A sneaky smoke was always the most satisfying one.

One February Stand-Easy Spider had us 'Fall-in!' and brought to attention. Our half-smoked cigarettes were nipped. He stood facing us and smiled his special 'bad-news' smile.

'Today, Monday The Twenty-Second Of February Nineteen Sixty, We Celebrate Something Special. Today, Her Majesty The Queen ... God Bless Her ... Has Issued An Instruction To Their Lords At The Admiralty.' He looked skywards. 'An Instruction To Her Favourite And most Senior Armed Service ... The Royal Navy ... To Splice-The-Mainbrace To Celebrate The Birth Of Her Fourth Child Last Friday The Nineteenth of February: As Yet

An Unnamed Boy And Third In Line To The Throne. Only The Royal Navy Can Splice-The-Mainbrace.' He paused and marched purposefully up and down the front rank smiling to himself. 'For All Eligible Personnel Who Draw Their Rum Ration They Will Be Issued With An Extra Tot Of Rum Today. Those Ineligible To Draw Rum Will Be Issued With Two Extra Free Bottles Of Beer.'

All of a sudden Spider had my undivided attention.

'You, My Lucky Lads, As Junior Seaman Second Class Under Training, Have Not Been Forgotten By Her Majesty. You Have Been Issued Free, Gratis And For Nothing ... An Extra Sticky Bun.'

Our expression said it all.

'In Appreciation Of Her Majesty's Gift, Keppel Nine Mess Will Give Her Majesty Three Rousing Cheers. Hip Hip ...'

'Hooray,' we slurred ... three times.

Our second instructional period of the morning finished about 12:30 and we were marched to the GMG for dinner. Our starting position in the queue depended on what the last instructional period had been and whether we had to change back into the dress-of-the-day. Normally Keppel 9 mess ended up near the back. Dinner always consisted of good, honest high-calorie food that would fill the stomachs of young lads who had probably spent the entire morning in physical activity of some kind or other. There was always a main course with a choice of vegetables followed by a suet-based duff (pudding) of some kind with sturdy, lacklustre custard. The only problem was, because we were either late or queue-jumped in the early days, we spent most of our dinner-hour queuing and by the time we got back to the mess it was time to fall-in again to be marched to our first lesson of the afternoon.

Wednesday afternoons were different: Wednesday was the day of the week when Ganges showed its competitive colours. The Navy traditionally called Wednesday afternoon a 'Make & Mend'. Guns explained that it was a term dating back to the days of sail to denote a period allocated so that the crew could make or repair any items of kit, or ship's equipment. At Ganges however, 'Make & Mend' meant Inter-Divisional sporting competition. On the acres of green, well-maintained sports fields, in the pool, on the rivers, on the assault-course, on the heaving-line ground, in the boxing ring and almost everywhere else something competitive took place with organised enthusiasm. Where more than one person congregated, a hyper-ventilating, enthusiastic PTI could be found attempting to turn something into a competition. The whole place was awash with running on the spot, star-jumping or bouncing PTIs screaming encouragement to anybody within earshot.

Cups, platters, salvers, trophies or just plain points, were awarded for absolutely everything: from football to blowing a Bosun's call there was a Ganges standard, a league table and an inevitable champion. There were some strange bits of chrome-wear: the 'Pulling Regatta Aggregate Trophy', known as the PRAT Trophy, and The Bunn Whaler Cup among them.

At the opposite end of the trophy scale, there were a number of unofficial prizes that weren't recognised by the establishment. Much celebrated was recognition for the longest, continual fart; second only in popularity to the celebrity status accorded to the individual who produced the largest unbroken turd.

Before tea at 17:30 we had to be showered and dressed in night-clothing (number 2 suits with a silk but no collar), our hair had to be combed and our boots shiny. We were marched to the Parade-Ground and mustered as for morning Divisions, quickly inspected to make sure that we were dressed correctly and then marched to the CMG for tea. As the Junior class at the back of the parade, this procedure ensured that we got our last meal of the day after everybody else. Tea was another substantial, hot meal sometimes finished off with a slab of fruitcake. It was a much more relaxed affair than dinner and we were allowed to amble back to the mess when we'd finished, sometimes clasping a filched slice of fruit cake to nibble later. The removal of any food from the CMG was highly illegal ... and punishable of course.

After tea, our evenings were filled with washing and ironing in preparation for the following day and for any of the many kit musters. Boots had to be polished, gaiters cleaned and the mess, the bathroom and night heads cleaned and ready for the evening inspection carried out by either the Duty Instructor or an Officer at 19:30. At this time, everybody was expected to be in the mess and correctly dressed. The level of inspection depended solely on the mood of the Inspector and was yet another opportunity for an individual's appearance, general demeanour, bed-space and locker to be scrutinised. After evening rounds those fortunate enough to have time on their hands would go for a walk or just lie on their beds. There wasn't much else to do: there was no radio to listen to, or TV to watch.

It was during this relatively relaxing time that I became addicted to my Seamanship Manual. I'd read and re-read the section on Ships' Boats; their types, classes and purpose. I couldn't wait for my next Boatwork session. I'd also studied the small section on page 100 about heaving-line throwing, but it didn't tell me anymore than I already knew. I was naturally drawn to the section on bends and hitches, but found it difficult to understand exactly when the Navy required us to use a Clove Hitch, a Running Bowline, a Sheepshank or a Monkey's fist. In the Navy it wasn't just a matter of knowing how to tie a knot but when to tie it. At the moment, splicing was an unknown quantity but it was something that I was to become fascinated with: not only did it have a purpose, it was strangely attractive when done correctly.

The mess lights were switched off at 21:30 and Class Instructors ensured that we were all correctly pyjama'd and turned-in. The final head-count of the day was taken and all hell would break loose if anyone was missing. Although it never happened in Keppel 9, there were stories of individuals using the evening's short period of free time to escape.

After my success in the Annexe boxing tournament I fancied myself as a bit of a boxer. During February I occasionally changed into my sports gear after evening rounds and went over to the gym to knock the hell out of a swinging punch-bag for half an hour or so. However, after the bag outwitted me two evenings in a row I decided that boxing wasn't for me.

At the end of our first month, 173 class were marched over to the Shooting Range, to be faced with a Chief Petty Officer with crossed gun badges on each side of his collar. His boots were huge and they crunched the gravel with practiced ease. 'My Name Is Chief Petty Officer Gunnery Instructor Remington. This Is My Shooting Range ... My Shooting Range. You Are Here This Morning So That We Can Assess Your Capabilities As Marksmen.'

This would be good.

'Follow My Instructions Without Hesitation And To The Letter And We Will Have No Problems. Don't Forget: You Are Not Playing Cowboys And Indians Now. This is for real ... Clear so Far?

We nodded.

'IS THAT CLEAR SO FAR?'

We mumbled 'Yes.'

'Good! You Will Shortly Be Given A Rifle And Ten Rounds Of Live Ammunition ... Clear?'

We mumbled something.

'IS THAT CLEAR?'

We jumped. 'Yes sir.'

'These Are Not Bullets,' Chief Petty Officer Remington bellowed as he held one up for us all to see. 'In Her Majesty's Armed Services These Are Referred To As Rounds: And These Are Real. What Are They Called?'

'Rounds,' we all repeated.

'AND ARE THEY REAL?'

'Yes sir.'

'Correct ... Real Rounds. Don't Let Me Hear Anybody Refer To Them As Bullets.'

Most of us nodded. There were some who replied 'Yes sir.'

'And Are They Real?'

Mumbles. Under my breath, I said, 'If you say so sir!'

We were ushered onto the shooting range where we were each given a Lee Enfield .303 rifle, and shown how to load and shoot it. Our targets were life-size pictures of scowling German soldiers running towards us brandishing serious-looking firearms.

As a child, roaming the badlands of West Yorkshire, my two-fingered gun had picked-off many a Red Indian; I had been famous in Pudsey for my accuracy over long distances. However, given a real weapon, my hand-eye coordination was rubbish: either that or I'd been given a badly misaligned gun. I managed to hit my target twice with my ten rounds, but missed my German completely. Upon close inspection, I found two holes on my target, one on the very edge of his right boot and one a few inches from his right shoulder. I suppose they could have strayed from my neighbour Norman who hadn't managed to hit his target at all.

The group who had scored zero or less were ushered away to a darkened corner of the range as far away from the advancing German hordes as possible. We were classified as useless and marked down as individuals who should never be entrusted with a weapon of any kind. Naturally, there was a small group who were crack shots and were able to stop their German with tight groups of puncture holes to heart or head. From a respectful distance, we who lacked the necessary coordination watched admiringly as our class marksmen were issued with more and more rounds until the very best in the class were identified. Bogey had an uncannily accurate eye and he subsequently became a valued member of the *Ganges* Shooting Team.

That night, staring at the rafters, I wondered if I had a real problem with my hand-eye coordination. I would have liked to have been a crack shot today: that would be something interesting to tell Mum. It would also impress my brother who, at the age of 12, was fascinated with guns. I suppose that during the last war the Ministry of Defence procured loads of German targets. That's obviously why, 16 years later, we were still shooting at life-sized pictures of our aggressive-looking European allies.

The following day started badly. The Petty Officer charged with getting Keppel 9 mess out of bed that morning was a particularly foul-mouthed individual who had much to say about our parentage ... or lack of it. Once he had pulled the blankets off two boys who slept near to the main door, the rest of us swung our legs out and sat on the edge of our beds staring blankly at the floor while this unknown and unpleasant individual passed us by.

He stopped at the foot of Bungy's bed and bellowed 'Last Man Up! Take Your Hand From Inside Your Pyjamas. Report To The Gatehouse Correctly Dressed In Ten Minutes!' He looked inside the hat that was on top of Bungy's locker and noted down his name. Mention of the Gatehouse was all we needed to get us moving.

Bungy eventually joined us at breakfast. When asked what had happened he explained that he had mustered at the Gatehouse along with about a dozen others and pushed a car down the road outside.

'Push a car?'

'To start it,' explained Bungy.

'Why?'

'To ferkin start the bastard of course,' explained one of the Arry boys.

'Did you get it to start then?' asked Tug.

'Yeah.'

'Whose car was it then?'

'I don't know.'

Conkers and Stumpy strolled into the CMG for breakfast with a pronounced swagger. They had both successfully scaled the mast to the Half Moon. Congratulations all round: it was the only good part of a bad day.

The day normally got off on the wrong foot whenever it started with Parade Instruction. Today it was particularly difficult as it was the day that Spider was scheduled to teach us how to 'Form Two Ranks'. Transforming ourselves from the standard three ranks into two ranks proved to be an unbelievably complicated manoeuvre. It took an hour of continuous practice before we could all understand what we were required to do. Spider was beside himself with frustration at times. We were pleased when a couple were detailed off to collect the Kye and Stickies, as this signalled the impending end to the session.

As we doubled back to the mess, Guns joined us at the top of the Long Covered Way. We were halted outside the mess and instead of being dismissed, we were kept standing to attention outside in the still-cold wind while both our Instructors disappeared inside.

They emerged stone-faced.

Spider coughed into his hand. 'It's An Unofficial Tradition In HMS Ganges That On The Morning That A Class Leave For The Last And Final Time ... They Trash A Mess. Today Keppel 9 Mess Has Been Trashed. When You Have Finished Your Kye And Bun You Will Enter The Mess And Tidy It Up As Though Nothing Has Happened. I Shall Inform The Schoolie That You Will Be A Quarter Of An Hour Late For Your Next Instructional Period!'

I didn't enjoy my Kye or my bun. Guns and Spider stood guard by the door to prevent any of us entering. They issued whispered instructions to Johnnie.

The mess looked like a bomb had hit it. All the beds were upside down, bedding and the contents of all the lockers were strewn over the deck. Our Burberrys had been removed from the pegs at the back of the mess and thrown over the rafters. All the damp kit that had been in the Drying Room had been removed and placed in the bathroom sinks that were now full of water: white items had been mixed with blue items. The spit-kid and the mess dustbin were in the night heads full of wet kit. Tins of metal polish from the cleaning-locker had been opened and their contents poured over our polished wood deck. Windows had been smeared with Pusser's Hard.

It took me ages to find some of my kit. I didn't have the time to fold and stow everything away correctly, so I just dumped everything I could find on top of my bed before we were marched off to school. The first cigarette of the morning's classroom session was a welcome and calming smoke. It took all of our dinner hour and most of the evening to return Keppel 9 to something like its normal state before evening rounds. The Bluebell (metal polish) was the most difficult thing to sort out: once the dried liquid was removed from the deck the smell lingered for ages. Then of course the stained part of the deck had to be re-polished by an army of us on our knees. Personally I had to re-wash a blue collar and a sea jersey and I never did find one of my blue woollen sports socks.

There was no time to spend staring at the rafters this evening: I went straight to sleep, my raw hands still smelling of dried, ingrained Bluebell.

After breakfast on Saturday morning we mustered outside and allocated our cleaning duties. The worst job by a nautical mile was cleaning the heads: they didn't clean themselves apparently. This job was usually given to whoever had upset the Instructor most during the previous week. A small team were responsible for cleaning the rafters: Conkers and Stumpy, our newly accredited mast climbers, were the newest recruits to the rafter team. Another group would clean windows inside and out. There would also be teams allocated to the washroom, the drying room, the Divisional Office, the outside front and the deck. The mess gear (dustbin, a pair of spitkids and the 'fanny') were polished until they shone inside and out.

By 10:00 the mess and associated outbuildings sparkled, all the windows were open at a precise angle, locker doors were similarly opened, mattress covers pulled tight and a sparkly clean towel draped over the end of the bed with name showing. Each mess had their own individual way of making a tiddly display of something or other on locker-tops. We learned that these final touches were known as Naval Bullshit, and it was these little

Keppel 9 mess cleaned and ready for your inspection SIR

things that made the difference between winning and losing a cake. 'Bullshit Baffles Brains, Lad,' so our Mess Instructors proclaimed. 'Bullshit Baffles Brains!'

Did it really? Hopefully someone would explain to me exactly what Bullshit was.

Once the mess was ready for inspection Johnnie remained behind with one of the Class Instructors while the rest of us were allowed to wander off to the Gym which, on Saturday mornings, was turned into a makeshift cinema. A large white screen was dropped at one end and rows of those low, uncomfortable gymnasium benches were arranged as seats.

On both sides of the screen was a large piece of advice entitled 'IF' written by a bloke called Rudyard Kipling.

It started ...

If you can keep your head when all about you
Are losing theirs and blaming it on you,
If you can trust yourself when all men doubt you,

And finished on the opposite side of the screen with ...

Yours is the Earth and everything that's in it,
And – which is more – you'll be a Man, my son!

The films that were shown were generally rubbish, but we all enjoyed the cartoons. The Royal Navy had a surprisingly strange relationship with a bloke called Fred Quimby. Fred was the artistic director of the Tom & Jerry cartoons and whenever his name appeared on a cartoon credit, the audience would shout 'Good Old Fred!' It was the Royal Navy's way of acknowledging Fred's genius, but why this verbal salute always took place, I don't know. In later years I would salute Fred in the prescribed Royal Naval manner while watching cartoons with my embarrassed young children.

When the cartoons were over there was a rush to the Gym's exit door and a cigarette. I would then either go for a stroll down by the foreshore, or for a swim. It was a strange relaxing time, about an hour before dinner. Saturday dinner was at 12:30, after which we all returned to our mess to find out if we had won a Mess Cleanliness cake or not. More often than not, Keppel 9 mess hadn't. We got a cake if we won; if we didn't, we got a bollocking. It was as simple as that. It took a while for us to figure out that the cakes were awarded in a complicated Ganges rotation ... and weren't that nice anyway.

Saturday afternoon was ours, providing we weren't under some form of punishment or didn't have a lengthy name to sew-in. According to Guns there were plenty of 'Pursuits' available to us should we be interested in obtaining our Duke of Edinburgh silver award. In reality, nobody in Keppel 9 mess bothered with any of them at this early stage of our training. One strange activity that was only read about in the Shotley Magazine was The Ganges Hornpipe Display Team: nobody I knew had ever seen it, heard of it, or believed it really existed.

Despite having an extra quarter of an hour in bed, Sundays were a panic as we had to prepare for Sunday Divisions, which followed the same pattern as weekday Divisions except we paraded in our best suit with silk, lanyard, tape, collar, un-wrinkled jacket and a sparkly clean cap. The prospect of being picked up for something that was not perfect was vastly increased and individually we were fortunate if we got away without a comment being logged in the Instructor's book. The Class Instructor was always equipped with a small brush to remove any dandruff or stray hair from collars and a pair of non-Naval issue scissors, the type that could cut, to trim the ends of anything that was ragged or considered too long, including stray strands of hair.

After the march past, providing we didn't have to 'Go Round Again!', we were marched to church. Outside the C of E church the Roman Catholics were dismissed to make their own way to their place of worship. Big mistake. This anomaly in the Ganges routine gave those of us who were genuine RCs, along with a large band of temporary converts, the opportunity to slope off somewhere for an hour or so. As long as we weren't spotted by anybody in authority, we generally got away with it. On a good day I went for a stroll along the foreshore: I don't remember what I did on bad days: maybe I went to church.

After our first Sunday Divisions, still dressed in our best suits, we were marched over to Mr Fisk's Studio, a small building from where he operated a very profitable photographic business. This morning he took a head and shoulder portrait of each of us. As the official camp photographer, we would get used to seeing Fiskie and his camera everywhere. No matter where we were, on Divisions, in the pool, up the mast, on the athletics track, rowing a boat or in the laundry, he would invariably appear with his clicking camera. He would print all his pictures, number them and display them on a board inside his studio. For a relatively small amount we could order a print of any picture on which we appeared. During my time at *Ganges* I amassed pictures of myself doing my dhobying, swimming, clambering over hurdles on the assault course, or as part of a team of some kind.

Once every six weeks or so, Sunday Divisions became a Passing-Out-Parade when families of those who were about to leave *Ganges* were invited to see what their young men were up to. Seating was arranged in front of Nelson Hall for all the visitors: it was a rare chance for us to see girls; girls in bright colours

... girls! As one of the junior classes we were at the back of the parade, so in our early days we never got to see or appreciate much up close.

Sunday dinner, the best meal of the week, was the time when I discovered new things to eat, like a swede and turnip combination, onion rings, small Yorkshire puddings and a red jelly sauce. We always had a crumble on Sunday – apple, rhubarb, raspberry or blackberry – and I learned that the best and most crumbly bits were those darker brown pieces in the corners of the tray.

The time after Sunday dinner was ours. By the end of February, I was on top of my sewing ... only the dreaded belt to finish. It was the only day when we were allowed to officially lie on our beds and when the weather was bad I buried myself in the pages of that literary masterpiece: the Manual of Seamanship Volume 1.

Monday Morning's Stand-Easy Kye sometimes had a hint of Bluebell to it, if we hadn't scrubbed the fanny out with enough fresh water after Saturday morning rounds. It probably contributed to keeping us regular however.

In late February we heard rumours that there had been a Forces Pay Review and that everybody was to be awarded an increase in basic pay. This was great and unexpected news: I'd only been in the service of Queen and Country for a couple of months ... and I was already eligible for an increase in my salary.

Spider fell us in outside the mess, unfolded a sheet of paper and smiled briefly. This was not a good sign. 'Her Majesty Has Agreed To Increase The Pay Of Those Who Perform A Useful And Effective Role Within Her Armed Services!'

This sounded interesting. Concentration button locked-in.

Spider coughed into has clenched hand, sniffed and grimaced, 'I Have To Inform You That Juniors Under Training Are Not Yet Classified As Useful Or Effective And Will Therefore Not Receive Any Significant Increase In Pay.'

Bugger! In reality, it came as no surprise. Any increase in my pay after only two months in the job was never going to happen was it?

Inevitably, collectively and individually we were beginning to fall foul of one of the countless *Ganges* rules. Doubling was the most popular and most applied form of instant punishment. Doubling with a Lee Enfield rifle on your shoulder was an uncomfortable variation: we'd done that a couple of times already, particularly when we transgressed while on the Parade-Ground. As a class we were finding a relatively short doubling session on the flat easy to deal with, but *Ganges* did have its ascents and descents in the form of Laundry Hill, the Long Covered Way itself and, the Instructional staff's favourite, Faith Hope and Charity. At any time of the day there was at least one *Ganges* class pounding up and down one of them. A sadistic twist was doubling while wearing our gas mask. Fortunately, this was banned the following year following a fatal incident.

Once a term each Division had an Expedition (Exped) weekend. The whole Division took part and we were divided into teams headed by Officers from the Instructor Branch or Divisional Instructors. It was a welcome opportunity to escape the surroundings and routine of *Ganges* for a couple of days. It was also a chance for members of the Division, both senior and junior, to work together. The Exped could be a trip on the MFV to somewhere exotic on the Suffolk coast, a rowing or sailing event up one of the rivers, an initiative test to see how far you could get without any money, or just a simple route march.

My first Exped was a simple route march to a campsite in the lower south-eastern reaches. Our group was headed by the Class Instructor from Keppel 3 mess: a Chief Petty Officer known unofficially by the name of 'Bracket' as he had bandy legs.

The Ganges Exped Store was similar to the Oilskin Store, except that it reeked of well-worn foul-weather clothing and the strange smell given off by damp, heavy canvas tents and groundsheets. Another unfriendly civilian, who had probably seen many, many thousands of Nozzers parade past his counter over the years, assessed our size and tossed a khaki rucksack and a set of limp, well-worn foul-weather clothing at us. We were also issued with a survival ration pack and some well-used eating utensils. Once outside we checked that our jacket and trousers fitted reasonably well. It was a Ganges tradition, of course, that the junior members of the Division had the job of carrying the heaviest loads, so the tents, groundsheets, pegs and associated rigging were evenly distributed amongst those of us from Keppel 9. We were told to take only essential items of personal kit and washing items with us, in order to reduce our load.

With sprightly step and some nervous humour we boarded the MFV which took us across the River Stour to a point just west of Harwich, where I set foot on the shore of Essex for the first time in my life. Then, as an out-of-step bunch, we trudged through the narrow lanes of a weather-beaten and thankfully very flat countryside. It was typical March weather, windy and cold with the ever-present threat of rain and other miseries in the air. For hours we made our slovenly way down quiet country lanes, high-hedged on both sides, devoid of traffic and through slumbering, seemingly deserted villages. I was looking forward to seeing a girl or two now that I was outside in the normal world: it was disappointing that all the Essex girls obviously knew that it was the Keppel's Exped weekend and had decided to lock themselves away.

We had a couple of laneside breaks when we were told exactly what to eat and drink. I suppose this was the sensible thing to do as Bracket had obviously done this particular Exped before. I noticed that the strange little can opener that came as part of my ration pack had on it a Pusser's arrow and the date 1944. Whatever was inside my tins and cans could be as old as me, so it was with some trepidation that I opened one of the small gold coloured tins marked 'Processed Cheese'. Those who had been on Exped before assured me that the contents would be OK and they were right. Despite playfully resisting my initial removal attempts, it tasted wonderfully mature: I liked cheese. The drizzly Essex rain turned to wet and heavy rain as the afternoon progressed and I realised that Naval Exped clothing was useless when pitted against anything wet: I had pyjamas that were probably more weatherproof.

Eventually we made it to our allocated camping ground at a place called Furze Hill to the west of Mistley village and just short of Manningtree. Tired and wet, and lacking much of the humour with which we'd started, we pitched the tents. The Essex light was disappearing behind western treetops as those of us from Keppel 9 mess were sent to scavenge for firewood while the more senior members of the team were organising cooking facilities and ensuring that the tents were erected correctly.

As total darkness descended like a cold, damp blanket we got a reasonably good fire going and sat around it watching the contents of a large can slowly come to a simmer. Water from a nearby stream was boiled and we made refreshingly drinkable tea; probably the first bromide-free brew I'd had since leaving Manchester. The dishing out of the stew, to which we had all contributed a can of meat, vegetables or processed cheese, was supervised by Bracket. It was delicious. With full stomachs we retired to our smelly tents. There were three or four of us to each tent and I crawled into my musty sleeping bag without taking my damp, tacky No 8s off. Knackered as I was, I didn't sleep immediately and lay awake staring at the ridge of the tent for a while.

I must have dropped off because we were awakened from profound slumber by someone banging on the side of our tent. I crawled out to find everybody standing around wrapped in their sleeping bags and watching a couple of grovelling Badge Boys from the senior mess trying to re-erect Bracket's tent. Apparently the guy ropes had been undone and the tent pegs removed. A note was found tied to an adjacent tent on which was scrawled a message from another Exped group who had identified themselves as the Wrabness Team, whoever they were. Bracket, who had the luxury of a tent to himself, explained that we should have posted sentries as he had half-expected something like this to happen. After Bracket's tent was re-rigged, Keppel 9 mess were given early morning sentry duties, while the rest of the team retired to their warmish sleeping bags. As sentries we wrapped our sleeping bags around our shoulders and stared out into the bleak, cold countryside, looking for the next wave of marauding individuals bent on waywardness. They never returned: obviously they had done what they wanted to do and were now snuggled up somewhere – even a Junior Seaman Second Class could figure that one out. As sentries, we didn't get relieved and remained watchful as the chalky pale light slowly emerged from behind the trees to the east of us. A couple of lads designated as early morning fire-lighters managed to relight last night's fire. As we were already halfway there, we sentries were eventually detailed-off to scavenge for yet more firewood.

After a hearty breakfast of stewed sausages and beans, we packed everything up and prepared to leave. Unwashed and unshaven, we ensured that everything was left as it was when we arrived and that the fire was properly extinguished: the early morning drizzle ensured that it was well and truly out.

I was given Bracket's groundsheet to carry back to *Ganges*: it was a little lighter than the one I had carried yesterday. Once again, the parents of all the available Essex girls had decided to keep their daughters safely indoors as we retraced our way back towards Harwich. Probably the right decision, as we were a dishevelled looking bunch.

Back at *Ganges*, a late Exped Sunday tea was organised for us. We queued in our damp, smelly foul-weather gear in a strangely empty CMG and piled our plates as high as possible. Before entering the mess we left all our foul smelling Exped clothing out on the Long Covered Way to be dealt with the following morning.

As we returned our Exped gear the following morning we learned that the Wrabness Team had been headed by Guns and the night attack had only been done for a laugh. Bracket pledged retaliation next term.

Mum made a point of writing to me at least once a month. It was always nice to hear what was going on at home: normal things like who was shopping in our shop, why Tony was getting into trouble etc. There were a small number of individuals in the mess who never crowded round the Instructor when the mail was being dished out because they never appeared to get any. Surprisingly, it was generally the Arry boys, and it was many months before I learned that *TS Arethusa* was a training ship for some abandoned or orphaned boys. I looked on them in a very different way from then on. My red letters from Christina always generated some comments from Spider or Guns.

'Is She A Looker Then, This Girl Of Yours From Switzerland?' asked Guns

'Yes sir.'

'Age?'

'Sixteen I think ... sir.'

'Legal Then?'

'Pardon sir?'

'Legal Then?'

'Suppose so, yes sir.'

'Is It A Serious Relationship?'

'Not really sir.'

'Platonic Then?'

'Pardon sir?'

'Don't Tell Me You've Never Heard Of Plato, Lad.'

I sniffed and went for it. 'It's a dog sir.'

'A What!'

'A dog sir: in the Disney cartoons.'

'You Are Kidding Me Aren't You, Junior Seaman Broadbent?'

'Yes sir ... sorry sir. Plato was a bloke: a Greek philosopher sir.' Thank goodness for a Grammar School education.

'You Can All Read Your Letters In Your Own Time. Fall-In Outside!'

Occasionally some of us received a parcel-chit that meant we had a parcel to collect from the Mail Office. I suppose I was luckier than most: having a shop meant that a lot of the goodies were available to Mum at wholesale prices. My Spring Term parcel proved popular: it contained loads of sweets and chocolates and anything else Mum thought I might be short of. Parcels had to be opened in the presence of the Regulating Petty Officer who ran the Mail Office. He would examine the contents and remove any item he considered unsuitable. After-shave lotion was always confiscated. It may have been a coincidence but the chins of our Instructors always smelled good, if you had the misfortune to get that close. It was rumoured that after-shave lotion contained alcohol and there had been instances of rowdy, sweet smelling over-indulgence amongst Juniors in the past ... allegedly.

From the top corner of the mess came a sound of someone kicking the front of his locker. It was Conkers from Wolverhampton who was screaming 'Bloody, sh-shit arsed women, bloody sh-shit arsed ba-bastard women, bloody ferkin Phyllis ... the ferkin cow ... the c-cow!'

Conkers was red-faced, slavering and stuttering. A couple of his neighbours eventually calmed him down. He wasn't the first one in Keppel 9 mess to receive a 'Dear John' but he was the first to take his frustrations out on his locker door.

'We were g-going to get engaged at Easter.'

'You weren't were you?'

'Yeah.'

'Blimey.'

'Fat ... fat c-cow.'

'Was she fat ... was she?' asked Lash.

'Phyllis? ... a little bit yeah!'

'You're better off without her then, Conkers.'

'Suppose I ferkin am yeah. I am, yeah.'

'Don't want to get engaged to a fatty do ya?'

'Suppose not no.' He gave the swinging locker door another kick.

'Bloody women eh, Conkers?'

'Bloody ferkin ... women!'

'You tell her, Conkers!' shouted someone from further down the mess. 'You ferkin tell her!'

The following day Conkers was informed that he had been charged 15 shillings for the repair of his locker door.

I'd told Christina in my last letter that we had had our portrait photographs taken, and she asked me, very politely, if I could send her one. I promised to send her one of the small ones: the large one I had reserved for Mum.

The gymnasium was a large imposing place that always smelt of horse liniment, a popular PTI enhancement. For those with no sporting interest it was a place of torture, hardship and pain. All the walls were covered with the dreaded wall-bars and dangling from the ceiling were the equally frightful climbing ropes. Climbing the rigging remained a Naval tradition and it was considered important that every one of us were able to climb a rope to the rafters and to control our descent without suffering rope burns. Nothing happened at a normal civilised pace in the Gymnasium; everything was done 'Atta Double!, 'Fast-As-You-Can!' or 'Chop-Chop!' It was here that we were introduced to team games like deck-football and deck hockey, both fast five-a-side games during which the prospect of injury was guaranteed.

After a couple of circuits one day in the gym PTI Shawcross invited us to participate in an unscheduled run across the Suffolk countryside. Bugger!

'Two And A Half Miles That's All,' Short-arse said, as he bounced up and down on the spot outside the gym in front of us, a tired and mainly disinterested group of shivering individuals. 'Two And A Half Miles ... I Normally Do Twice That Before Breakfast Each Morning!'

Well, bully for you Short-arse!

He did a swift about-turn and sprinted off towards a distant hedge. The Navy had a way of controlling a group of unenthusiastic Cross-country runners. The leader would lead by setting a pace slightly faster than our best runner. Two other PTIs, known as 'arse-kickers', would bring up the rear and, with a range of physical and verbal incentives, encourage the tail-enders of the class to 'Bunch Up There!'

After what seemed like hours of me placing one disinterested foot in front of the other we were halted in a narrow lane alongside a wreck of a barn.

'That's It Then!' Short-arse did a couple of star jumps followed by a series of upper-torso twists. 'Two And A Half Miles In A Little Under Twenty Four Minutes. That's The Time For Your Last Man To Arrive!' He bounced up and down as though he was on elastic. 'Not Good Enough! Not Good Enough!' He sprinted on the spot. 'The More Observant Of You Will Have Noticed That We Are Not Back At Our Favourite Gymnasium!' He bent over to touch his toes, up again and down again. 'So We'll Make Our Own Way Back ... At Your Own Pace!' He did a series of star jumps followed by another lengthy on-the-spot sprint. 'The Gymnasium Is Exactly Two And A Half Miles Distant And I Would Like To Welcome You Back There In Less Than Twenty Minutes.' He held his stop watch aloft. 'In A Lot Less Than Twenty Minutes ... Off You Go ... Thata Way!'

So off we went, retracing our strides alongside Suffolk hedgerows, down muddied tracks and across cold stubbled fields. The *Ganges* mast in the far distance, slowly, ever so slowly, looming larger. As expected Blacky brought up the rear. PTI Short-arse referred to him as the Canteen Boat. Eventually Blacky staggered into the space outside the gym, almost collapsing just ahead of a couple of palpitating PTI arse-kickers.

PTI Short-arse was running on the spot. 'Anybody Who Wants To Be Sick ... Do It On The Rose Bush!' he shouted and waved an arm towards an isolated rose stem that looked as though it was had struggled out of a small piece of brown earth by the side of a gymnasium wall. 'The Only Carrot Coloured Rose Bush In The Country! ... It's Called The Pride Of Shotley Gate!'

'What was our time sir?' asked someone who was interested.

Short-arse looked at his watch, shook it and put it to his ear.

'Don't Know Lad. Appears To Have Stopped.'

We left Blacky retching over the rose bush as Johnnie marched us back to the mess.

For some inexplicable reason my name appeared on a hockey team sheet one Wednesday afternoon and I lined up to take my position against a team from Collingwood Division. In West Yorkshire, blokes didn't play hockey: hockey was a girls' game.

Half an hour each way was far too long. This hockey business proved to be the most aggressive and potentially damaging of games when played under *Ganges* rules and I vowed never to play it again. Hockey sticks wielded by over enthusiastic and undisciplined opponents could, and did, injure you.

The pool was my environment, and my breaststroke talent was recognised at our first Inter-Divisional Swimming Gala. For quite a few months my name was on the large poolside record board for both the 25 and 50 yards breaststroke: until a boy from the recruitment before me, bettered my 50-yard time by a second and a half.

Surprisingly, we still had Lash and Mucker who hadn't yet passed the Naval swimming test. They were woken early two or three times a week and with towel and trunks under their arms were marched over to the swimming pool before breakfast. *Ganges* was understandably proud of the fact that nobody ever completed their training without having learned

No 1 breast-stroker!

to swim, or jump off the top board, which I suppose simulated jumping over the side of a sinking ship. I still couldn't understand why anybody who was unable to swim would join the Navy in the first place.

Both Lash and Mucker were a little embarrassed about their extra lessons, but we did check on their progress. Lash had almost cracked the swimming and treading water bit. Mucker suffered from something called water-vertigo and froze when he got anywhere near the top diving board.

After tea one day we were marched over to Mr Fisk's place to collect our portrait photographs. We waited in a well-behaved, patient line while we were handed a brown envelope which contained one large photograph on a hinged board and four smaller copies: they were free. Then we were marched back to the mess. My picture was awful; my expression was terrible, my hair too short, the lighting was unsympathetic, in fact it didn't look like me at all.

Most of the other lads were happy with their portraits. I was undecided whether to send one of the smaller ones to Christina as promised. I convinced myself that maybe she would see something in the picture that I didn't, so I sent her one.

I don't know what it was like in other parts of England, but in Pudsey in the 1950s, I rarely heard foul language; certainly it was never heard at home or at school. The *Ganges* environment was completely different: from the moment we arrived in the Annexe, all boys together and out of earshot of our parents, our method of communication developed a colour and character all of its own. Apart from all the Naval slang and terminology, we quickly learned how to swear. I lay in bed at night pondering the meaning and/or significance of some of the previous day's expletives. Gradually however, I realised that you didn't necessarily have to know what each word meant or signified, you just had to know where to place it in your dialogue. For instance there was no longer just plain 'Charlie'; our early morning trill on the bugle, was 'ferkin-Charlie' and seamanship was similarly prefixed. The more accomplished swearers split multi-syllable words somewhere in the middle, so we had 'seaman-ferkin-ship'. The Instructors would feign attempts to moderate our swearing with threats of 'Washing Our Mouths Out With Pusser's Hard!' But we knew it was an idle threat: after all, they were sailors too. There were degrees of swearing, of course. The ever-popular, and oft' used 'fu©k', was at one end of the scale and words like bollocks, twat or arsehole were at the more acceptable end. I learned very quickly that the use of certain expletives was strictly reserved for the messdeck, and definitely not to be used outside *Ganges*, unless of course you were in a pub and you wanted to impress your mates. It was a well known fact that sailors could swear with more style and humour than anyone else.

Easter Leave was looming and thoughts of long doing-nothing days, just lying in bed ... and girls ... invaded my consciousness. Junior Seaman Norman Commander suddenly became popular with all the lads who lived in and around a place called Sunderland. Apparently he had three beautiful, unattached sisters, all over the ages of 16 and 'gagging for IT!' I calculated that Pudsey was too far away from Sunderland for me to profit from this information.

One late March morning we all found it more difficult than normal to drag our bodies out of bed. Guns informed us that while we had been snuggled up beneath our blankets, the clocks of the United Kingdom, the Commonwealth and the rest of the so-called civilised world, had been pushed forward an hour.

Clocks-forward-day was the traditional day for the last Inter-Divisional cross-country competition of the season. Those who knew the ropes had long worked on their excuses to avoid participation, and were posted as Course Marshals alongside a battalion of freshly charged-up PTIs who considered clocks-forward-day to be the pinnacle of the term's sporting calendar. The rest of us mustered on football pitch number three, resplendent in Divisional colours at 14:15 for a 14:30 start. Despite my pre-race preparation of a heavy dinner followed by three fags, I doubted that I would impress any cross-country scout: I knew my limitations.

The *Ganges* 'A' cross-country course was a mixture of mud, slime, grass, bog, sand, and a section of pot-holed roadway. It snaked between Suffolk's head-high hedges, through bramble-edged paths, over rickety bridges, through cold flowing becks and waterlogged marshes, past an army of arm-waving PTIs and was one hundred ferkin percent horrendous.

As expected, I finished well down the field with mud-caked gym shoes and splattered shorts that would be an absolute bugger to clean. We even had to wash the splattered Divisional shirts before handing them back in. When the final results were published, I'd finished about 20 minutes behind the winner. If I read everything correctly, Keppel Division were a disappointing tenth overall.

Parade Instruction was an ever-present and integral part of our curriculum: we were subjected to a couple of hours of it four or five times a week. We practised and re-practised marching, turning, wheeling, reforming, dressing and rifle-flinging in all its forms. Our class Instructor normally took us for Parade Instruction, but just occasionally we would be drilled by someone unknown to us: someone for whom Parade Instruction was important.

Tug had still not figured out that the front rank was the most dangerous place to be. He was one of those unfortunate individuals that the more sadistic of Instructors automatically homed in on. 'Are You A Party?' Our Parade Instructor this morning had a large hooked nose, a blotchy complexion and a large warty growth, the size of a sixpence, on his cheek. He stood rigidly in front of Tug.

'Pardon sir?' asked Tug

'Pardon, Lad ... Pardon? ... You'll Be Saying Balls To The Padre Next. Are You A Party, Lad?'

'Sorry sir ... I don't understand the word Party sir.'

'Are You A Girl, Lad?'

'No sir.'

'Because You Ruddy Well March Like One.'

'Sorry sir.'

'You Need To Clench Your Buttocks, Lad.' Warty-Face bent forward at the hip and glared. 'You Swing Your Stern Like That When You Are Onboard A Ship, My Lad ... And You'll Be In Real Trouble. Do You Understand Me?'

'I've recently been circum ... something sir.'

'You've Been What?'

Johnnie, who was standing behind Warty-Face, mouthed 'cir ... cum ... sized'.

Tug spluttered. 'Circumcised sir ... sorry sir ... I've recently been circumcised.'

'Aargh ... Aargh,' Warty-Face partially closed his evil eyes. 'That Explains Everything Then.'

'Thank you sir.'

'I'll Be Keeping My Eye On You, Lad! I Want To See A Good Deal More Buttock Clenching From You In The Future, Young Man, And Less Rear End Fluttering. Do You Understand Me?'

'I think so sir.'

'You Think So?'

'I understand sir. Thank you.'

'Class ... Class ... Ten Shun! Tin To The Right In Threes ... Right Tin!'

Tug was the only one to turn left. Bastards that we were becoming, we all sniggered.

'Think It's Funny Do We? Think It's Ruddy Funny Do We?' Warty-Face spluttered. 'Twice Around The Parade-Ground ... Class ... Class ... Tin To The Right In Threes ... Right Tin! ...'

Oh bollocks!

'Double March!'

Have I mentioned that the Parade-Ground covered two acres? Over the far side and out of earshot of our Instructor, Tug asked, 'I don't march like a girl do I?'

'A little bit yeah,' replied Chinless.

'Now that you mention it ... you do a bit,' said Slattery.

'Bugger!' said Tug 'I'm going to have to sort that out then.'

'More buttock clenching practice that's what you need,' Johnnie confirmed.

It was the first day of April. I was already awake as Spider burst into the mess to announce that we had been granted a full day's rest and that we could stay in bed for as long as we liked. 'The Duty Chef Will Be Around Shortly With A Cup Of Fresh Hot Tea For Each Of You!' He then smiled, turned about smartly and left us.

I looked, open-eyed, at Tug.

Tug snuggled down and farted.

I responded in kind.

Spider returned a few moments later. 'April Fool! Get Out Of Your Manky Pits ... Show A Leg! ... Show A Leg! ... Show A Stinkin' Leg! Fall-In Outside In Exactly Twenty Five Minutes. After Divisions Keppel 9 Mess Are Going To Experience The Ganges Assault-course! Twenty Five Minutes!'

How sadistic was that, not only an April Fool but the dreaded Assault-course to start the day. The Assault-course had a reputation: stories of life threatening injuries were *Ganges* legend. In the Dining Hall I stuffed myself with as much fried stuff as I could muster. If I was going to go down, it would be on a well-lubricated stomach.

The Assault-Course was the exclusive domain of the largest, fittest, loudest, ugliest, most sadistic PTI that *Ganges* had on their books. He was the same PTI who had been in charge of the Annexe boxing competition. Physically he looked like a cartoon super-hero: wide of shoulder, narrow of hip and square jawed.

We stood 'Hatta Ease!', while he introduced himself: 'My Name Is Chief Petty Officer PTI Ruffles. This Assault-course Is Mine! I Have The Honour Of Preserving The Finest, Most Demanding ...'

Demanding? Oh no!

'The Most Demanding Assault-Course In The Royal Navy.' He stomped up and down the front rank. 'I've Seen Everything On My Assault-Course: I Joined This Man's Navy When Long John Silver Only Had An Egg On His Shoulder!'

I think some of us smiled. Not me.

Chief Petty Officer PTI Ruffles expanded his already massive chest and continued. 'On The Other Side Of My Record Board Is A List Of The Fastest Three Runs Over This Course Since It Was Designed. On the 14th October 1949 A Class From Rodney Division Completed This Course In 19 Minutes And 22 Seconds. This Time Has Never Been Bettered. Me And My Staff,' he waved his cane at a group of barrel-chested PTIs puffing at attention only a short distance away, 'Wait Patiently For A Team Of Young Men To Rewrite History And Write Another Top Line: A Record That Will Go Down In History ...'

My knees were beginning to shake: I was staring at a large brick wall, draped with long knotted ropes, it was obviously a dividing structure of some kind. Guns and Spider stood to one side with expectant smirks on their faces.

'Let Me Take You On An Assault-course Adventure. Your First Obstacle Is The Wall. The Red Brick Structure That You Can See In Front Of You. One Of My Staff Will Explain To You The Method Of Scaling This Structure ...'

I didn't pay much attention as he explained each of the obstacles in terrifying detail. I switched-on again as he was explaining the last bit.

'After The Final Obstacle It's A Relaxing 50 Yard Sprint To The Finishing Line During Which, Some Of Your Accumulated Mud And Shite Should Drop Off Your Little Bodies. Your Class Time Is Taken When The Final Class Member Crosses The Finishing Line.'

Chief Petty Officer PTI Ruffles stood to attention with his whistle in his mouth. He took a deep breath and blew.

Simultaneously, his team of PTI assistants began to shout encouragement and scattered to all parts of the course. A noisy, palpitating team of four PTIs congregated at the base of the wall. As it was the first obstacle, we all managed to scramble over it after a fashion, then things got progressively difficult. On the other side of the wall we crawled through netting, through pipes half full of stagnant, green water. We balanced ourselves on wooden planks spanning more waist-high green water and swung ourselves over gaping chasms on the end of elderly, knotted ropes. We climbed frames and balanced our way between structures high above the ground ... and finally, finally ... we repeated the last three obstacles and, almost dropping with exhaustion, we collected a 20-pound sandbag which we carried the last 50 yards to the finishing line. Chief Petty Officer PTI Ruffles stood watching, stop-watch in hand as, one by one, we stumbled over the finishing line and dumped our sandbag at our feet. He didn't look impressed.

Blacky was the last to finish.

Ruffles clicked his watch and stared at it in utter disbelief. 'Class Fall-in!'

I stood there on the end of the middle rank, water, mud and sweat flowing from my soaked, sagging sports gear. My hair was gunge-plastered to my head. My plimsolls were black and awash with Assault-Course mud and green slime. I had a kit muster in two days! I was shivering, I was cold, tired and I smelled of something unimaginably rancid. I wiped my nose: it had picked up something dark green and slippery.

Chief Petty Officer Ruffles waved a slip of paper at us. 'The Good News Is That You Have Done Something That No Other Class This Year Has Achieved. You Have Smashed The Thirty Three Minute Barrier. You Have Recorded The Slowest Time For A Class This Year: A Staggeringly Slow Thirty Three Minutes And Seventeen Seconds.' He went for a 20-yard Super Hero strut, part way to the wall and back. 'My Granny Can Do It Faster Than That ... She Needs Some Help To Get Over The Wall Because She's In A Ruddy Wheelchair!'

We hung our heads.

Spider appeared from the other side of the wall, he didn't look very happy.

'Take Them Back To The Mess Petty Officer ... At The Double ... Liven Them Up A Bit.'

I've never enjoyed a shower so much. Clean water revealed a number of cuts and other marks on my legs. It took a while for the stagnant smell to wash away. As if this wasn't enough, our next session was Parade Instruction. What sadist had put today's schedule together?

After lights out, staring at the rafters, I decided that the day hadn't been a complete disaster. For tea this evening I had devoured a plateful of Cheese Ush.

I eventually managed to get my white Assault-Course plimsolls clean and blanco'd ready for the end of term kit muster. Most of us passed by the skin of our teeth, including Bungy. People were learning to help each other and individual skills were being improved. I had finished my red silk sewing; the final article, the belt, had proved to be a real challenge. The blue sports shirt I had worn on the Assault-Course still had a whiff of stagnant water about it despite having been washed twice in 'New & Improved' sparkly blue Daz. On the packet it clearly stated that it washed everything to a new level of cleanliness now that it contained a new and improved detergent formula. Well, it certainly wasn't man enough to sort out my blue sports shirt.

We had a few minor kit muster failures. Those who significantly failed kit-musters were occasionally made to lay their kit out in Nelson Hall; a favourite place because it was near to the Instructor's mess. Since arriving in the Main establishment I had seen individuals laying their kits out on the Athletic track, the Assault-Course, the end of the jetty and the rifle range ... sometimes in the rain!

A few days after our last kit muster of the term, Guns spotted blood on Conkers' bed sheet. After further examination he discovered a series of self-inflicted marks on the insides of both his upper arms: Conkers had been cutting himself. A search of his belongings uncovered a blood-stained razor blade wrapped inside a handkerchief inside his brown case. Conkers never really fitted in with any of the mess groups that had formed themselves over the past months, and regularly commented that he wanted 'out of this ferkin organisation'. However, he hadn't yet worked out exactly how to do it. Ever since the Dear John letter from Fat Phyllis he had lost interest in almost everything.

While we were at breakfast, Conkers disappeared. A few days later his locker was cleared and he left us.

We were left unsupervised for less than five minutes outside the Seamanship Block. It was an unusually sunny April day and our sap was on the rise. We had discovered a pile of freshly mown grass cuttings piled up to the right of the main entrance doors and stuffing a handful of grass down the neck of your mate's shirt was a great idea that quickly developed into a class brawl.

'Fall-In!' yelled Guns.

Flapping our shirts and smoothing our collars, we did as instructed.

'Full Of Energy Are We ... Full Of Excess Energy?'

Nobody answered of course. It wasn't that type of question.

'Make Sure Your Boot Laces Are Tight!' He stood there until we all checked our laces. 'Tin To The Rayt In Threes ... Rayta Tin!'

I had a good idea where we were heading.

The pain of last month's trial run was but a distant memory. Guns took up position on a small concrete blister located on the right hand side between the top of Faith and the bottom of Hope. We stood to attention at the bottom staring upwards at Charity's top step, still distant and sharp against the clear blue sky.

'Class ... class ... Double March!'

I suppose everybody dealt with the ups and downs of the following quarter of an hour in their own individual way. Me, I counted steps: Faith had 21, Hope also had 21 and Charity, as befits her name, only had 20. We soon learned that Charity had a characteristic that more than made up for her missing step: her top step was a few inches higher than the others and it caught-out many a Keppel 9 shin. Descending Hope was the worst; her steps were slightly shorter and required an unnatural twist of the booted foot. We stumbled up and down, Guns screaming the dreaded 'Haybaht Tin!' as we reached the bottom again ... and again ... and again ... and again. Each time we reached the bottom we would look to see if Guns was still on his blister: if he was, it would indicate that the punishment would continue.

Eventually, time was our savour: and we were marched, coughing, spluttering and weak of leg and/or thigh back to the mess and a welcome fag. A couple of deep drags put my searing young lungs back into working order.

Blacky claimed to have heard someone say that his class had bunny-jumped up Faith, Hope and Charity. Because it was Blacky, none of us believed it ... or took any notice.

That night I stared at the rafters trying to remember the new seaman-type phrases and words I had heard that day, but there were far, far too many. One of my calf muscles wouldn't stop twitching. It was an uncomfortable night.

The following morning all the class stumbled to the bathroom; everybody was feeling the after-effects and my legs, hips and upper body ached. The morning Suffolk light was starting to appear as we crawled out of our beds these mornings. Was this a sign of the long anticipated summer?

Lash came bounding in and tossed his swimming gear into an empty bowl. He spread his arms wide 'You see before you a qualified ferkin swimmer.'

We all congratulated him, then got on with our morning ablutions.

Haircuts were a nuisance: along with being told to 'Take Your Hands Out Of Your Pockets!', the instruction to 'Get Your Hair Cut!'

or 'Get Your Ruddy Hair Cut!' were probably the most feared and the most regularly used phrases in *Ganges*, particularly as Main Easter Leave was looming. Along with many others, I tried to keep as much of my hair as possible, plastering it with water to make it look shorter and pulling my cap well down. But I didn't get away with it: I was rumbled at the first April Pay Parade along with everybody else. I suppose the Instructors knew exactly what we were trying to do with only weeks to go before leave. 'If You Think We're Going To Let You Go Home To Mummy With Hair Like That My Lad, You're Mistaken! Name And Mess Number!'

I waited my turn within Shotley's shearing-shop for the third time in as many months. It was rumoured that Shotley came from Brighton and that if you told him that you also came from Brighton, you might get away with having slightly less cut off. I tried it, but my broad West Yorkshire accent was a dead give-away. His barbering skills were time-constrained and I came out with most of my removed hair inside my shirt, and looking like I had been sheared by a sight-impaired maniac.

Our main Easter leave was from Friday 15 April until Monday 9 May: three weeks and a weekend, giving us a 23-day break. The week leading up to leave had a slightly different feel to it. We Juniors could be excused our excitement, but Guns and Spider were also different somehow and I suppose they were looking forward to a break from us as much as we needed a break from them. Throughout the final week of the term, not an hour went by without someone mentioning something to do with leave. What we planned on doing to imaginary girlfriends was a popular subject of conversation as was food and long periods of lying in bed. The training curriculum was changed slightly as leave approached, with activities that involved possible injury being toned down. Nobody was seen climbing the mast.

The final days of term appeared to go on forever and no matter how tired I was when I got into bed I didn't sleep well. I spent hours staring at the rafters, imagining what I would say to my mother and what I would say to my friends who were still at school. Would I wear my uniform or would I go in civvies? I wondered if the pony-tailed girl who lived up the road would say yes if I asked her for a date.

We were scheduled for Boatwork on Wednesday morning and I must admit I wasn't too keen on playing galley slave again. It was a surprise when we fell-in outside the sail locker. Petty Officer Miserable-Shit, who dished out the oilskins, also dished out masts, sails and rigging that had to be carried down the jetty to our allocated boat. Today I was in Whaler number four and shouldering the heavy end of her mainmast. In the winter and early spring the sails never had a chance to dry out between classes, and those carrying the half-dry mainsail struggled.

Spider was our coxswain and it took us a while to get everything rigged. In particular the main mast was a bugger to get stepped correctly and the stiff mainsail was difficult to unfurl. We were given our crew positions and duties: I was placed on the starboard main-sheet, close to Spider and the tiller. It felt very, very strange as we slowly drifted away from the jetty, wind-powered for the very first time. We were about to put many hours of theory into practice.

We sliced through the waters of the Rivers Stour and Orwell and, as with pulling, we quickly improved. Spider obviously enjoyed his sailing. I was immediately enthralled: as we made our way out towards Harwich a bone-chilling south-westerly caught us almost putting us on our 'beam ends' but Spider had it all in hand and was quick to issue the necessary instructions. Before we knew it, we were skimming north-east with a following wind and our tautened sails straining manfully. For a brief while we were able to secure the working end of our sheets and enjoy the experience; no wonder sailing was popular! Our return trip westwards was a much more complicated affair. Spider had to explain to us again how a sailing craft could travel into the wind and all the co-ordinated work required to achieve this. I was one of the three or so class members to be given a turn on the tiller and I must admit that I did a little better than Misty who didn't have much sense of the wind direction or the messages relayed by the sails. In fact when Spider took over the tiller as we were approaching the pier I personally received a whispered 'Well done!' and something like a nod of approval.

Back on the jetty I overheard Guns telling Spider that Tug was a born sailor who had lived all his life in Cowes on the Isle of Wight. Spider responded by telling him that I had promise and could read the elements well. Tug and I would have to have a chat: I suddenly understood what a difference a bit of encouragement made. We unrigged everything and secured it in the prescribed *Ganges* fashion before trundling it all back down the jetty to the sail locker where another class were waiting to be issued with all the equipment for Whaler number four. It would have been a simple matter to have left our boat rigged for the following class: but that's wasn't the *Ganges* way.

Later that evening I managed to get Tug on his own. 'Heard that you impressed Guns this afternoon.'

'Probably: I've been sailing ever since I can remember. But these boats are a bit different.'

'Spider told me I had promise. I nearly brought the boat back in towards the jetty ... all by myself ... nearly.'

'Hard work eh?'

'Yeah. Misty was given a spell on the tiller but he was rubbish.'

'Looking forward to next term when we can really get on with the sailing.'

'Me too,' I agreed.

Later that night, before lights out, I got my nose into Chapter 7 of the Seamanship Manual. Of particular interest was page 199 that explained to me the meaning of Beating, Reaching, Running, Tacking, Wearing, Gybing and being Close-hauled. Brilliant stuff, although I had to read it a number of times before it sunk in.

The normal Pay Parade following Divisions on Thursday morning didn't take place. We were told that our accumulated leave pay was equivalent to the average worker's wage for a fortnight. To have 2,000 young, excitable boys with that much money in one place shortly before being dispersed to all corners of the country was considered too much of a risk. We would be paid the following morning when we were issued with our railway tickets and our Paybooks.

Paddy, who came from Londonderry, Northern Ireland, was allowed to go home a day before the rest of us. Along with a small group of others he left dressed in the civilian clothes that he had arrived in. The clothes belonging to the Northern Irish lads hadn't been sent home during the first few days in the Annexe, but had been kept under lock and key somewhere. Apparently, wearing Her Majesty's uniform in Northern Ireland was considered too risky.

That afternoon, along with a number of other classes, we were assembled in the gym to watch a film: it was the same colourful VD film that we had seen in the Annexe ... but on a much larger screen and more sharply focused. If it was meant to put me off girls, it failed completely.

We didn't have much in the way of personal gear to take home with us and we only had our Little Brown Cases in which to put everything. My packing was easy: yesterday's underwear and a clean white front. I also had a small collection of Fiskie's pictures to show Mum and Tony. I took another look at my portrait photograph and disliked it even more, but packed it anyway. It was regrettable that Fiskie hadn't been in the Annexe during my finest moment to capture action pictures of me in the boxing ring. However, I did pack my boxing certificate: that would impress Mum. The opening and closing of Little Brown Cases was heard throughout the mess until the early hours as individuals remembered something or other. I decided, before I fell asleep, to take my Seamanship Manual home.

In the very early hours the Tannoy crackled and we were out of bed before the first notes of 'Charlie' were bugled. Dress of the day was our best 'going-home-on-leave' uniform and shiny boots, as for Sunday Divisions. The CMG had flashed-up early and we ambled across the Quarterdeck ... yeah; we ambled across the Quarterdeck ... for breakfast. There wasn't much queue-jumping this morning. The noise was unusually shrill ... as we tucked in to our last *Ganges* meal for 23 days, I wondered if Mum could do deep fried bread.

I made my bed for the last time for 23 days. Washed, dressed, fed and watered we were all herded into the gym where each mess was allocated a section of deck where we squatted and squirmed to await developments.

Spider explained that we would receive our leave pay of seven pounds ten shillings plus an extra six quid Ration-Allowance that the Navy paid to our Mothers for feeding and looking after us for the forthcoming three weeks. 'This Is Not Extra Money For You To Flitter Away On Sweets, Cigarettes And Wild, Wild Women. This Money Is For Your Mummies ... Directly From Her Majesty. So Make Sure That You Hand It Over ... Understand?'

Along with our Paybook we were given a third class return railway ticket to the station nearest to our home. I suppose the Paybook was a form of identification; after all it contained that shocking picture of me with my towel wrapped around my chest. Unfortunately it also contained my date of birth so I wouldn't be able to use it to get myself a drink in a pub.

'Do Not Sit There And Count Your Money ... The Amount Will Be Correct. Stow It Away In Your Belt Pocket!'

'Yes sir.'

We noticed that the Arry boys weren't with us and they hadn't collected any leave money. It was rumoured that some didn't have homes to go to and would spend their leave in *Ganges*, poor sods!

After what seemed like ages, sitting on the gym's wooden deck cuddling our Little Brown Cases, those of us who were to travel north via London were corralled onto a fleet of local double-decker buses. Once through the Main Gates I felt that I was really on my way to Ipswich Railway Station ... and home! It was still dark and I was fascinated by the sight of civilian houses, some with dim yellow lights glowing through drawn curtains.

This was 'Civvy-Street', where life was going on as it always did and where nobody realised what we had been put through during the past 14 weeks. There were few people about: no doubt they were all still snuggled up in their nice warm beds. They had no idea that we were passing by and what we had suffered in the service of Queen and Country.

A couple of Instructors travelled on the bus with us to make sure that we caught the correct train at Ipswich. The initiative part of our young, immature brains had been de-activated 14 weeks ago and it was going to take a while before that function kicked in again.

Our train from Ipswich to London Liverpool Street was a *Ganges* special. Hundreds of excitable uniformed boys with bags of energy to expend couldn't be expected to travel with normal East Anglians, could they? Many of us, mainly those who hadn't been on leave before, just stared blankly out of the window as the watery April sun slowly appeared behind us. Fields, hedgerows, trees, houses, cars, garages, shops and people flashed by. We rummaged in our Little Brown Cases and our money belts. I counted my money: including what I had saved during the past month and a half, I had over 15 quid in notes and coins.

London was busy. Waiting for us outside Liverpool Street Station was a fleet of Blue naval buses and, along with a load of others I got on the one that was marked Kings Cross.

There were girls everywhere. Girls in a rush, girls just standing around, girls in skirts, girls in coats, blonde girls, dark-haired girls, tall girls, small girls. Girls wearing hats, girls without hats, girls with handbags, girls with suitcases, girls with long hair, girls with shorter hair, beautiful girls in high heeled shoes, girls in tan stockings, girls everywhere!

At Kings Cross, *Ganges* boys queued at a small tobacco kiosk and quickly bought its entire stock of cigarettes. Standing in a group with our Little Brown Cases held firmly between our ankles, we enjoyed our first London smoke. We were an isolated, uniformed group with a dense cloud of exhaled smoke hovering above us: already a breed apart. I wondered what all the girls ... all those girls thought of us!

Individually we drifted away to catch our respective trains. Mine was all stops to York and the north-east coast as far as Scotland. We were very much on our own now: no Instructors in evidence for the first time since we had left Shotley. I shared a compartment with a group of other boys, most of whom, judging from their badges, had been at *Ganges* longer than I had. We all puffed away and had to open the window regularly to clear our compartment of accumulated smoke: real sailors we were, continually joking, swearing, telling each other sea-stories and ogling every girl who walked down the narrow corridor outside our window. As we pulled out of Kings Cross, simultaneously our stomachs informed us that it was Stand-easy and time for mid morning Kye and Stickies, so a couple of us made our way to the Dining Car where we made a significant dent in the train's stock of pork pies, sausage rolls and Cornish pasties.

Our numbers decreased the further north we travelled. As we chugged out of Doncaster one of the lads, sporting a number of badges, suggested that we go and get ourselves a beer from the dining car. The oldest looking amongst us tried his persuasive best, but both the blokes behind the counter flatly refused to serve us. 'We've been told that all you Ganges boys are under age. More than my job's worth: sorry lads.'

Eventually the train trundled through the outskirts of Leeds. I recognised landmarks; nothing had changed since I'd been away. Along with a group of other Leeds lads, I grabbed my case, put on my cap, and gave the toes of my boots a quick rub on the back of my trousers as our train pulled in to Leeds City Station. We swung our doors wide open before the train came to a complete halt, not wanting to waste a precious second of our time at home.

I was the only *Ganges* boy on the Pudsey Greenside train.

With my cap positioned a little further back on my head than was allowed and swinging my Little Brown Case I made my way down familiar streets and lanes towards home. Mine was a quick, expectant walk, a relaxed march maybe. I turned a few heads, but didn't pass anyone I knew, not that they would have recognised me anyway, in my uniform and with my short hair and ruddy, weather-beaten Suffolk complexion.

I rubbed the toes of my boots on the back of my trousers again before I entered my front door. Home at last! Mum was serving in the shop; the TV in the corner was on. With her customer gone she bounded up the stairs into the lounge ... and there I was: uniformed son, home from the sea, well ... Suffolk. There were lots of cuddles, tears and the inevitable question 'When do you go back?'

Mum admired my uniform; she said that I filled it out well. I explained the significance of the seven horizontal creases in my trousers. I couldn't remember what the black silk represented but my sparkly white rope lanyard had something to do with guns. I didn't mention that I didn't have shoes. Between customers, I also explained that I was skilled at doing my own washing, drying and ironing and I was really looking forward to putting on some comfortable underwear, my drainpipe trousers, my suede shoes and my coat. Mum said I looked older, I'd grown and that I looked the picture of health. I think she exaggerated a little, as Mother's tended to do. She admired the red silk sewing and said that she was surprised that the Navy went to all the trouble of sewing our names onto our kit for us. I didn't say anything: if Mum wanted to think that the Royal Navy had done it for me, then so be it. She told me that the lady who owned the haberdashery shop down the street had died, that the girl whose parents owned the fish and chip shop over the road had gone off to Stage School and that Mr Ramsden had broken his leg again. That was good news: Mr Ramsden and I had never seen eye-to-eye, mainly because he was a foot smaller than me.

'Did you know that while you've been away the Queen has given birth to her fourth baby, a boy called Andrew, and this coming weekend there is going to be a large demonstration planned in London against Nuclear weapons?' Mum asked.

'We haven't got a radio or a television in *Ganges*.'

'Haven't you?'

'I heard about Andrew: we had an extra Stickie for that, but I haven't heard about the Nuclear Weapon stuff.'

'What's a Stickie?'

'A bun that's sticky.'

'Right you are. I thought the whole of the country could receive television and radio signals now.'

'Not *Ganges*.'

The lady from next door had seen me arrive, and had joined us.

'Your hair's a mess,' stated my younger brother. He was right: in an era of fashionably styled hair for boys of my age, my Shotley-shearing looked severely out of place.

I described as much Naval stuff as I thought would interest everybody, but realised that unless you'd been through the *Ganges* mill, it didn't make much sense. I showed them my boxing certificate which impressed them all. Mum told me that my Granddad, Ernest Large, had been a great boxing fan and had served with The Royal Horse Artillery in the First World War, but she never imagined in her wildest dreams that her shy, stamp-collecting son would develop into a boxer of some distinction.

I also explained that last week, I'd developed a passion for sailing.

'Sailing?' Mum and the next door neighbour asked, wide-eyed.

'Yeah, sailing. In fact I've brought my Seamanship Manual home with me so that I can do some swotting while I'm home.'

'You must be keen then.' The shop door bell rang and Mum skipped away. Our shop bell had been interrupting family conversations for as long as I could remember.

My Mum saw something in Mr Fisk's portrait photograph that I didn't, and placed it on top of the Welsh dresser where it stayed for the next five years, until she sold the shop and moved south to Wakefield.

I warned both Mum and Tony that I might occasionally refer to the floor as a deck and that I had started smoking seriously. When Mum left to serve another customer I went upstairs to the bedroom that my brother and I shared. He asked me for a cigarette but I refused, saying that he was far too young to smoke. I hung my uniform jacket up, folded my trousers in the prescribed Naval fashion and removed my Pusser's underwear. Even Tony laughed at them as I twirled them around my head and sent them flying into a darkened corner of the room where they slapped against the wall and landed on the floor with a resounding 'thunk'. My civvies had a strange feel to them. My favourite black shirt with the white stars was a little tighter than when I left, but the drainpipe trousers fitted perfectly as did the suede brothel-creepers. In civvies, I felt like a completely different person.

I huddled into my green-grey gabardine coat and went for a walk. I half expected things to have changed since the start of the year, but they hadn't: Pudsey was exactly as I had left it. It was only me who had changed; now I walked with a more upright, shoulders-back swagger. A number of neighbours miraculously appeared, all to look at the developing young man they once knew and to ask me the same question 'When do you go back?'

'Three weeks.' I replied.

'What ship are you on then?'

'*HMS Ganges*.'

'Is it a big ship?'

'Massive.'

That first evening I couldn't wait to tune into Radio Luxemburg to listen to what were the most popular records. Reception hadn't improved and it took a little time to get the radio tuned in. Long ago I'd worked out that putting it at the top of the stairs with the aerial next to an exposed water pipe gave the best signal. Top of the Hit Parade was a record called *My Old Man's a Dustman* by Lonnie Donegan which, after hearing it more than once, started to grow on me. Over a late supper, after Mum had shut up shop, I explained what the food was like in the Navy and how much choice we had. I also described 'Train smash', 'Cackleberries', 'Cheese Ush' and 'Shit on a raft': the last one made Mum wince. I made a little ceremony about giving Mum the six quid Ration Allowance the Navy had given her for feeding and accommodating me for the forthcoming 23 days: she was chuffed to bits. We almost stood and sang *God Save The*

Queen over the dining table... but didn't. I half expected Mum to give me some of it back for my own use, but she was an East Yorkshire girl ... and didn't.

The pony-tailed girl who lived up the road came in the shop that evening. She looked even more gorgeous than I remembered and I was more than a little embarrassed. I was determined to ask her out on a date ... but not just yet. She asked me when I was going back and this time the question sounded different.

'I've got 23 days leave,' I said proudly, as though I'd earned it.

It felt strange sleeping in a well-mattressed bed with the prospect of a Charlie-free morning.

The first morning I was determined to stay in bed until noon, but I didn't; I was wide awake early and itching to get up and do absolutely nothing for an entire day. Dredging my Dung-Hampers from the corner of the bedroom, I gave them to Mum for washing: old habits die hard. I explained at some length my newly acquired Naval washing, ironing and sewing skills and actually showed Mum how I ironed and folded my uniform. Was she impressed? I don't know, but she was definitely surprised.

For the rest of my first full day at home I did absolutely nothing, watched television and played some of my record collection. I accused my brother of using my record player while I had been away; he said he didn't, I said he did, he said he didn't, I said he did, he said he didn't, I said he did ... that's how our arguments always started. I went out and bought myself the latest edition of the *New Musical Express* from the paper shop down the road, studied what was in the Hit Parade and decided what records to buy. The important things in my life today were records and girls, not in that order of course.

Pudsey is the kind of place where the entire household's weekly wash is shamelessly displayed on outside washing lines every Monday without fail. It's a West Yorkshire tradition, and a form of communication going back many generations. When the lady at number 61 visited the local lingerie emporium next to the bicycle repair shop last July, everybody immediately knew. Similarly, when the bloke at number 56 bought himself a pair of two-toned Y-fronts he was immediately branded a Fop and a Dandy by the inhabitants of Robin Lane. An old guy, who lived by himself, was discovered collapsed because a neighbour noticed that his weekly underwear hadn't been pegged-out at the normal time: he was taken to hospital and subsequently made a full recovery. The lady over the road hoisted a trio of capacious brassieres and matching pink bloomers every Monday which, when the wind was in the east, strained her washing line posts almost to breaking point.

Unfortunately the most sophisticated detergent of the day had little effect on my Dung-Hampers. Amidst items that gently wafted in the drying West Yorkshire wind, my greyed monstrosities, manufactured from material impervious to weather, sagged miserably unmoved. They were to tax my mother's washing and drying skills to the limit.

On my first Monday I put my uniform on and caught the bus from outside the shop into Leeds; a 40-minute journey. I suppose I'd suddenly become rather proud of my uniform because I was probably the only sailor in town and, with my new-found Suffolk confidence, I wanted to show myself off. Sitting on the upper deck of a double decker bus, directly above the driver, and enjoying a cigarette, I was asked by a number of ladies (not attractive young girls unfortunately) if they could 'touch my collar for luck'. It was obviously something to do with the war and the olden days. Some of the old dears actually staggered the entire length of the bus to stroke my collar. As I strolled through the centre of Leeds towards the large record store I received more requests from ladies. I decided that I would have to find out more about this strange custom. After stroking my collar the ladies always smiled and said thank you ... it was strangely gratifying and I felt I was doing something socially significant.

In the basement of a large electrical retailer was the largest and most popular record shop in Leeds. Along one wall were small booths where customers listened to records prior to buying them. I had money to spend and asked one of the girls behind the counter if I could listen to a Fats Domino EP that the *NME* had said was popular. She smiled at me: I was probably the first sailor she had ever seen.

'Booth number five sir.'

She called me sir ... called me sir! She didn't want to touch my collar for luck, nor did she ask me when I was going back. I closed the door to booth number five and listened to the familiar rounded voice of Fats, but I was disappointed with his latest release and ended up buying *Running Bear* by Johnnie Preston and *Poor Me* by Adam Faith. I also bought myself a small brush contraption that I could stick on the stylus arm of my record player to clean the record grooves. I casually removed a couple of pound notes from my bulging wallet to pay: I felt good. Maybe the girl behind the counter thought that sailors, after long overseas journeys, were well paid for what they did in the name of Queen and Country. As I turned nonchalantly away to leave, she called me back ... 'Excuse me sir.'

'I turned and smiled. 'Yes?'

She held out her hand full of coins. 'Your change.'

Sod it!

The Pudsey sun appeared long enough to dry most of the moisture entrapped within my 'Hampers'. Mum transferred them indoors to the clothes-airer that hung from the ceiling directly above the coal fire. The clothes-airer was a popular feature of the time and was a series of wooden slats raised and lowered by a simple pulley system. The 'Hampers' hung there motionless and uninviting, blocking out much of the reflected Yorkshire light until Mum, with an expert rub of her two fingers, finally declared them 'dry and aired' some days later.

On Easter Tuesday I went to Elland Road to watch Leeds United scrape a well-deserved 2-1 win against Preston North End. Elland Road hadn't changed at all. Despite the fact that our team was now in the First Division, our toilets didn't look as though they'd been properly cleaned since my previous visit last year. Unfortunately, the opposition in the First Division was much tougher and we were firmly entrenched in the bottom half of the league.

The following day was the only day of the week when my mother could officially close the shop at dinnertime; so we went to Leeds together. I was in my uniform, at Mum's request, and once again a number of ladies asked if they could touch my collar for luck. I bought Mum a meal; the first meal I had ever bought anybody. She thoroughly enjoyed the halibut, but was concerned about the cost: she's an East Yorkshire lass. Not for the first time she said that I should be careful walking around with so much money in my wallet.

During my free time I dipped in and out of my Seamanship Manual. I learned that the boat I had sailed for ten minutes was called a Montagu 'K' Whaler, 27 feet long, clinker-built construction and yawl-rigged. It weighed three quarters of a ton and its life saving capacity was 27 men: no girls or women I noticed. It had a foresail, a mainsail, facility for a mizzen sail, whatever that was, and a drop keel. I dog-eared page 199: I was determined to fully understand all about the beating, reaching, running, tacking, wearing, gybing and close-hauled business. I wasn't looking forward to going back to Shotley, but there was a part of me that couldn't wait to go sailing again.

My mother took the unprecedented decision on the final Friday of my leave to close the shop for a few hours to watch the wedding of Princess Margaret (the Queen's younger sister) to a bloke called Anthony Armstrong-Jones on TV. I couldn't have been less interested. My highlight was that I eventually plucked up the courage to ask the pony-tailed girl for a date. She agreed, but it turned out to be a bit of a disaster. Standing up against a rusty stomach-bar in the crowded Scratching Shed end of Elland Road watching Leeds United beat Nottingham Forest 1-0, obviously wasn't her idea of an afternoon out. I suppose, if you weren't a Scratching Shed type girl ... you weren't a Scratching Shed type girl, and there was no changing that. What really put the mockers on the day was that, despite the win, our relegation to the Second Division was confirmed. I'd had better days.

The three weeks and a weekend were over far too quickly and I spent a sunny, Yorkshire Sunday morning sitting in the lounge pretending to spit and polish my boots ready for my return. I'd ironed a razor-sharp crease down the centre of my white front as we had been instructed to do. Before going on leave we had been told by Spider that the Navy in the Home Fleet changed from winter to summer clothing on the first day of May regardless of the weather. As we were technically members of the Home Fleet and were on leave on that date we had to ensure that when we returned from leave we were wearing a white front, otherwise we could be charged with something or other. I packed my electric razor, my mother-washed sea-jersey, 'hampers' and a couple of pairs of civilian underpants in my Little Brown Case underneath all the sweets and packets of cigarettes.

Ganges Juniors converged on London from all over the country and swamped the scheduled train from Liverpool Street to Ipswich. A train full of quiet and thoughtful Juniors de-trained at Ipswich where a fleet of blue Navy canvas-backed trucks and buses were waiting for us. For a moment, the normally peaceful Ipswich Station was packed with stumbling, morose looking young boys in Naval uniform. A battalion of Instructors corralled us onto transport. With our Little Brown Cases firmly held between our feet, it was a depressing and uncomfortable journey down the narrow roads and lanes back to Shotley and in through those dreaded Main Gates.

I had a sinking feeling in the pit of my stomach. Another 14 weeks was a daunting prospect, particularly as we would be straight into the dreaded 12-week examinations.

6

PROMOTION AND A PAIR OF SHOES

Our truck pulled up outside Nelson Hall and we were lined up to have our Little Brown Cases searched. My illegal imports were a tub of Brylcreem and a small plastic bottle of Old Spice talcum powder that Mum must have sneaked into my case. My mother was a keen advocate of a snowy application of talcum powder after every bath.

My Inspector sniffed the top of the tin. 'This Is Serious 'Foo-Foo' This Is.'

'Pardon sir?'

'This Talcum Powder Is Seriously Fragrant.'

'Mum must have put it in my case without me knowing ... sir.'

'I'm Not Going To Allow You To Take This Onto The Messdeck, Young Man.'

'OK ... sir.'

My Pifco electric razor and a spare pair of civilian underpants were closely examined and for a moment I thought I would lose them as well, but I didn't. He pulled a face when he found the Seamanship Manual in the bottom of the case.

'You Took Your Seamanship Manual Home?'

'Yes sir.'

'For Any Particular Reason?'

'To learn about sailing while on leave sir. We only had one sailing lesson before leave.'

'So You're A Bit Of A Sailor Eh?'

'Yes sir.'

He closed my case and I think he smiled. He placed the talcum powder alongside the Brylcreem on the bench behind him. 'Next ... Chop Chop Then!'

In the corner of Nelson Hall were a group of lads who had returned from leave wearing their sea jerseys. I noticed Misty among them.

The mess and my bed-space were exactly as I had left them: it was as though I'd never been away. I wondered if any of the Arry boys had stayed in *Ganges* for the whole leave period. Guns welcomed us back by telling us what the 12-week examinations consisted of; I wished he hadn't said anything. When he asked me if I had enjoyed my leave, I took the opportunity to ask, 'Why is it, in Leeds I had old ladies asking to touch my collar for luck ... sir?'

Guns stood at the foot of my bed. 'Leeds Eh? I've Heard That They're A Funny Lot In Leeds. Did It Happen Often Then ... This Touching Of Your Collar?'

'Yes sir, quite often.'

'You'll Have To Watch Those Leeds Ladies.'

'It was just touching my collar sir.'

'You're Lucky That You Don't Live In Portsmouth, Lad. The Ladies Of Portsmouth Do It Differently.'

'Pardon sir?'

'In Days Gone By, Sailors Used To Get All Their Pay Once They Had Returned To Their Home Port From A Long Sea Voyage. With Me So Far?'

'Yes sir.'

They Went Ashore With Their Pockets Bulging With Hard Earned Money. Still With Me?'

'Yes sir.'

'And Who Do You Think Would Be Waiting On The Jetty For Them When They Arrived Back In Portsmouth?'

'Their family sir.'

'No, Not The Family, Lad ... Definitely Not The Family. The Pompey Girls Were Waiting For Them.' He winked suggestively. 'The Pompey Girls.'

'Right sir.'

'And Can You Guess What They Were Waiting For?'

'No sir.' There were sniggers from those in adjoining beds.

Guns snorted. 'They Would Compete With Each Other To Entice A Sailor With Promises Of Sexual Pleasures.' He took a deep breath. 'You Have To Remember, Lad: The Sailors Had Been At Sea For Many A Long Time In Those Days.'

'I understand sir.'

'This Was Known Locally In Portsmouth As Touching Up A Sailor.'

'Right sir.'

'The Plan Being To Get Their Grubby Little Hands On As Much Of The Sailor's Hard Earned Money As Possible.'

'Right sir. To steal their money sir?'

'Not Exactly Steal It.'

'Not exactly sir.'

'To Exchange It .... For Sexual Favours.'

'I understand sir.'

'That, Young Man, Is Where The Tradition Of Touching A Sailor's Collar Comes From. In Future, Be Careful When You Turn Your Back On Those Ladies In Leeds.'

'Right-o sir.'

'And When You Get To Portsmouth ... Watch Out.'

Looking at the rafters this evening I wondered why that bloke had called my talcum powder 'Foo-Foo': it sounded a bit Chinese to me.

The time of Charlie hadn't changed: it was still at 06:00. We had two empty beds in the mess, Paddy's and Bungy's. The truth about Norman Commander's sisters was revealed. Lash had called round to Norman's place during leave in the hope of seeing his three unmarried sisters. It turned out that he only had one 14-year-old sister and she was 'No oil painting!' according to Lash.

Despite there being no noticeable improvement in the weather, their Lords at the Admiralty had decreed that Royal Naval summer started officially after colours on the first day of

May. Apart from changing our warm blue sea jerseys for flimsy white fronts, we also lost our Stand-Easy Kye. Instead we had cold milk. Apparently we would have to wait until the first day of October before the stimulating properties of Kye would once again be available to us.

Naval bathrooms are great levellers: there are few physical secrets in communal bathrooms. A number of us noticed that Stumpy Borrowdale had returned from leave with a large plaster on his upper arm and we were curious to know what was hidden beneath it.

Ever so slowly Stumpy removed one side of the plaster to reveal part of a scabby Heart, Anchor and entwined Ribbon tattoo. 'Got to keep it dry for two weeks,' he said.

We all looked on in admiration.

Someone whistled approvingly. 'How much did that cost ya?'

'Three pounds two and six.'

'Ferkin hell.'

Stumpy tapped his plaster. 'Got special waterproof sticky tape and everything.'

That evening both Paddy and Bungy returned. Paddy had missed two Belfast ferries and had caught the wrong train at Liverpool. Bungy said he had woken up on Sunday feeling ill and didn't feel like he could travel all the way back to Ipswich as he 'had the runs'. Both were charged with 'Returning Late From Main Easter Leave' and had already been seen by the Officer of the Day: they both had to see the Commander in the morning. Misty had been made to do a couple of circuits of the Parade-Ground and given a severe bollocking because he had returned from leave wearing his sea jersey, but he hadn't been officially charged.

We started our 14-week term with sailing. Despite it being a cold, damp Suffolk day the oilskin store was now officially locked until the first day of October. Petty Officer Miserable-Shit, wearing an unseasonable oilskin and a thick woollen scarf, dished out masts, sails and rigging for our allocated boat. I was excited: I'd studied the sailing characteristics of the Montagu Whaler while on leave and had memorised many of the craft's good points and some of her disadvantages. Given another opportunity to get my hands on the tiller, I'd show 'em.

Unfortunately my boat for today was a Cutter, which was much bigger than the Whaler and the masts and stuff weighed a good deal more. Only 24 hours ago I had been wrapped up in a nice warm, comfortable bed with the smell of Sunday morning bacon and Yorkshire sausages wafting up the stairs. Now, here I was dressed in shorts, sports shirt and plimsolls shouldering a good proportion of the weight of a solid oak mast on my young shoulder.

An unknown Petty Officer with a large purple nose was our coxswain today. We secretly christened him 'Schnoz'. It took ages to rig our Cutter, a single dipping lugsail rig with two training sails. The mast was a bugger and took most of the crew to get it stepped. On the main mast was a device called a traveller that was attached to the top of the mainsail by a yard. Once rigged, Schnoz positioned his crew; quietly and without criticism he explained what we would be required to do and when. We drifted gently away from the jetty. From astern I noticed a monstrous, dense black Suffolk cloud sneaking up on us. It followed us until we were in mid-channel with no means of escape, before dropping its watery contents on us. Schnoz was wearing a white roll-neck submariner's jersey and watertight trousers tucked into his seaboots. We were wearing next to nothing and no socks. As the rain strengthened Schnoz instructed us on how and when to dip the yard which took a minimum of two of us to manoeuvre. If we dipped it too early, the billowing sail could trap our fingers; too late and the sail and the yard could have our head off. Tug and I were on the mainsheets as near to Schnoz as we could be, but neither of us got a go on the tiller as Schnoz was enjoying himself too much. Because the Cutter was a much wider boat we would have expected her to be more stable than the narrow Whaler, but she wasn't: she had a smaller drop keel, so easily keeled over when the wind was anywhere near the beam. However, in Schnoz's expert hands she skimmed over to Harwich and then back towards Shotley before losing our following black cloud long enough for us to unrig and return all the equipment to

Petty Officer Miserable-Shit's Boat Equipment Store. Everybody, apart from Schnoz was wringing wet, cold rain water running down our pinked legs from our sodden sports gear. A couple of cigarettes followed by a warm shower put me back in reasonably good working order.

I was becoming addicted to my Seamanship Manual. It was a formidable but fascinating book, brimming with strange, exotic terminology. It depicted fully rigged sailing ships and named every single item of rigging. It showed me how to tie a bewildering range of knots and when and where to use each. A Turks Head was apparently of no practical use whatsoever, nor was the Matthew Walker knot. The reef knot, clove hitch and the bowline appeared to be used everywhere. I wondered what Matthew had done to have a knot named after him. Signal flags were displayed on colourful pages. The book was to become my bible and I loved it and longed for the day when I could officially get my hands on the sequel: BR67 The Manual of Seamanship Volume 2.

Paddy and Bungy were both on Captain's defaulters this morning while we had been sailing. At dinnertime, we all crowded round to find out what punishment they had received: they had both got 14 days Number 9s and stoppage of leave for the remainder of the term. Paddy had been cross-examined on his ability to read a ferry and train timetable. Bungy had been asked about his general health and wellbeing.

We were getting ready to turn-in when Guns noticed Stumpy's plaster, which was looking a touch ragged around the edges. 'And What Do We Have Here, Junior Seaman Borrowdale?'

Being addressed by your full name and rate normally signalled trouble.

'A plaster sir.'

'And What Is Underneath The Plaster. An Injury Perhaps?'

'No sir.'

'What Then, Junior Seaman Borrowdale? What Is Lurking Under Your Plaster?'

'A tattoo sir.'

'A Tattoo!' yelled Guns clasping his hands together in mock excitement. 'Let's Have A Look At It Then!'

Slowly Stumpy peeled back the plaster to reveal one anchor fluke and part of a trailing yellow ribbon.

'Well, Well, Well. And When Did We Decide To Tattoo Ourself, Junior Seaman Borrowdale?'

'When I was on leave sir.'

'And Where Did You Spend Your Leave?'

'At home sir.'

Guns took a deep breath. 'And Where Is Home, Lad?'

'Blackpool sir.'

'Blackpool?'

'Yes sir. It's in Lancashire. Up north.'

'Yes … I Know Where Blackpool Is, Lad! So They Have Tattoo Parlours In Blackpool Do They?'

'Yes sir.'

'Lets Have A Proper Look Then.' He helped Stumpy to gently remove one side of the plaster. 'And What Does Your Tattoo Represent, Junior Seaman Borrowdale?' Guns smiled before grabbing the remainder of the plaster and ripping it from Stumpy's arm in one swift movement and tossing it on top of his locker.

Stumpy winced and covered his tattoo with his free hand. There was a glint of a tear in both eyes.

'Hands Down By Your Side, Lad.'

Stumpy stood up straight his hands down by his side, his fingers in line with the seam of his pyjama bottoms.

'What Is It Then, Lad?'

'It's an anchor and a heart entwined with a yellow ribbon sir.'

'Very Artistic. And What Is This Writing On The Ribbon?'

'My Mum's name and my girlfriend's sir.'

'Very Good. And What Is Your Mum's Name Then?'

'Mum ... sir.'

Guns looked at the mess rafters and inhaled deeply. 'And The Name Of Your Girlfriend Is?'

'Cynthia sir.'

'And How Old Is Cynthia?'

'Almost 16 sir.'

'How Almost.'

'Pardon sir?'

'How Old Exactly?'

'Fifteen years nine months and 19 days exactly sir.'

'She's A Virgin, Verging On The Verge Is She Then?'

'Pardon sir?'

'Never Mind. Are You Sure That Whilst You Are Here In The Service Of Queen And Country Cynthia Is Not Baring All For Another Spotty Young Lad From Blackpool.'

'She won't be doing that sir.'

'What Will Happen To The Name On Your Tattoo When Cynthia And You Are No Longer Together?'

'That won't happen sir.'

'Why? Is Cynthia A Bit On The Doggo Side?'

'Pardon sir?'

'Doggo. Ugly!'

'No sir.'

'Attractive Is She?'

'Yes sir.'

Gun picked up the plaster in two fingers and offered it to Stumpy. 'Put Your Plaster Back On, Junior Seaman Borrowdale.'

'Thank you sir.' There was an expression of relief on Stumpy's face.

'Get Dressed,' yelled Guns. 'Night Clothing And Your Cap.' He smashed the bed with his cane. 'Muster Outside The Gatehouse In Five Minutes. You Will Be Charged With Self Inflicted Injury ... In Other Words, Having A Tattoo In Contravention Of Queen's

Regulations And Admiralty Instructions, Which Clearly States That Junior Seamen Under Training Are Not Allowed To Tattoo Themselves. Understand?'

Stumpy's eyes widened and he grabbed his uniform trousers from the inside of his locker.

'Do You Understand, Junior Seaman Second Class Borrowdale?'

'Yes sir, I understand.'

Guns strode up and down the centre of the mess. 'Let This Be A Lesson To You All. You Are Not Allowed To Get Yourself Tattooed Under The Age Of Sixteen Or ... Or Whilst You Are Under Training At HMS Ganges ... So If Any Of You Have The Urge To Disfigure Yourself Whilst On Leave ... Think Again!'

There were murmurs of understanding as Stumpy laced up his boots and picked up his cap before scampering away towards the door.

Guns waited until Stumpy had gone. 'And When You Are Old Enough To Have A Tattoo, Never ... Never Be Stupid Enough To Have The Name Of The Latest Girlfriend Engraved Permanently Upon Your Body!'

Staring at the rafters this evening I remembered the Cheesy-Hammy-Eggy I had for tea. Another Naval delicacy, consisting of melted cheese on a slice of toast topped with a slice of ham with a fried egg on top. Naval Haute-Cuisine at its very finest.

Summer term at *Ganges* was definitely more comfortable than the previous term. Afternoons and evenings on the sports fields were slightly more enjoyable and because we were far from the Junior class now, we got our meals quicker as we were able to queue-jump. We were also beginning to understand the place, its people and its routines which enabled us to cut some of the corners.

Our 12-week exams added a degree of uncertainty to our days as we didn't know exactly what we were being assessed or examined on: it could be anything, but passing these exams would guarantee our promotion to Junior Seaman First Class. Along with a rise in status and pay, we would then be eligible for shore leave on either a Saturday or Sunday afternoon, have a star badge to sew onto our right arm, and best of all ... we would be eligible for shoes ... a pair of ferkin shoes!

The tests and examinations were coming at us thick and fast. We pulled and sailed regularly, we laid our kit out twice a week to show how we could improve by having our kit kicked all over the deck because of something ridiculously ridiculous. Failure of any aspect of our exams would result in being back-classed.

Stumpy, still in his best suit, slumped against the top of his locker.

'What did you get, Stumps?'

He tossed his cap onto his bed. 'Combination of things.'

'Go on then,' encouraged Misty.

'Captain gave me a lecture on ferkin tattoos.'

'Another lecture?' I asked

'Exactly the same. We're not allowed to have them whilst under training.'

'Is that true then?'

'Yeah'

'So what did you get then?'

'7 days number 10s.'

'That's steep,' exclaimed Slattery.

'And I've got to report to the Sickbay after tea each day to have it checked.'

'Every day? Why every ferkin day?'

'Check on the scabbing process and for any possible infection. Apparently something in the yellow ink can sometimes cause problems.'

'Blimey!'

'Then one of the Reggies had a go at Cynthia ... another one telling me I was an idiot for having my girlfriend's name tattooed on mi arm.'

'Right.'

'He doesn't know anything about Cynthia does he?'

'He doesn't ... no.'

'Or anything about our relationship?'

'Suppose not, Stumps. Suppose not.'

'Sod 'em all.' He ripped off his silk and lanyard and tossed them onto his bed.

Like Stumpy, all of us unwittingly did something that contravened one of the countless *Ganges* rules. My first taste of recorded Naval punishment was bread-related. One thing that was never available in the CMG, and greatly missed, was toast. All the bread was pre-buttered and piled at the end of the serving counter. It was the height of bravado to purloin a couple of slices and take them back to the mess where they were turned into crispy, brown toast.

When correctly dressed in night clothing we had to have the cuffs of our uniform jacket fully buttoned. Having the cuffs undone and folded back was in contravention of the *Ganges* dress code. I was unfortunate to be spotted one evening as I was leaving the CMG after tea with one of my cuffs unbuttoned. I was called over by a member of the Regulating staff, known to everybody as 'The-Scots-Git'. The timing couldn't have been worse: *Ganges* was in the middle of the latest bread-smuggling crackdown and I had a couple of slices of buttered white crusts stuffed inside my jacket.

'Do Your Cuff Up, Laddy!'

The jacket distortion wouldn't have been noticed had I been in a crowd but standing alone in front of the Scots-Git was my downfall.

'What's Have You Got Inside Your Jacket, Laddy?'

'Nothing sir.'

'Nothing Sir?' He tapped my chest and recognised the sound of secreted bread. 'Truth, Laddy ... Truth. What Have You Got Inside Your Jacket?'

'Bread sir.'

'Taking Food Out Of The Dining Hall Are You?'

I could only nod.

'You Do Know That Removing Food From The Dining Hall Is In Strict Contravention Of Ganges Standing Orders Don't You Lad?' he bellowed, holding up my pair of crusts wrapped carefully in a handkerchief that I had taken to the CMG specifically so that the butter wouldn't stain the inside of my jacket.

'Yes sir.'

'And One Of Your Cuffs Was Undone! If Both Your Cuffs Had Been Correctly Fastened You Would Be Back In Your Mess Making Toast By Now ... Undetected!'

'Yes sir, sorry sir.'

'As It Is You Are In The Rattle, Lad. Report To The Gatehouse In Five Minutes With Your Cap! You Will Be Charged With Removing Food from the CMG And Lying To A Member Of The Regulating Branch ... Namely Me!'

Five minutes later, I stood outside the Gatehouse while my charge was read out to me 'Did, In Contravention Of Her Majesty's Ship Ganges' Standing Order Number Blah, Blah, Blah, Remove Food From The Central Mess Galley, Namely Two Slices Of Buttered White Bread Crusts. Do You Understand The Charge?'

'Yes sir.' I was worried; this could mean something serious. He handed me my butter-stained handkerchief. I was marched over to the Quarterdeck where I stood lonely to attention waiting to be seen by the Officer of the Day. The Scots-Git paced impatiently up and down with his clipboard under his arm.

I reflected on what I had learned about the various *Ganges* punishment options.

Fortunately, the more traditional Naval punishments such as Walking the Plank, Keel Hauling and being Flogged Around the Fleet had been discontinued, but others remained. Official punishments would range from the relatively easy extra work required by number 10s to lots of extra work, doubling and the removal of any spare time required by a period of number 9s. Usually 14 days' number 9s was the worst most people received.

The punishment that was constantly threatened, but rarely imposed, was Shotley Routine. This was an officially sanctioned mess punishment that was used by Instructors in the very worst of circumstances. It included all the worst aspects of number 9s combining lengthy periods of drill, additional kit musters, physical exercise as well as being woken up at irregular intervals during the night and doubled everywhere. Those under Shotley Routine wore green tin hats without chinstraps. It was awarded in whatever duration the Instructor and Divisional Officer thought necessary. More than three days of Shotley Routine was considered excessive.

The ultimate punishment, and the only one left from the days of Nelson, was 'Cuts'. This was a caning awarded by the Captain and administered by the Master-at-Arms in a special room behind the Gatehouse. As far as I know, *Ganges* was the only place that still used this form of punishment. Apparently Cuts were not administered at the other Junior's training establishment, *HMS St Vincent* in Gosport Hampshire, as it was situated close to the centre of a town and employed many civilian staff. The maximum number of cuts had reportedly been reduced over the years and currently stood at twelve. However, when applied accurately, six were sufficient to draw blood, ruin a perfectly good pair of white sports shorts and made the recipient walk like a duck for a week or so afterwards. Of course, cut marks were considered a special badge of honour.

I was eventually marched up to a small table behind which stood a stern-faced officer who had a small piece of mashed potato stuck to his chin.

'Defaulters ... Off Caps!' bellowed Scots-Git.

Fortunately we had recently been taught how to remove and replace our cap in the standard Royal Naval fashion and I removed my cap correctly: up ... two ... three ... down!

Details of my charge were read out to me.

'Why did you take bread from the Central Mess Galley when you knew it was against *HMS Ganges* Standing Orders?' asked the Officer with mashed potato on his chin.

'To eat sir.'

'Why didn't you eat your bread while you were in the Central Mess Galley?'

'Don't know sir.' It wasn't a good response.

Scots-Git coughed and clicked his heels together, 'Excuse me sir. It is a well known contravention of Standing Orders for boys under training to remove slices of bread from the CMG and take them back to the mess to make toast.'

'Toast?'

'Yes sir, toast.'

'They have toasters in the mess?'

'No sir, they use irons.'

'Irons?'

'Yes sir.'

'What type of iron exactly?'

'Clothes irons sir, flat irons.'

'To make toast?'

'Yes sir.'

'How do they do that?'

'They switch the iron on and when it becomes hot they iron the slice of bread ... on both sides sometimes.'

'And that makes toast?'

Scots-Git inhaled. 'It does sir, yes.'

'I'll be damned. Why don't they make the toast in the Dining Hall?'

'There are no toasting facilities in the Central Mess Galley for Juniors under training sir.'

'No toasting facilities?'

'No sir.'

The officer looked at me with an expression of disbelief, 'Is that what you planned on doing,' he looked down at the charge sheet, 'Junior Seaman Second Class Broadbent? ... toasting your bread with the mess iron?'

'Yes sir.'

The Officer shook his head and the piece of potato fell onto my charge sheet. He looked directly at me with a serious expression. 'Rules are there for a reason. If the rules say that ... '

I had heard something similar many times before and my concentration levels ceased until it came to the important part when the details of my punishment was announced.

'Two days number 10s for the bread-smuggling offence ...'

Only two days: I'd got away with it!

'And an extra five days' number 10s for lying to a Senior Rate: seven days number 10s in total. Make the appropriate arrangements, Regulating Petty Officer.' Then the Officer looked directly at me, 'Don't let me see you in front of this desk again young man!'

I had the foresight not to thank him.

Scots-Git clicked his heels together. 'Two Days Number 10s On The First Charge And Five Days Number 10s On The Second Charge. On Caps ... Right Tin ... Qwuick ... A ... March! Eft ... Rayht ... Eft ... Rayht... Eft ... Rayht! Wait For Me Outside The Gatehouse!'

My first visit to 'the table' as a defaulter was over. At the Gatehouse I was issued with a Man-Under-Punishment-Card on which were the dates of the start and finish of my punishment routine. I was also given a well-worn board on a length of string that I was to hang on the bottom of my bed so that I could be given my early morning shake starting from tomorrow.

For a brief moment, when I returned to the mess, I was the centre of attention. In a strange way I was quite proud of my board on a length of string and hung it centrally on the rail at the bottom of my bed before staring at the rafters.

I watched one of the Arry boys as he finished ironing the last of his slices. It smelled wonderful.

'That smells nice,' I said.

'It'll ferkin taste nice too,' he replied as he walked back to his bed-space waving his golden slices. 'I'll clean the iron when I've finished mi toast.'

Today's phrase was 'In The Rattle' which meant being hauled in front of an Officer for breaking some rule or other. I lay there and wondered what number 10 punishment routine would be like: hopefully it wouldn't involve a lot of doubling or marching and anyway, in seven days it would all be done with.

In the morning I was prodded awake by a 'Reggie' and told to muster on the Quarterdeck in the dress-of-the-day in half an hour. I gave Stumpy a thumbs up as he too crawled out of his bed: brothers under punishment.

On the Quarterdeck, dressed in Number 8s, boots, gaiters and cap, our names were called and we were divided into those under number 10s and those under number 9s.

I soon learned that number 9s were serious as that squad were doubled away in the direction of the Parade-Ground. Number 10s were slightly less serious and we were dispatched to the far reaches of the establishment to skirmish (pick up litter) for three quarters of an hour. We weren't supervised so it was a bit of a 'loaf' really. Appropriate or what?

One advantage of being under punishment was that at dinner and tea time we were able to go to the front of the CMG queue so that we could muster on the Quarterdeck and be given our extra work. Only once during the next seven days, were those of us on number 10s drilled on the Parade-Ground. During the following week I found the early morning, dinner and tea-time skirmishing sessions rather enjoyable. Getting up early meant that Stumpy, Paddy, Bungy and I had the bathroom almost to ourselves, which was a nice change from the normal mad jostling for a morning sink. Almost everybody, at some time, earned themselves a period of number 10s: it was considered an integral part of the training curriculum.

'You Will!' screamed Chief Petty Officer PTI Ruffles, 'Improve On Your Last Pathetic Attempt On My Assault-Course ... You Will!'

We were standing to attention in three ranks, smallest in the centre, tallest on the flanks. We all knew what to expect and I was a little apprehensive.

'The Submerged Pipe Section Has Been Extended And Fresh Cold Slurry Has Been Added ... This Very Morning. The Sprint Distance To The Finish Has Been Shortened By A Couple Of Yards To Compensate.'

Someone on the front rank snorted ... then covered it up with a cough.

'You Need To Get To Grips With This Assault-course. Kick It ... Punch It ... Swear At It ... Spit On It ... Piss On It ... Shit On It ... Show It Who's Boss ...'

Guns and Spider stood to the side; they were wearing seaboots. At a nod from Chief Petty Officer Ruffles, now known as 'Truffles', Guns came over and divided us into two teams. 'Those Of You Who Live On The Port Side Of The Mess Will Form The Port Side Team. The Remainder Who Live On The Opposite Side Will Make Up The ... ?' He looked around and pointed directly at me, 'Will Make Up The ... ?'

I wasn't to be fooled. 'The starboard side team sir.'

'Clever Boy, There's No Flies On You Are There?'

'Not at this time of year sir.'

'Don't You Back Chat Me, Young Man.'

To be addressed as 'young man' could mean trouble. 'Sorry sir.'

'Fall-In In Your Teams. Port Side Team Will Be The First To Go!'

I was in the port side team and along with all the others we bounced up and down in mock anticipation. A few performed sarcastic PTI-type star jumps. Tug and I did a five second running-on-the-spot sprint.

'On My Whistle!' yelled Truffles.

And then we were off. Over the wall, then a crawl under the netting and through the partially submerged pipes and the fresh, cold slurry, across a series of wooden planks spanning waist high green water, an arm-wrenching swing over a gaping chasm, up and over a greasy climbing frame and a balancing act between structures high above the ground. Then we repeated the last three obstacles, before collecting our sand bag, which we carried the last 48 yards to the finishing line.

Truffles stood with his stopwatch in his outstretched hand as the final member of the port side team staggered in. Truffles snorted and nodded at Spider to get the starboard side team under way. I'd lost all sense of time, I was wringing wet and had collected a fair amount of the slurry that was starting to congeal. Inhaling only when completely necessary, I hand-wiped myself and picked off some of the solids that had stuck to me.

We waited in a disorganised heap until the starboard side team staggered home.

Truffles took a deep breath and ran his finger around the inside of his collar. 'The Port Side Team. Your Time Was Six Minutes And Seven Seconds Quicker Than Your First Attempt. Still A Long Way Short Of My Grandmother's Worst Time. You Should Kick The Arse Of The Team Member Who Was Last Over The Line.' He flicked his paper. 'The Starboard Side Team Would Have Been Fastest If It Hadn't Been For Their Last Man Who Needs A Brace Of Crackers Up His Arse. He Let You Down. Now That You Know Who The Weakest Members Of Your Teams Are, You Should Be Able To Work Out How To Help Them Improve Their Performance. I Shall Expect A Significant Improvement For Your Next Attempt!' He turned to Guns and Spider 'Take Them Away, Petty Officers!'

Halfway up Laundry Hill, Guns had to admit that the fresh slurry smell was wicked ... and that we should concentrate on getting any stains out of our sports gear as soon as possible. He promised an extra block of Pusser's Hard to those who wanted it.

Later that evening, as we were turning in, Blacky explained that his poor performance on the Assault-Course was a result of a cartilage problem he has suffered with ever since his playing days at Preston North End. This provoked a series of dismissive comments from some members of the mess, including me.

Being caught in possession of any item of kit or personal items belonging to someone else was a serious offence. The threat of having our backsides caned was sufficient deterrent for us to be very careful, particularly when collecting our drying from the Laundry or the Drying Room. We all helped each other and it was relatively easy to collect someone else's dry laundry and unintentionally misplace or keep an item not belonging to you. There were many hundreds of kit items being washed, dried, ironed and folded within the mess, so it was bound to happen occasionally. One particular Sunday morning I had a problem. I was next in the ironing board queue and had my blue uniform collar folded over my arm ready. When I opened it flat I discovered a dark blue stain on the upper side. Obviously someone had hung something dark blue and wet over one of the rails above my collar and it had dripped. My other collar was wet and there was no way, even with my depth of laundering expertise, that I was going to get this stain out and the collar ironed in time for Divisions.

So I had no choice but to borrow one and I went to Sunday Divisions wearing a uniform blue collar belonging to G. Commander, and clearly marked as such. Just my luck, it was a rather windy day and if there is one item of kit that is liable to misbehave in even the slightest breeze it's the flappy blue collar. If I was spotted wearing someone else's collar I would be 'In The Rattle ... In Deep Shit'.

Each Division was inspected by the Captain of *Ganges* during Sunday divisions at least once a term, although exactly which Division was a well-kept secret until the last minute. From a lowly trainee's point of view the Captain's Inspection was the pinnacle of panic. Today, because I was wearing someone else's blue collar, the number one man himself was going to inspect Keppel Division.

The Captain arrived at our Class followed by a fawning retinue of people with less gold rings on their arms. Our Divisional Officer saluted and reported. Like many others I hoped that the Captain wouldn't ask me anything.

The Captain homed-in on Tug.

'Where are you from, young man?'

'Keppel 9 mess sir.'

'Where does your family live?'

'Cowes sir.'

'On the Isle of Wight?'

'Yes sir.'

'Have you done any sailing before?'

'Yes sir. Thank you sir.'

Guns clicked his heels and took a large lungful of air. 'This particular Junior Seaman is developing into an exceptionally good Coxswain sir.'

The Captain nodded and asked Tug: 'Are you enjoying life in the Royal Navy?'

'I think so sir. Some days yes ... and some days no sir.'

The Captain blinked and turned to our Divisional Officer, said something and walked on.

There was one point during the Parade, when we were being inspected, when a gust of wind flapped our collars and Guns skipped along the middle rank flattening them down for a few of us. I couldn't wait to give George his collar back.

Once our class inspection was over Guns plonked himself directly in front of Tug and spoke directly into his starboard ear. 'When The Captain Or Any Other Person Of Higher Rank Than Your Miserable Self ... And That's Everybody ... Asks You If You Are Enjoying Life In The Royal Navy, The Correct Answer Is Yes Sir: Do You Understand? Yes Sir Is The Only Acceptable Answer. Capiche?'

'Yes sir,' replied Tug looking straight ahead.

'Some Days Yes And Some Days No' ... What A Pathetic Answer That Was. Makes Us All Look Like A Bunch Of Pathetic Fairies. What Does It Make Us Look Like Lad?'

'A bunch of fairies sir.'

'What Kind Of Fairies, Lad?'

'Er ... pathetic ones sir.'

'You Will Lay Your Kit Out In Nelson Hall This Evening And I Will Inspect It At Precisely Twenty Hundred.'

'Yes sir, thank you sir.'

The Bugle band struck up a rousing, slightly out of tune, tune. It was the signal for Guns to reposition himself at the front. Tug exhaled, pulled a resigned expression and stared unblinkingly straight ahead.

One important decision I made towards the end of the month was to join the Bugle Band. I hadn't exactly made my musical mark in Pudsey's Cub Band and my decision was based on the fact that I knew how to spit into the end of a bugle and make a noise. Secondly, and more important, it was a way of avoiding Divisions with the rest of 173 class. As the rest of the class were fallen-in outside the mess to be marched to the Parade-Ground each morning, I would remind Guns or Spider that I was a member of the Bugle Band and they would wave me away.

Down in the Bugle Band practice room we were fallen in outside and marched as a Band to the Parade-Ground. At the head of the band was a Royal Marine bandsman with a big elaborate stick who took the band thing very seriously. On the Parade-Ground, we weren't subject to a Divisional Officer's inspection and we didn't do the march past. We just stood there and made a musical noise. Some band members were passable musicians but the majority of us were there just to enhance the volume. If you didn't fancy blowing your bugle you could stand there and pretend: it was a doddle compared to the stress of normal Divisions. Being a member of the Band did involve a little extra Parade Instruction in the evening, which was a bit of a drag, but worth it. I didn't discover the perfect way of avoiding morning Divisions until the following month.

At the beginning of June most of 173 class were promoted to Junior Seaman First Class and we were issued with our badges. We quickly sewed our first class stars onto the right arm of our No 8 shirts and a red one on to our best No 2 suit jacket. It was during this process that I learned what a 'homeward-bounder' was. A homeward-bounder was a sewing stitch that was considered oversized and which had to be removed and re-sewn. Once we had our badge sewing and position approved we were fallen-in outside the mess and marched to slops where we were issued with a pair of Royal Naval shoes! Bliss; though we could only wear them on Saturday and Sunday afternoons and on a weekday evening when we were dressed in Night Clothing.

Unfortunately we didn't all gain promotion at the same time: there were individuals who were still on the various failure lists. Although Mucker had learned to swim he still hadn't done the jump from the high board, and Stumpy had still not managed to negotiate the Devil's Elbow. Those with less than average kits didn't get shoes either. Those who failed to come up to the mark in more than one activity were back-classed. With uncharacteristic *Ganges* consideration, those leaving the mess were allowed to clear their lockers while the rest of us were out doing something else. The first indication that someone had left us was when gaps appeared in the lines of rolled-up and taped raincoats on the back wall of the mess. It says a lot, for both the new-found pride in our mess and the acceptance that messmates come and messmates go, that the raincoats were immediately rearranged so that no gaps appeared and the empty beds were moved to the far end of the mess.

Being a First Class Junior had a number of tangible benefits. Sporting our badge certainly gave us credibility around the place: it identified us as individuals who had done at least 16 weeks and gave us a degree of precedence in the CMG queue. After five months of weekly washing with Pusser's Hard our Number 8s were fading nicely, and we were beginning to look like proper Sailors. Some tried to accelerate the fading process of blue items by adding bleach to the water when doing unsupervised hand washing, but if you were caught, or it didn't come out right, you were in deep shit. It was like most things Naval; if you did it gently and under cover of darkness you could probably get away with it. I decided that I'd take anything I wanted fading home to Mum: she'd know how to do it.

Tug had struggled through almost everything. In particular he was awkward on the Parade-Ground, but he had been promoted because he was a natural coxswain. Apparently he had been sailing since he was four years old. Everybody in the mess was glad that Tug remained with us because he had a wicked sense of humour and smiled through everything: even the Assault-Course.

As a Junior Seaman First Class my pay was increased. Unfortunately I still wasn't much of a wage-earner. My gross weekly salary was now 52/6d, my deductions remained the same but my pocket money was increased to 17/6d which gave me a weekly credit balance of 29/4d.

As a First Class Junior Seamen we were issued with a whistle called a Bosun's Call, a piece of traditional Naval equipment that predated electricity and the Tannoy. As members of the Seaman branch we were required to master this whistle and learn how to play a whole range of different tunes. Room number 7 in the Seamanship block vibrated to the sound of Class 173 as we learned how to produce a variety of high-pitched, unmusical sounds. When we thought we had mastered it, we were shown how to trill. This required good co-ordination of lips, hand and tongue and was completely beyond the capabilities of some. Needless to say there was a *Ganges* Piping Competition, an opportunity for First Class Junior Seamen to whistle and trill in front of judges. The supreme champion, and a few runners up, were awarded a long metallic chain on which to dangle their whistle and which proudly replaced their rope lanyard when dressed in their Sunday best uniform. They were designated *Ganges* 'Call Boys'.

Tug and I were designated Keppel 9 mess coxswains for the Inter Divisional Pulling and Sailing regatta, which this year was held on a Saturday in atrocious weather. We both selected good crews, which gave us the edge as we were fully crewed with First Class Seamen: there wasn't a Stoker, a Communicator, or a Blacky in either of our boats. We ensured that we carried no dead weight, and exposed ourselves bravely to the elements as we triumphed over almost everybody. We flew our divisional burgee proudly as victory followed victory. When all the points were totted up Keppel Division were top in Sailing and runners up in Pulling.

The following Thursday the weather was good and everybody congregated on the rising banks that surrounded the well-skirmished Athletic track. As my previous cross-country performance testified, I wasn't designed to run lengthy distances. With this in mind I'd put my name down for any of the short-course events in the Inter Divisional Athletics Competition. The entire flock of *Ganges* PTIs fluttered and star-jumped around flapping their arms, yelling instructions to groups of Juniors who stood around in competitive groups waiting to be told where to go, what to do and when to do it.

I came second in the 100-yard hurdles, I came somewhere in the middle of the field who scampered a long 200 yards and I also came second in the high jump. The Chief Petty Officer PTI in charge of the high jump and the long jump for the day, commended me on my scissors-jumping technique and encouraged me to practise.

At the end of a long athletic day, as the Suffolk sun was setting behind the hammer-throwing netting, we gathered in tired class groups while the Divisional scores were calculated. Fiskie had spent the afternoon clicking away with his camera at anything that moved; now he photographed gathered groups at rest.

The PT Officer announced the results: Keppel Division had come third overall, which was a great surprise to all our assembled Divisional Instructors and the Divisional Officer. We received a small silver-coloured cup that would be placed alongside the much larger platter that Tug and I had helped to win at the Sailing Regatta.

By this time, other badges were being earned. Boydie had been promoted to Leading Junior and Johnnie had been elevated to the position of Petty Officer Junior and now had a crown above his stripe. A number of badges that denoted specialist skills were sewn on the cuffs of our blue serge suits. Coxswain's badges were the most respected: they were awarded to those who had a particular skill in either pulling or sailing. Tug was the first to get his Coxswain's badge. Second in importance was probably the rifle badge that was awarded to those individuals who could shoot straight. Members of the Bugle Band could earn themselves a rather stylised bugle badge, if they wanted it.

I thought someone had made a terrible mistake when my name was included on the bottom of the Divisional .303 Shooting team list along with Stumpy's. Neither of us had displayed any shooting ability whatsoever. Guns explained to us both that we weren't shooting: we were to accompany the team as support members. We were the lads who stuck coloured sticky tape over the holes in the target after each round of shooting. It wasn't a bad job, but the sticky tape, which we had to lick, tasted awful and both Stumpy and I suffered from a ferocious dose of the Shotley-shits for a day or two afterwards.

Spider stood in the middle of the mess holding up a full page colour photograph of Brigitte Bardot wearing a skimpy orange bikini. 'Will The Pervert Who Had This Pinned Inside The Lid Of His Little Brown Case Step Forward ... Now!'

Surprise, surprise! The one who eventually owned up was an Arry boy by the name of Glover. He strolled down the centre of the mess and stopped just out of Spider's arm-striking distance.

'So, Young Lad,' said an unsmiling Spider holding Brigitte's picture aloft. 'From Where Did You Obtain This Picture?'

'Reveille magazine sir.'

'You Buy The Reveille Magazine?'

'Only when I'm on leave sir.'

'What Does The Reveille Magazine Do For You, Junior Seaman Glover?'

'Er, don't know exactly sir.'

'Does It Give You A Thrill?'

'I just like the pictures sir.'

'Are You Aware That Having Such Pictures In Your Possession Whilst You Are Under Eighteen Years Of Age Contravenes Queen's

Regulations And Admiralty Instructions And Is A Punishable Offence In This Man's Navy?'

'No sir.'

'Young Men Of Your Tender Years Could Be Scarred For Life By Such Pictures.'

'Sir?'

'This,' he waved the picture of Brigitte in front of Glover's face. 'Can Do A Lad Of Your Tender Years Irreparable Harm!'

'Sir?'

'I Don't Have To Explain Why ... Do I Junior Seaman Glover?'

'Yes sir.'

'Don't You Back Chat Me, Young Man!'

'Aye, aye sir. I mean no sir.'

That was a disappointment: I wanted to know why a picture of Brigitte Bardot in a skimpy bikini could be harmful to us at 16 years of age, and not when we were 18.

'Pictures Like This, Young Glover,' he wafted Brigitte again, 'Are No Good For You. Understand?'

'No sir.'

'Let Me Tell You Young Man. Impure Thoughts At Your Tender Age Drain You Of Energy. And Whilst You Are Onboard Her Majesty's Ship Ganges You Need All The Energy You Can Muster. Does That Make Sense?'

'Yes sir.'

It rang a bell with me also.

'So What Shall We Do With This Picture Of Miss Bardot?'

'Don't know sir.'

'As I Am A Touch Over Eighteen Years Old You Could Legally Give The Picture To Me!'

'Could I sir? Thank you sir.'

'You Could, Young Glover. You Could!'

'Right then sir.'

'Do I Take It That This Picture Of Miss Bardot Is Now Legally Mine To Do With As I Wish Then?'

'Yes sir.'

Spider carefully rolled Brigitte up and left with a noticeable spring in his step.

The main benefit of being a First Class Junior was shore leave. Each Saturday or Sunday afternoon, we were able to leave the camp between 13:30 and 20:00. Although theoretically it was a major breakthrough, in reality it was beset with problems. The first hurdle to overcome was the filling out the official 'Leave Request Form' stating where you were going and why. It was tempting to write 'To get out of this crappy place for a while' as a reason for requesting leave but nobody ever did: instead we wrote something ridiculous like 'To go for a walk' or 'For a change of scenery'. Once filled-in we would hand our forms to either Guns or Spider who would be the first to remind us that 'Leave Is A Privilege ... And Not An Automatic Right!' Providing that we were free from any form of personal, class or mess punishment they would sign and pass the Leave Request Form to the Divisional Officer who had the authority to approve our request. The penultimate obstacle to overcome, before we were allowed out of the camp, was mustering on the Quarterdeck to catch the Liberty Boat. If we didn't muster on the Quarterdeck within five minutes of the pipe, we missed the opportunity completely. Resplendent in best suits, all the Liberty Men would be inspected by the Duty Regulating Petty Officer, well known for their doggedness. If we didn't pass the inspection, and at least 50 percent didn't for some reason or other, we were sent back to the mess, our Leave Request Form destroyed and our leave cancelled.

Once ashore we all experienced an unusual sense of freedom. We didn't escape the *Ganges* influence completely: the populace of the surrounding area knew that all the *Ganges* Boys were under 18 and this effectively closed all licensed premises to us. Many *Ganges* staff lived and shopped in the vicinity and would make themselves known if we so much as removed our cap or rolled our jacket cuffs back. There were four destination options: Ipswich, Harwich, Felixstowe and for the really unadventurous ...

Shotley Gate itself. Naval transport to Ipswich was provided but it was a relatively uninspiring town and not very sailor-friendly. Harwich and Felixstowe, both with maritime connections, were a short MFV trip across the river. On a blank week, a wander around Shotley or Ipswich was all we could afford. If we had money in our pocket, we headed for the bright lights of Suffolk's answer to Las Vegas: Felixstowe. Felixstowe is a coastal holiday resort that had, among its list of attractions, a fairground. Once in the centre of pulsating Felixstowe we would immerse ourselves in the seaside atmosphere, the music and the girls. Our uniforms, and the fact that we were in a group, gave us added confidence and we would try and 'chat-up' girls, but it was an uphill struggle. The Felixstowe girls knew as much about *Ganges* as we did: they knew that we had to catch the 19:00 MFV back over the river and that we were banned from pubs. Consequently they weren't interested in us. I never heard of anyone forming a relationship with a girl they had met while on Felixstowe leave.

I hadn't received a letter from Christina for over a month now. I wondered if it was something to do with that dreadful portrait photograph I had sent her.

Another relationship that came to an abrupt end was that between Stumpy and Cynthia. Cynthia, who had just celebrated her 16th birthday, had written Stumpy a short note telling him that she had found someone new and he needn't bother knocking on her door when he was next home on leave. He was devastated and spent the following few

I sent this picture to Christina ... and she never wrote to me again

days in a lovelorn daze. Guns was surprisingly understanding … for a while. It wasn't the first 'Dear John' letter to be received in the mess, but it was the most noticeable. Every time we saw Stumpy's tattoo, we saw Cynthia's name. I suppose it underlined what Guns had told us: don't tattoo the name of your current girlfriend on your body, no matter how much you may want to.

I didn't get the chance to play cricket. By July my swimming skills were being fine-tuned. Inter-Divisional swimming galas were regularly held, and although the lad from 27 Recruitment always pipped me over 50 yards, I always won the 25 yard sprint. No matter how hard I trained and practised, I couldn't gain the extra yard I needed over two lengths. Our reward for all our efforts and time spent training was never anything more motivating than a bar of Cadbury's Milk chocolate, retail price 6d.

I was pleasantly surprised when it was arranged for the *Ganges* Swimming Team to go to Southend to compete against a team from a Police Training College. The Gala took place in a pool on the pier and I clearly remember my shock when I dived in, took a mouthful of water, and almost choked: it was a cold, salt-water pool! When I got over the shock, I won my sprint. Despite the freezing water I enjoyed the trip as it earned me my *Ganges* Swimming Colours which I was very proud of. I sewed them on the front of my blue sports shirt.

Getting to sleep was slightly more difficult in July as the Suffolk sun still shone through our sparkly clean windows casting strange rafter shadows across the ceiling. It wasn't unusual for me to recall the day and try to recount the number of times the mess or class had been on the receiving end of a spluttered bollocking. I also recalled the number of times that I had been individually chastised or castigated. Slowly, I was learning how to deal with denigration and not to let it worry me.

Our Parade Instruction was improving as was our rifle drill. We would start each Parade-Ground session outside the far end of Nelson Hall in front of the Armoury door and nearest to the Instructor's mess. There was a class groan if we were told to draw rifles. None of us enjoyed carrying an antiquated and relatively heavy piece of equipment around the Parade-Ground: it was difficult enough dragging our own body weight around sometimes. Rifle drill, particularly with bayonets, was never enjoyable and, if you were standing behind Tug, it was dangerous. Each session on the Parade-Ground involved learning a new and more complicated manoeuvre. Parade Instruction was one of those things that continued until the very end of our time in *Ganges*. Like logarithms or algebra: it was something we Seamen rarely used once we left.

One bright sunny morning, having been dismissed by Spider, I decided to take the longer route from the mess to the Bugle Band Hut. My route skirted some sweet smelling scrubland adjacent to the shooting range and I decided to take a stroll in through the gorse. I followed a natural pathway between the shoulder-high bushes that unexpectedly led to a clear area of ground up against a section of a red brick wall that I assumed was the Shooting-range boundary. Up against the wall lay a large bark-free log. I made myself comfortable on the log and lit a cigarette, inhaling slowly and deeply and enjoying the solitude. Apart from short periods in the sitting-down heads this was the first time since I had been at *Ganges* that I had been completely by myself ... and nobody knew where I was. By the time I'd finished my first cigarette I could hear the sound of the Royal Marine calling the Bugle Band to attention away down to my left. To my right, over the roofs of the messes on the Short Covered Way, I could hear the shouted commands of the Parade GI. I knew exactly what was happening: morning Divisions were getting underway. I decided that if I was missed by the Bugle Band, I was in trouble anyway, so I may as well sit back, enjoy the moment, have another cigarette and deal with the consequences later. There was a possibility of course that I had discovered an imperfection in the *Ganges* morning routine. The wall reflected the morning sun nicely, I stretched my legs out, and stared at my polished boots. In my silent surroundings I watched ants working, butterflies drifting around and in the distance I heard the sounds of *Ganges* at Divisions. I recognised the music that accompanied the first march past and listened for the occasional scream from the Parade GI, 'Go Round Again That Class!' I placed my cap on the grass alongside me, closed my eyes and just listened: I could hear birds. Up until now I couldn't remember hearing a bird in *Ganges*. I smoked a few more cigarettes until I heard the Bugle Band marching on the road towards the Band Hut where they would be dismissed. Time to leave.

With my shoulders hunched so that I was below the level of the surrounding gorse, I retraced my steps and made it back to the Long Covered Way just as my class were being mustered outside the mess to be marched to the first lesson of the day. Nobody said a word; nobody noticed anything different. I was on edge for the remainder of the day.

That evening I was amazed that I had apparently got away with my little diversion. I spent some time staring at the rafters, trying to work out if there was a flaw ... but I couldn't find one.

The following morning I joined up with the Bugle Band for Divisions; nothing was said about my absence yesterday. So, the next day I was on the log again, and the day after, and the day after that. It became a habit, a longed-for part of my daily routine. I decided that if I went to the Bugle Band occasionally there was more chance of being missed when I didn't go, so more often than not I sat on my log, even when the weather was dull or damp. My time on the log helped me through *Ganges*.

It wasn't a natural place for a log to be. Someone must have placed it here. Someone had discovered and used this place before me: I wondered who he was, when it was and if he had enjoyed his brief periods of solitude as much as I did.

After tea one evening I went to the Bugle Band Practice Room and discovered that there was a list of local village functions on the noticeboard to which the Band had been invited. This was something not to miss and I made sure that I kept an eye on the Band noticeboard so that I knew of any of the summer out-of-camp activities. About once every three weeks or so the Band made itself available to march around a field blowing our bugles and banging our drums at some Suffolk village fête or other. The Band did it for free; I don't suppose for one minute that anyone would pay to hear us ruin perfectly good pieces of music. It meant getting dressed in our best uniform and white webbing but it was worth it in order to get out of *Ganges* and see some girls!

A few weeks before summer leave, *Ganges* held its annual Parents' Day. It was on a Sunday and a tiered seating structure was constructed in front of Nelson Hall. Divisions took place in the afternoon after dinner to enable relatives from distant places to get to this remote part of Suffolk. Naval buses ran a shuttle service from Ipswich Railway Station. Sunday morning was spent in cleaning the mess, as our families would be invited to see where we lived after we had finished on the Parade-Ground. I had arranged for Mum and Tony to come down, driven by a family friend, who had a racing-green Morris Traveller.

We paraded for the benefit of our guests who sat straining their necks in order to identify their young man. There were lots and lots of girls and women who added a welcome splash of colour to the drabness of Nelson Hall and our surroundings.

At one stage of the proceedings, awards were presented to those Juniors who had shown a particular aptitude for something or other. The award that would surely have caused the most confusion was the *Ganges* Call Boy Champion who was presented with a Silver Bosun's Call by the Captain, no doubt making his parents extremely proud: confused ... but proud. The finale was Manning-The-Mast when a select group of volunteer trainees climbed the mast in time to the music of the Royal Marine Band. One of the group, a particularly courageous trainee known as the Button-Boy, would shin to the top of the mast, stand to attention and salute on a circular platform about a foot in diameter with only a flexible lightning conductor stuck between his legs for support. He apparently received a special crown-piece from the Captain in recognition of his achievement.

Then we marched past to a series of rousing Naval tunes played by the Royal Marine Band while the Captain took the salute. There was no Parade GI to send us round again on Parents' Day.

Once Divisions were over, we and our guests were shown to the NAAFI or the CMG where trays of finger-food were laid out. Divisional Officers and Instructors mingled and chatted with mums, dads, brothers, sisters, uncles, aunts, family friends and girlfriends. For us it was a time to get a look at the girlfriends of our classmates. Lash's mother was a very good-looking woman. The girl who was introduced to me as Slatterey's girlfriend was a bit of a dog ... more than a bit of a dog if I'm being truthful. I proudly gave my Mum, Tony and the family friend a tour of Keppel 9 and a few other interesting places, all of which had been tarted-up in preparation. Those of us who had guests were given the remainder of the day off and we made our way to Ipswich where we spent a couple of uninspiring hours and had something to eat.

Later that evening, when we were on the quiet roads leading back to Shotley, the family friend asked me if I would like to have a drive. He must have been a very persuasive man because Mum, a conservative and careful lady by nature, agreed. My adventurous button was pressed and I enthusiastically took the wheel. The fact that I was far too young to hold a driving licence, had no insurance or any driving experience whatsoever didn't cross my mind. I was driving and it wasn't that difficult. I followed instructions from the family friend as I gingerly negotiated the narrow, and fortunately empty, country lanes of rural Suffolk. By the time I arrived in Shotley I considered myself semi-proficient! Unfortunately I hadn't fully mastered how to stop and I came to a rather snatched and screechy halt at the end of Caledonia Road only feet from the *Ganges* gates. The aroused Regulating staff looked through the gate wide-eyed as I emerged from the driving seat, thanked the family friend for the experience, kissed Mum goodbye, gave Tony a friendly tap on the shoulder and waved the Morris Traveller a fond farewell.

I spotted Conkers in the CMG queue with a bunch of Nozzers who hadn't been in the Navy very long. I decided to have a word as he looked happier than he had looked when in Keppel 9 mess.

'How are ya mate?'

'Brilliant thanks.'

'Haven't seen you around for ages.'

'Spent a bit of time in the Sick Bay, then I got transferred to a place called Netley down south somewhere. Spent a while there: brilliant place, absolutely brilliant. Changed my life.'

'Changed your life how?' I asked, a little bewildered.

'Taught me that girls aren't all that important.' He sniffed.

'Aren't they?'

'Naah.'

'No more girl trouble then?' I asked.

'Who needs 'em?'

'Well ...'

'I've decided to become a Homo.'

'You what?'

He leaned on my shoulder and whispered in my ear. 'I'm goin' to be a Homo.'

'A what! Why?'

'Won't have any more women troubles then, mate.'

'That's true I suppose, but ...'

'Don't tell anyone though will ya.' Again he leaned closer. 'Apparently it's illegal in the Navy.'

'Is it?'

'So one of the blokes at Netley told me.'

'Fancy.' I was getting hungry: it was time for me to go.

For our summer term Exped weekend we were once again issued with a well-used khaki rucksack, rank smelling foul-weather clothing, a ration pack and cooking utensils. Surprisingly we weren't given a tent, which was a bit disappointing as Keppel 3 were now the junior mess in the Division and would have been used as the pack-mules. We tried on, and exchanged, items of our Exped clothing until we were all reasonably satisfied with what we had. Then we had dinner and lounged around waiting for what Spider referred to as our limousine, to arrive. Some of the more senior Division members were issued with plastic-covered maps and a compass. Someone whispered 'Cambridge': I didn't know if that was where we were going or the model of our limousine, as there was a spacious car with that name at the time.

Our limo turned out to be a Royal Naval three-ton, canvas-backed truck, into which we were herded and trundled away to Suffolk's northern pastures. My bum was aching as the truck eventually ground to a halt in the United Kingdom's most isolated lay-by. No sooner had we all disembarked than Spider slapped the back of our truck and it spluttered away leaving us stranded. I looked around; there was nothing, only flat green fields and an empty road. To our right was an elderly wooden gate, partially collapsed and leading to a barren field.

Spider waved his plastic-covered map. 'Fall In, Tallest On The Flanks, Shortest In The Centre.'

So we did exactly that, in a Suffolk lay-by.

Spider inhaled and continued. 'Pay Attention Everybody! Those Who Have Maps Stand Over There To My Right.' He pointed towards the road. 'The Rest Of You Divide Yourselves Into Groups Of Four! No More Than Two From The Same Mess In Any Group!'

Eventually, with help, we divided ourselves up in accordance with Spider's instructions. Tug and I chose a couple of Nozzers from 3 mess. Once assembled, we were joined by a senior Junior from 5 Mess who had a plastic-covered map.

'All Of You Who Make It To Our Objective Before Nightfall Will Be Rewarded With A Hot Supper And A Well Sprung Mattress To Sleep On,' Spider explained. 'Those Of You Who Don't Make

It Before Nightfall Will Sleep Under The Stars And Go To Bed Hungry! The Door Will Be Locked At 20:30 Exactly!'

Sleep under the ferkin stars ... me?

'My Team Come With Me!' Spider's team slunk over towards the collapsed gate. We watched them as they strode smartly away across the barren field and out of sight.

Our team leader from 5 mess had a well-faded No 8 shirt under his anorak. He introduced himself to us as Jim and told us to stay exactly where we were until all the other teams had gone. We watched as the penultimate team stomped away: we were all alone. Jim told us to take the weight off our feet and stretch out on the adjacent grass verge. He told us that his home was on the outskirts of Cambridge and he knew exactly where we were, and more importantly, he knew where we were heading. Apparently it was a good three-and-a-half hour trudge for anyone wishing to walk it. If we all agreed, he would call his Uncle Ernest, who ran a small transport business, to give us a lift in one of his vans.

'Just one problem lads,' said Jim. 'The nearest phone box is just around that corner up there ... a five minute walk.'

Five minutes later we were sitting comfortably in a partially roofed bus shelter while Jim called his Uncle Ernest.

'Not only is my Uncle Ernest willing to give us a lift,' spurted Jim as he emerged smiling from the phone box, 'he will also supply us with something to drink for the journey. He'll be here in about half an hour. Relax.'

And that's exactly what we did.

We piled all our equipment into Uncle Ernest's van and jammed ourselves into the back as best we could. Jim, of course, had the passenger seat and was busy showing his Uncle where we were to go.

'Got it. You're going to the old waterlogged schoolhouse,' said Uncle Ernest. 'There's a couple of bottles of Dandelion & Burdock in that crate in the back lads ... if you're thirsty.'

One of the Nozzers turned his nose up at the offered refreshment, but the rest of us polished a couple of bottles off in short measure. Our youthful burps made Uncle Ernest smile.

After half an hour of not seeing another vehicle on the narrow roads, Ernest came to a halt in front of a rusted metal gate leading to a field that dipped away. 'The old schoolhouse is just down there.' He turned and nodded in the opposite direction to a thick wall of trees. 'Behind those trees is the remains of a village which was abandoned at the turn of the century.'

'Why was it abandoned?' I asked.

'Don't know.'

'Because it didn't have a pub probably,' said Jim.

'Probably,' agreed Uncle Ernest.

Jim packed his map away. 'I used to play in these woods as a kid. We don't want to be the first to arrive, so we'll find ourselves a nice shaded spot from where we can see the schoolhouse and wait until one or two of the other teams have arrived before strolling down. Don't anybody mention Uncle Ernest right?'

The place we decided to rest and stand lookout for the afternoon was wonderfully quiet and shaded with a perfect view of the old schoolhouse and its approach-ways. My excess of Dandelion & Burdock ensured that I nodded off.

Three and a half hours after Spider had left us in the lay-by, the first team headed by one of the 5 mess Leading Juniors, shuffled down a distant pathway. They lounged against the shaded wall of the schoolhouse until Spider's team appeared some 20 minutes later.

Ten minutes later Jim jumped to his feet. 'Let's go. Remember to look as though you've just completed a long trek ... knackered. And no mention of Ernest.'

We followed Jim through the wood, over the road into a small patch of waist-high bushes through which a small overgrown path led us down into the open fields bordering the schoolhouse. As we reached the bottom we all developed limps, shortness of breath, pained expressions and stitch. Theatrically we all removed our rucksacks and collapsed against the schoolhouse wall next to the main door.

'Better tell Spider we've arrived safe and sound,' said Jim as he hoisted himself slowly to his feet.

'Good Effort Lads,' said Spider as he came out of the door followed by a smirking Jim. 'Anything Less Than Four Hours For

That Distance Is To Be Commended, Very Good Effort Indeed. Particularly From The Two Nozzers From 3 Mess. Well Done All Of You!'

The old schoolhouse was ancient. The floors were stone-flagged, doors and windows were rotting away and the brown painted walls of the four large rooms were badly flaking. Each room was lit by a totally inadequate single, fly-encrusted light bulb. The kitchen was a small butane gas burner; the worktop was a couple of planks supported by a pair of wooden trestles and seating was a pair of tubular canvas chairs. As instructed, we placed our Ration Packs in one large pile whilst Spider tried to light the gas burner. Eventually it exploded into life, taking Spider and a fawning Leading Junior completely by surprise and almost blowing Spider's woolly hat off.

The two rooms on the upper floor were furnished with double banked Naval beds. I threw my rucksack onto one of the top bunks; I'd always wanted to sleep on a top bunk. Tug flung his rucksack onto the top bunk next to the window and the Nozzers automatically took the bottom bunks. Despite what Spider promised, the bunks didn't have mattresses, so I spread my smelly foul weather gear over the springs and rolled my sleeping bag out.

The team lead by Johnnie was the last to arrive, but well before the 20:30 curfew.

'That was one heck of a walk we did today sir,' said one of the team leaders as we sat on the floor of one of the downstairs rooms eating a can full of stewed meat and beans.

'This stew is great sir,' said a snivelling Nozzer.

'How Did Your Team Find Their Way Across The Ford Without Getting Wet?' Spider asked Jim.

Jim didn't flinch. He finished whatever he had in his mouth and looked at the ceiling. 'A farmer with a flock of sheep came by and we watched as they were herded up behind the RAC phone box where there was a hidden bridge sir. So we just ...'

'You Just?' interrupted Spider.

'Sorry sir. We followed the sheep. Follows to follow the locals sir, they know all the short cuts.'

Spider scanned at us all in turn. 'That, Lads, Is What We Call Initiative. Look Around You At All Times. Don't Be Blinkered.'

Jim winked at Tug and me.

After a breakfast of canned sausages, beans and Bromide-free tea we all mustered outside on the springy damp grass to be given Sunday's task. 'I Have Arranged Transport Back To Ganges For 17:30 This Evening,' explained Spider. 'We Have Been Selected To Do Something Rather Special For This Isolated Community And For The Owner Of This Building Who Kindly Lets Us Use It Throughout The Year.'

We waited for further details.

'We Are Going To Paint The Walls And Ceilings Of The Upstairs Rooms. Split Into Two Teams, We Will Clean And Then Paint Each Room. This Is Not A Competition! I Will Supervise Both The Cleaning And Painting!'

Each member of our team was issued with a bucket of cold water containing foul smelling Tepol, a scrubbing brush, a cloth and told to 'Scrub!'

Within hours the upper floor rooms were cleanish. We were given paint pots full of sickly pale-green paint and a brush each. Spider gave us a quick three-minute painting demonstration: showing us how to hold our brush, fill it with the correct amount of paint, how to apply it to a vertical or overhead surface and how to smooth-out brush marks. Apparently the skill required to paint properly was all in the wrist action.

My wrists ached as we were loaded onto the canvas-backed three-ton truck for our journey back to Shotley. We were tired and most of us fell asleep sitting on the hard, slatted wooden seats. Some spent the entire journey scraping pale green paint from their hands. I had been one of a small group who had been told that soaking your hands in a bucket of cold Tepolled water would remove any dried paint ... and it did. I wasn't warned what effect a lengthy application of Tepol would have on my tender skin: it wasn't pretty and took many days to un-wrinkle.

We made it back to *Ganges* before dark. The CMG had laid on a meal of scraps for us ... and a slab of very dry, un-iced, brown cake with hard bits in it.

With summer leave on the horizon, I began to look after what I had left of my hair. With liberal applications of Suffolk water, I carefully stuffed as much of it up inside my cap as possible and avoided being capless whenever possible. I also tried to lengthen my sideboards a little but the facial hair in that particular area wasn't that plentiful, so it wasn't a success.

As leave got closer, and my hair grew longer, I was convinced that I was going to go home looking reasonably decent this time, but I underestimated the sadistic streak that ran through those members of the Regulating Branch who manned the Main Gate. Three days before summer leave I was Duty Bugler. Without my consent, I'd been classified as a proficient bugler and joined the ranks of those who had the dubious honour of getting up half an hour before everybody else and playing 'Charlie' over the main Tannoy at the Gatehouse. I hung my bugle on the end of my bed so that a member of the Gatehouse staff could wake me 45 minutes before Reveille. This gave me time to wash myself, comb my hair, stuff it under my hat, grab my instrument and double across the Quarterdeck to the Main Gate while the rest of the camp slept. I settled myself next to the main Tannoy and with my moistened bugle mouthpiece hovering close to my dry, nervous lips, I waited for a signal from the duty Regulating Petty Officer who was watching the Gatehouse clock. Being Duty Bugler was a nerve-wracking experience: blowing a bugle at this time in the morning wasn't easy and Reveille wasn't the easiest of tunes to get right.

Click.

Thankfully I managed to play 'Charlie' more or less in accordance with the Duty Bugler standard. I had almost escaped the Gatehouse, pleased with myself and glad it was all over, when one of the Regulating Petty Officers placed a restraining hand on my shoulder and flicked my cap off. He was the one who had witnessed my return from Parents' Day leave. Things were taking an early-morning turn for the worse.

'Now Then, Stirling Moss, What's All This Then?'

I responded in the required fashion. 'Don't know sir.'

'Name, Mess And Ships Book Number!'

This was official.

He noted down my details on a sheet of paper and finished with a very deliberate and heavy-handed full stop. 'Get Your Hair Cut Today. Report To Me Personally ... Here At Exactly 18:00 This Evening With Your Hair At A Regulation Length. I Will Let Your Class Instructor Know!'

Shotley himself looked at me sympathetically as I shuffled into his shop after tea. He asked me who had picked me up and when I told him that it was a Reggie, he smiled. I think I received a Shotley Special; a cut that removed almost all of my hair and piled it up around my feet, leaving the irritatingly tickly bits inside my white front.

At 18:00 I reported to the Reggie at the Main Gate. With a beaming smile, he removed my cap and looked admiringly at my butchered locks. 'Perfect, Absolutely Perfect. I Must Send A Special Message Of Congratulations To Your Hairdresser. With A Haircut Like That You'll Have All The Girls At Home Swooning At Your Feet! Where Is Your Home Town, Where Does Your Mummy Live?'

'Pudsey sir.'

'Pudsey! What Kind Of A Name Is That?'

'Just Pudsey sir.'

'JUST?'

'Sorry sir.'

'And Where Is Pudsey When It's At Home?'

'Yorkshire sir. West Yorkshire, between Leeds and Bradford.'

'Well Those Pudsey, West Yorkshire Girls Will Certainly Be Looking Forward To Seeing You During Your Leave ... Won't They?'

'Probably not now sir.'

'Pardon?'

'Probably not now sir.'

'Still ... You'll Be Able To Take Them For A Ride In Your Car Won't You?'

'I don't have a car sir.'

'Back To Your Mess.' He handed me my cap. 'Put Your Cap On, Prevent You Catching Cold!'

Even my messmates looked upon my haircut with a degree of sympathy. However I gained a couple of respect points by explaining that the Reggie who had picked me up was the same one who had seen me getting out of the driving seat of the Morris Traveller on Parents' Day.

'You ferkin didn't?'

'I ferkin well did!'

'It's still a ferkin awful haircut though, mate.'

My hair was traumatised and it stopped growing completely.

The Main Leave morning routine was similar to before except we were all assembled in Nelson Hall to await the buses, apparently because it was officially Naval Summer Time ... and windy ... and raining.

Once again, we were chaperoned via Ipswich to London and across town to Kings Cross. This time I acted like a seasoned traveller. We First Class Juniors had a bond of experience and we smoked, swore and joked our way north, the smoky atmosphere within our compartment discouraging any civilian passengers to share with us. Even the ticket inspector did what he had to do very quickly.

I got a taxi from central Leeds all the way to Pudsey; it was about eight miles and was an extravagance that not many 16-year-olds could afford. I enjoyed lounging on the back seat taking in all the familiar views. I had 21 pounds, two shillings and eight pence burning a hole in my pocket, less the taxi fare, and three weeks and a weekend to spend it all.

I rubbed the toes of my boots on the back of my trousers before I entered my front door. Home again. Mum wasn't serving in the shop, she was watching something on television. There were lots of cuddles and tears.

'Welcome home my love, when do you go back?'

'Fifth of September.'

'And what have you done to your hair?'

'Me? Nothing.'

'It's terrible.'

'I know.'

'Have you brought your book home again?'

'Yes. They're going to give us a new edition of the Seamanship Manual sometime next year.'

'Are they love?'

Mum, Leeds, Pudsey, and home were relatively unchanged: Tony looked a few months older and an inch or two taller. I soon fell into the relaxed routine of being home, but in a strange way I missed the *Ganges* routine. With nobody telling me what to do and when to do it, I constantly had to decide how to fill my days. Mum said that I looked slightly more mature, I'd started shaving every other day and she was sure that I'd grown a bit.

The pony-tailed girl who lived up the road knew I was home because Mum had told her, but she didn't come into the shop. I was glad about that; despite combing what was left of my hair into something resembling a style, I still looked like an escaped convict who had been dragged backwards through a field of nettles and over a barbed wire fence. I noticed that Mr Fisk's portrait photograph was still on top of the Welsh dresser. Over dinner I once again made a little ceremony about giving Mum the Ration Allowance money the Navy had given her for feeding and accommodating me for the next three weeks. She was chuffed to bits as she never expected that the Navy would give it to her a second time.

I was awake early on the first morning that was a typical Pudsey day, dull and dreary. The Rome Olympics were on TV so I stayed inside and watched it. The quality of the pictures, all the way from Italy, fascinated me.

The following day I caught up with the latest popular music releases as broadcast by Radio Luxemburg and went into Leeds to my favourite record shop. It was the same girl behind the counter but she didn't recognise me, probably because I wasn't in uniform. I bought *Apache* by The Shadows and my first LP (Elvis Presley's Greatest Hits). I paid casually with a smile but I think it was my haircut that let me down; she didn't look at me directly as she gave me my change, nor did I get a smile.

I watched a lot of the Rome Olympics because the weather during my first week at home was terrible, and when it's terrible in West Yorkshire it's best to stay indoors. It brightened up midway through the second week and I spent most of a sunny Thursday and Friday watching our local cricket team. Pudsey was very much a cricketing place: we were the home town of perhaps the most famous English cricketer of the time, Sir Leonard Hutton. He was retired now but he still watched the local team, Pudsey St Lawrence, play. As a much younger boy I had once shared a wooden bench with Len, not realising who he was. On the drive home my father explained to me that the old bloke I had been sitting next to, and who I reckoned was a boring know-it-all, was Len himself. I always regret not having got his autograph; he was a schoolboy hero of mine along with John Charles of Leeds United and Wales, and Brian Close of Yorkshire Cricket Club and England.

I only went out in my uniform a couple of times. I wanted to show everybody that I had a couple of badges but I doubted if anyone would notice, or understand what they were for.

Leeds United beat Rotherham United 1-0. Football in the second division was different from the first division and even the names of our opponents didn't have much of a footballing ring to them. The crowds were sparser than last year, but the toilets were the same; exactly the same.

I went to the pictures once to see 'Saturday Night And Sunday Morning' because I had heard it was a bit raunchy, but I was disappointed. I was on my own and quickly became bored. I saw my father briefly and we arranged that he would visit me at *Ganges* for my passing-out parade in January and possibly take me to London if it could be arranged.

Once every year a patch of derelict scrubland next to the British Legion Club on Pudsey's Robin Lane was transformed when the Summer Fair came to town. From the comfort of my bed, I heard the familiar early morning rumble of the trucks and the caravans as they negotiated the narrowness of our Lane. By mid afternoon, the Waltzer, Dodgems, Swinging Gondolas,

Horses on Poles and an array of other colourful attractions were almost ready for us.

Rousing rock-and-roll music and flashing lights combined with the smell of diesel generators, toffee apples and candyfloss was a clarion call for all the teenagers of Pudsey to congregate and let their hair down. I didn't have that much hair to let down, but I converged on the fairground along with hundreds of similarly minded individuals. I loved the fairground atmosphere and had decided to fritter away a good proportion of my earnings on the slot machines, shooting ranges and hoopla stalls. I also intended to look at girls. I knew from long experience that the fair attracted Pudsey's fairest maidens in reasonably large numbers and I knew exactly where to watch them. If there was one piece of fairground equipment specifically designed to entertain and enthral testosteroned teenage boys it was the Waltzer. Its centrifugal force threw screaming, leg-flinging girls into wonderfully revealing positions, made more enjoyable by the fashion for hooped skirts that were almost impossible to control. Lounging on the undulating walkway that surrounded the Waltzer, I watched revolving cars full of whirling girls as they revealed much more than they intended. Having failed to preserve their modesty, most would stagger out of the cars at the end of their one and only Waltzer experience, but thankfully not all. There were girls with a more outgoing and gregarious personality who would part with their money to entertain us again … and again.

We lounged nonchalantly against the rails, smoking cigarettes and watching an ever-changing kaleidoscope of nylon-stockinged legs flash in front of us. Life didn't get any better than this.

I was encouraging a member of the Waltzer staff to increase the swing of a car containing a group of particularly immodest girls, when I was tapped on the shoulder. It was Barbara, a classmate of mine from fifth form art. She had matured significantly since I'd last seen her.

'Peter. Thought I recognised ya,' she said, screwing her nose up at the sight of my cigarette.

'Hello Barbs.'

'Haven't seen yew for ages.'

'I've been away.'

'Bin away, duwin wha?'

'I'm in the Navy.'

Barbara's slate blue eyes widened, 'Navy ... yewer not in t'navy are ya?'

'Yep, over six months now.'

'Where are ya then ... in t'navy?'

'Down south.' I needed to choose my words carefully: I could be in the process of being picked-up here. 'In Suffolk, near to Essex and London ... and Cambridge.'

'On a ship then?'

'Yes.' It was a lie: but all's fair in love and lust.

'What's it called then ... yewer ship?'

'It's a she, all ships are called she.'

'Why?'

'Dunno.'

'Ya don' 'arf sound posh.'

'Do I?'

'What's she called then ... this ship of yewers?'

'Ganges ... HMS Ganges.'

'Is it big?'

'Massive. Biggest ship in the Navy.'

'Is it really?'

'Yeah.' I noticed how her blouse was stretched and I could see the outline of her bra.

'What ya dun with yewer hair? Ya used to 'ave nice hair.' She gazed at Shotley's handiwork.

I had a flash of inspiration. 'This is the style down south, called a Caesar style. Everybody's got their hair like this ... in Suffolk.'

'Bit short init?'

'It's the fashion,' I flicked my cigarette over the railings, 'down south.'

'Been anywhere … yuh knaw … interestin' lyke?'

I tried hard to maintain eye-contact, but my gaze drifted downwards to the top of her blouse which periodically gaped to reveal a darkened chasm and a tantalising glimpse of frilly edged underwear. I coughed. 'Next year we're off on a round-the-world trip.'

'Round t'world … the whole world?'

'That's the plan, completely around the world.' I needed another cigarette: I wasn't a natural liar.

'Bet you'll 'ave a girl in every port then.' She laughed and one of her front buttons pinged undone.

'Yorkshire girls are the best though.'

'Naah we're not. I 'aven't bin any farther south than Donnie in mi lyfe. Been up north though: went to Newcastle wimi Dad once to watch United play.' She re-buttoned herself.

An opportunity! 'You support Leeds United then? I used to go to all their games before I joined the Navy. Still do when I'm home.'

'Naah … Ahm norra football fan really. I only went cos mi Dad wanted someone to go wiyim.'

I inhaled a large lungful of smoke and blew it out respectfully over my shoulder. 'If you give me your address, I'll send you some postcards whilst I'm travelling next year.'

'I Dunno, Pete.' There was a slight colouring of her cheeks as she looked away towards the setting Yorkshire blur which people from these parts call the sun.

'Just a postcard or two.'

'Mmmm.' She looked towards the setting sun and I took the opportunity for a good old ogle. What a chest … a generously proportioned West Yorkshire frontage.

'I'll 'ave to ask mi boyfriend.'

'Your boyfriend?' My stomach dropped.

'Oh you've bin away aven't ya? Ya don't knaw.'

'Know what.'

'I'm goin' out wi Norman Longbottom … ya know Norman.'

'Norman, the train spotter?' I asked.

'Yeah, that's im ... and that's not all.' She folds her arms across her frontage.

'Isn't it?' I ask.

'No.' She unfolded her arms.

'Go on then.'

'We're gewin on holiday together to York ... next week.'

'Crikey.'

'We've gorra Bed & Brecky together.'

'You're haven't?'

'We 'ave. We're goin' to sleep together and all that stuff for three days!'

'Blimey!'

'Then we're goin' tut Railway Museum place. Norman says we can go for two days on't trot if we like.'

'Blimey.'

'So I'm really looking forward to it ... losing mi whatsit and everything.'

'Losing your what?'

'You know ... thingie.' She glanced downwards and stroked her tummy.

I inhaled deeply: that's what a 1950s Grammar School education did for you. Over Barbara's shoulder I caught the eye of an old school friend who was drawing his fingers across his throat and shaking his head at me. I gave him an acknowledging wave.

'Looks like I've got to go, Barbs.'

'Look after yewer sen then.'

'Thanks. Will do.'

'What's t'name of yewer ship again?'

'HMS Ganges.'

Norman ferkin Longbottom, the train spotter, of all people! He was going to take her whatsit and everything ... why 'Arsy' Longbottom of all people?

The three weeks and a weekend flew by and before I knew it I was sitting in the lounge polishing my shoes preparing to return to rural Suffolk. I had ironed a razor-sharp crease down the front of my white front and ironed my suit. Packed in my Little Brown Case were sweets and numerous packets of cigarettes along with a couple of extra pairs of civilian underpants, still in their plastic wrapper.

Maybe it was the balmy Yorkshire weather but I really didn't want to go back this time. Dad didn't take me to the station because he was working, so I caught a bus into Leeds. I scraped enough money together for my fare; it had been an expensive leave one way and another.

7

FROM *HMS PETARD* TO A DATE WITH JAYNE MANSFIELD

The blue Navy trucks were waiting for us outside Ipswich Station and we were jammed onto them by a small battalion of Naval Instructors. I was back!.

We lined up in Nelson Hall to have our Little Brown Cases searched for contraband. This time I lost a bottle of Old Spice after shave and a cigarette-rolling machine that I thought would come in useful. I managed to get away with the extra underpants, although the Petty Officer did rip the plastic wrapper open to check inside.

Back in the mess exaggerated tales of leave abounded. If every story was to be believed, there wasn't a good looking female virgin with enormous tits left in the entire country: the boys from *HMS Ganges* had deflowered them all in the space of 23 days! Blacky trotted out the preface to a story about an encounter he had with twins from Wigan, but nobody took any notice. I didn't add to the bullshit. Spider and Guns paced up and down the mess encouraging us to 'Get Back Into The Routine ... Chop Chop!'

Summer was definitely finished: Charlie screamed at us in the Suffolk dark once again. There were two empty beds in the morning: Lugs and Glover had not returned. Glover arrived back on Tuesday evening, claiming he had fallen sick while at home, but had not followed the correct procedure and got himself a Sick-Onshore certificate from his doctor. Lugs was forcibly returned to us. On Thursday I saw him briefly, standing between a couple of policemen outside the Gatehouse; his locker was cleared and belongings removed from the mess. One minute he was our messmate and the next minute he was gone. We rarely saw Lugs after that: rumour had it that he had fallen into that strange, continual punishment cycle. No sooner had he finished one punishment session, than the session itself caused him to misbehave and he was given a further period of punishment. We missed him because he was an enthusiastic goalkeeper and good at rugby. Glover was given 14 days' number 9s and his leave was stopped for the remainder of the term: he had the distinction of being the first Arry boy in the Division to be hauled in front of the Captain's table.

Misty, Tug and I decided to try and escape ashore the first Saturday back from leave. Surprisingly, all three of us got our Leave Requests signed, without being given the standard 'Leave Is A Privilege' lecture. We passed the Quarterdeck inspection at the same time and caught the MFV over the river to experience the doubtful delights of Harwich. Between us we had less than eight shillings to fritter away.

Harwich didn't disappoint us: we'd heard it was a crap place for a run ashore ... and it was. If there were any girls living in Essex, they obviously had got something else to do ... indoors. We wandered around town, unable to find anything of architectural interest or anything that would broaden our minds. Even Essex pubs were out of bounds, so after an uneventful couple of hours we shuffled back to the waterfront to wait for the MFV back to Shotley. One of the shore-leave rules was that we weren't allowed to smoke while walking around town. So, dying for a smoke, we decided to visit a greasy-spoon café and splash out on three coffees. I had some loose tobacco and Tug had a packet of cigarette papers. During the previous months all three of us had developed our own method of rolling the contents of old dog-ends inside a cigarette paper and sticking it together without much of the tobacco falling out. It was a useful skill on a blank-week when recycling old tobacco was the only way of getting ourselves a smoke.

We were sitting at a table trying to manufacture a roll-up each when our feeble attempts caught the eye of a friendly, old gentleman who watched us for a while before coming over to sit with us. He knew how to roll a cigarette with one hand, a skill he said that he had perfected in the engine rooms of submarines between the Wars. Within minutes he showed us how to do it. He also explained why hand-rolling tobacco is called Tickler in the Royal Navy. It was because a company called Tickler was the first to provide jam and marmalade to the Navy in airtight jars, and the sailors quickly discovered that the empty jars were perfect for keeping their tobacco fresh and moist. None of us bothered to ask the old guy his name, but we did offer him a Tickler which he gracefully refused; his wife apparently had stopped him smoking some years ago. All three of us would be eternally grateful to him, particularly in forthcoming blank weeks. I came across very few other people during my time in the Navy who could roll a perfect cigarette with one hand: one was a fearsome Pompey girl who was a regular at The Lennox Public House on Portsmouth's Commercial Road. Maybe she had met the same old bloke sometime between the wars.

The MFV dropped us at the Suffolk foreshore in plenty of time, according to my wristwatch. I wanted to practise my hand-rolling skills, so I called in to the Shotley Village Store and Post Office to buy myself a small packet of hand-rolling tobacco and some cigarette papers. Tug and Misty went on ahead. As I left the shop I checked the time: I had five minutes before my leave expired. I stuffed my tobacco and papers into my pocket as I sauntered down Caledonia Road towards the Main Gate. Unfortunately, the Regulating Petty Officer on the gate was the same one that had seen me driving the Morris Traveller and who had made me get my haircut before Summer leave. 'Good Evening Stirling. Nice Of You To Return ... Eventually.' He waved an arm towards the Gatehouse. 'Be So Good As To Step Inside For A Moment!'

I checked my watch: I was bang on time.

Inside the Gatehouse my signed and stamped leave request sat all by itself on the desk. My least favourite RPO asked his assistant, 'What time does it say on the main gate clock RPO?'

'Twenty ten exactly RPO.'

I looked at my watch again. It showed exactly eight-o-clock. I opened my mouth. 'But sir I ...'

'You Don't Want To Be Charged With Insubordination As Well As Being Adrift From Leave Do You?'

'No sir.'

'Are You Questioning The Accuracy Of The Main Gate Clock, Lad?'

'No sir.'

'The Main Gate Clock Is Always Correct, Lad: Never Wrong.'

'Yes sir.'

'Back To Your Mess. Get Out Of Your Finery And Report Back Here In Five Minutes In Night Clothing ... With Your Cap!'

'Yes sir,' and I scuttled away. Back in the mess I told some of the lads what had happened. One of the Arry boys explained that it sounded like I was on the wrong end of the rarely used Gatehouse clock scam used by the Reggies when they were bored. That made me feel a whole lot better.

For the second time I was marched on to the Quarterdeck and stood outside the Officer of the Day's cabin alongside my favourite Duty RPO. Eventually one of the Instructor Officers appeared and the punishment process began.

'Off Caps!' bellowed the RPO as I stood in front of the desk.

The Schoolie ruffled some sheets of paper and looked up at the ramrod straight Petty Officer standing to my right, 'Read me the charge Petty Officer.'

'Sir! Did, In Contravention Of Queen's Regulations And Admiralty Instructions, Return From Sunday Leave Ten Minutes Adrift At Twenty Ten.'

The Schoolie stared at me. 'And what do you have you to say about the charge, young man?'

'Nothing sir.'

'Why were you adrift from leave?'

'I didn't think I was sir.'

'You didn't think that you were what?'

'Adrift from leave sir. My watch said that it was a minute before eight ... nineteen fifty nine exactly when I walked in the Main Gate sir.'

The Schoolie looked inquiringly at the RPO.

The RPO clicked his heels together. 'The correct time was twenty ten sir ... by the Gatehouse clock.'

'You are a First Class Junior Seaman,' the Schoolie said as he scanned the charge sheet. 'Broadbent. You have been at HMS Ganges long enough to know that leave is a privilege not a right. Leave is a privilege that is not to be abused young man. Commander's report.'

'Commander's Report!' bellowed the RPO. 'Hon Caps ... Right Tin ... Qwuick ... A March! Eft ... Rayht ... Eft ... Rayht... Eft ... Rayht! Wait For Me Outside The Gatehouse!'

The following day I was once again stood to attention on the Quarterdeck along with a small number of other lads waiting for the Commander of *HMS Ganges* to make an appearance.

As the door to the Wardroom Office was opened by The Master at Arms, our RPO stiffened. 'When Your Name Is Called March Smartly To The Table, Stand At Attention Facing The Commander And Wait For The Master At Arms To Order 'Off Caps'!'

The Commander was an elderly man with wisps of grey hair straying over his ears. His nose was hooked and he had penetrating green-grey eyes.

'This is not the first time you have been at the defaulters' table, is it Junior Seaman Broadbent?'

'No sir.'

'Twice in nine months is not a good record.'

'No sir.'

'Read the charge, Master at Arms.'

He read the same words as were read out by the duty RPO yesterday, but with more emphasis on the word ADRIFT.

My lecture began in the now familiar manner. 'Leave is a privilege Broadbent: not a right. As a training establishment where the best sailors in the world are trained we cannot tolerate individuals coming back from leave whenever they feel like it. The expiry time of leave at weekends is established so that you have the time to get changed and turned-in before lights out. Do you understand that, young man?'

'Yes sir.'

'Leave breaking is a very serious offence.'

Here it comes, I thought to myself, serious punishment.

'Seven days number 9s. Master at Arms. Leave stopped for the remainder of the term.'

For a second time I was issued with my Man Under Punishment card and a bed-board.

The following morning I mustered on the Quarterdeck with Glover and a dejected looking Lugs, along with all the other Men Under Punishment. For a short while the routine was exactly the same as before, until those of us under number 9s were marched over the armoury and issued with special punishment rifles. The rifles were heavier than those we normally used for class Parade Instruction. They had no webbing and definitely no bayonet. Had *Ganges* added extra weight to the punishment rifles? Naah, they wouldn't do that would they? The Duty Punishment Petty Officer was not happy; he started us off with an anti-clockwise double around the Parade-Ground. During one circuit I noticed those under number 10s ambling away to do their half-hour skirmishing.

As we were drawing to the end of our hour's drill, dribbles of early-morning risers were drifting towards the CMG for their breakfast. We returned our rifles to the armoury and were doubled across the Quarterdeck to do a couple of lengths up and down Laundry Hill to finish us off for the morning and to make the walk back to the CMG longer. I didn't double during the dinner hour; instead I was part of a team who scooped buckets full of heated food waste from the stinking troughs behind the CMG into large dustbins and transported them on wheeled trolleys to the pig-sties about half a mile away. After tea, those of us on number 9s were given an hour's community work: my first session was in the Wardroom pantry where I alone washed, rinsed, dried and put away all the crockery from whatever meal the Wardroom had recently consumed. The pantry had no washing-up machinery, only two large stainless steel troughs, one full of steaming hot soapy water alongside another full of tepid grease-filmed rinsing water. It was here that I first saw someone dry a stack of hand-held plates: top first then bottom; flip the top plate to the bottom of the pile and start again. I never forgot how to do that. I thought it was magic.

An alternative to working in the Wardroom Pantry was the Main Galley where we were used to clean encrusted work surfaces, cooking equipment and floors. A gentle skirmishing routine was a pleasant and unexpected alternative. Our punishment day ended with a final muster three quarters of an hour before lights-out. Depending on how quickly the Duty Punishment Petty Officer wanted to get back to the Senior Rates bar we would simply be mustered and checked before being dismissed, or subjected to a final goodnight double around the periphery of the Quarterdeck. Then I would get everything clean and ready for the following day without disturbing my mess mates before crawling into bed and hanging my Man Under Punishment board on the end.

The main event of our final full term was Sea Training. It was eagerly anticipated by everybody, because we were going to sea onboard a real Naval ship for the very first time. We were shocked to learn that there were no beds or bunks onboard the ship and that we would have to learn how to sling a hammock. The Arry boys smiled knowingly.

The hammock issue area of Naval slops was tucked away in a dimly lit corner. An elderly man wearing a grubby brown coat issued each of us with a piece of heavy-grade canvas about six feet long by two-and-a-half feet wide with eyelets on the shorter sides. His assistant plonked a thin, prickly mattress along with an array of ropes and rings on top of the canvas ... and that was it: apparently I now had the component parts of a Pusser's hammock. It was a heavy and cumbersome load to carry back to the mess and I thankfully dropped it at my feet on the Long Covered Way outside the mess. We were each allocated a pair of hooks that were welded to the main roof support stanchions. I made sure that I was next to Muddy who apparently knew all about hammocks as he had slept in one onboard Arethusa for yonks.

Spider, Guns and all the Arry boys taught the rest of us how to incorporate all the clews, rings and lanyards in order to produce something that vaguely resembled a standard Royal Naval 'Mick'. I reflected briefly on the number of boys who had learned how to sling a hammock from these very same hooks before me.

Once slung and secured, the most difficult and humorous part of the whole thing was learning how to get into it: even the Arry boys had difficulty, as there were no helpful handholds on the deckhead of the Long Covered Way. After many a tumble, much foul language and many a laugh, we all managed to get in and stay in. We enjoyed a brief swing before Guns ordered us out so that he could teach us how to lash-up and stow it.

'Distribute The Bedding And Other Contents Equally Over The Whole Length Of The Hammock, To Prevent It Looking Lumpy When Lashed Up. I Hope That You All Understand Lumpy?'

I struggled: not quite knowing what a lashed up hammock was supposed to look like.

'Roll Your Mattress Up Lengthways And Lay It Down The Centre Of The Hammock Ensuring That It Doesn't Overhang The Head Or The Foot.'

Rolling a mattress wasn't as easy as it sounds.

'Now Stand With The Right Arm Against The Hammock Looking Towards The Head ... Decide Which Is The Top Of Your Hammock ... And Pass A Running Eye Of The Lashing Line Clear Of The Bedding. Fold The Two Edges Of The Hammock Together To Enclose The Contents And Lash The Hammock Using Seven Equi-Spaced Marline Hitches. Secure The Final Hitch Making Sure That It Is Clear Of Any Contents. Check That None Of The Contents Are Protruding. Protruding Means Poking Out. Remember In The Event Of An Abandon Ship, Your Hammock Has To Pass Through A Standard Admiralty Pattern Scuttle And Once In The Water Should Be Capable Of Keeping You Afloat Until Rescued!'

'Wouldn't that depend on how far away our rescuers were sir?' Someone at the far end asked.

Guns strained his neck but couldn't identify who had asked the question. 'Don't You Come The Smart Alec With Me, Lad! Now Lay The Hammock On The Deck And Then Twist The Nettles, Clews And Lanyard Tucking Them Securely Under The Lashing Towards The Centre!'

Guns had to demonstrate how to do the tucking a number of times. He kicked a few hammocks that he didn't consider well lashed. 'Sling These Monstrosities Again And Lash Them Up Correctly!'

Once all the hammocks were correctly lashed we all re-hung them and left them hanging, as classes from the other messes began to arrive for their Stand-Easy.

After Stand-Easy we unlashed our hammock, stowed one of our blankets, a sheet and a pillow inside along with a spare set of number 8s, a change of underwear, socks, a clean towel and our washing gear. Then we lashed the whole thing up again. Once again Guns reminded us that a correctly lashed-up hammock had to pass through a standard-sized scuttle. Lash blinked at this information. We each tied a name-tag to our hammock. Obviously this was so that when we abandoned ship we could each swim around until we found the hammock that belonged to us ... with our name tag on it!

The usual ship used for Sea Training was not available, and we were to be the first class to use its replacement, the Frigate *HMS Petard*. We didn't know it at the time, but *HMS Petard* was a distinguished Second World War veteran, her crew having been credited with stealing the German Enigma codes. She was also the only Royal Naval vessel to have sunk a German, an Italian and a Japanese submarine, having been active in both the European and Far Eastern theatre of operations during the Second World War.

We didn't have to travel to *HMS Petard*; she came to us. On a bright, sunny morning she gracefully, without fuss or ceremony, came to anchor just off the *Ganges* foreshore. Her arrival was a touch disappointing for me, as I had been looking forward

Her Majesty's Ship Petard

to a trip to one of the big Royal Naval places like Portsmouth, Plymouth, or even Chatham.

We marched down to the foreshore, each of us with our sagging hammock on our shoulder. I felt a little like a real sailor as I staggered up the gangway onto the *Ganges* MFV and rolled my hammock onto the upper deck with all the rest.

After a short, spray-drenching trip our relatively small MFV made herself secure alongside *HMS Petard*, a monster of a vessel. There was definitely an art to timing the step from the bobbing MFV gunwale onto the bottom platform of *Petard's* accommodation ladder. I found it difficult because my ferkin hammock unbalanced me. Once we were all safely aboard we grouped around Guns and Spider who told us that they had tossed a coin and that Guns had lost and was coming with us for the week. I was beginning to appreciate just how much we relied on our Class Instructors to help us come to terms with those things we had never experienced before, and it looked like the forthcoming week was going to be packed to the gunwales with them.

Spider bade us a smiling farewell, skipped down the ladder and expertly stepped on to the MFV. He waved to Guns as the MFV silently drifted away leaving us marooned. We were at sea, really at sea! I looked around: *HMS Petard* looked like an elderly lady who had been through rough, tiring times and had obviously seen better days. There were brown rust streaks on the bulkheads, equipment and the deck; ropes and fenders were strewn everywhere in a most unseamanlike manner and there was a continual thump of throbbing machinery and a pervasive cocktail of strange smells.

With some difficulty we negotiated our way to the forward Seaman's mess, discovering along the way that we were much too large to pass through a standard Admiralty-pattern watertight door, with a hammock on our shoulder, without banging our head, grazing an elbow or scraping a shin. The doors were all clipped closed and designed for the passage of proper sailors without hammocks. We struggled along the narrow main passageway, which Guns explained was known onboard every Naval ship as the Burma Road. Grinning crew members, in well faded number 8s or grimy overalls stood to one side as we staggered past trying to retain our balance as *Petard* rolled us a welcome. At the far end of the Burma Road we squeezed ourselves, and our hammock, down through a narrow hatch opening.

Nothing prepares you for the forward Seamen's messdeck of a World War II Frigate. It's claustrophobically dim with a low deckhead of confusing pipes, valves, levers, trays, cables and trunkings. People milled about everywhere. There were smells that I could almost taste: cigarettes, dirty water, disinfectant, food, fuel oil, metal polish, overflowing ashtrays, seaboots, strong tea, Tepol, and wet oilskins. Everything appeared to be on top of us. It was a bleak, grimy and noisy place. Large circular trunks running from deck to deckhead separated our side of the mess from the starboard side. As we stood goggle-eyed, Guns told us that the port side of the mess had been partially cleared to accommodate us and that a small number of the ship's crew would sleep on our side to look after us. The ship's Seamen were accommodated on the starboard side and it was best that we stayed clear of them. He himself would be present at most times of the working day and could be contacted in an emergency in the Senior Rates mess at any other time. Standing shoulder to shoulder, each of us holding on to our bent and battle-scarred hammock, we tried to take everything in. I doubt if any of us believed that we could be comfortably accommodated in this space. *Petard* rolled unexpectedly and many of us lost our balance. From above came the sound of running feet and yet another item of noisy, clattering machinery burst into life directly overhead. The noise vibrated through the deck and made the deckhead lights fizz and crackle. Flakes of nicotined deckhead paint fluttered to the deck. At the ship's-side of the mess was a long Formica-topped table. Seats topped with burgundy coloured plastic cushions ran around the sides of the mess. What was it with the Navy and the colour burgundy? Our lockers were small stowage spaces underneath the cushioned seats; no wonder we had been told not to bring much stuff with us. Guns told us to stow our hammocks in a mesh enclosure in the corner with our name tags uppermost. My senses were reeling; everything appeared confusing and noisy. Before I had time to partially absorb the character of the forward Seamen's mess we were ushered out and up a series of ladders and out through the screen door leading to the forecastle. We were stood behind the breakwater, far away from what was going on forward of us. *Petard* clattered, squealed, groaned and vibrated while her anchor was hoisted from the murky depth of the River Stour. A bloke grappling with a hose washed down the anchor and, with a change of vibration, *Petard* pointed her bows towards the North Sea and slowly made her way east.

Once we hit the North Sea proper, she took on a seriously slow roll and pitched alarmingly in the sweeping grey waters. There was obviously a skill required in negotiating ships' ladders. As 173 Class climbed or descended ladders as a group, members of the ship's company waited patiently at the top or bottom. We watched admiringly as the crew appeared to fly up and down them without any apparent effort. We enjoyed a brief period on the upper deck by the port lifeboat whilst Guns explained to us that in the event of abandoning ship this is where we would muster in order to man the lifeboat. Abandon ferkin ship! We'd only just arrived.

Back in the mess, Guns pointed out the hammock bars: there were no hammock hooks onboard *Petard*, only black painted bars with strategically placed depressions.

'What are those hole things sir? Up there sir,' Syd asked, pointing.

'Those Hole Things, As You Call Them, Junior Seaman Harbour, Are Punkah Louvres. They Provide Fresh Air To The Messdeck.'

'Thank you sir.'

'They Can Be Adjusted If Required:, If They're Not Stuck With Paint That Is.'

Guns stood on a bench and tried to demonstrate how to adjust one ... but it was stuck solid. 'Now That You Know Where The Heads Are, The Bathroom, The Hammock Slinging Bars, The Galley And Your Abandon Ship Station, You Should Be OK For Now.'

We sat on our burgundy coloured bench cushions and listened while an unknown Petty Officer told us something about *Petard*'s history. She was a 'P' class Frigate built by Vickers Armstrong Ltd on the Tyne and was completed on Valentine's Day (14 February) 1942.

Some bloke in the main passageway was blowing on a Bosun's Call and shouting 'Fall out special sea dutymen. Hands to dinner. Cooks of the mess to the Galley.'

There was no CMG onboard; our food had to be collected from the main Galley by those members of each mess nominated as 'Cooks'. I was one of the unfortunate trio of Cooks nominated for the port side Seamens' mess because I couldn't hide quickly enough. Along with Slattery and an Able Seaman, I made my way aft, up a ladder onto the upper deck and the galley. We queued outside the hatched door of a steaming, incredibly hot compartment full of racks of brown encrusted trays full of food. Because the forward Seamens' mess was the largest onboard, we had the most trays. We each had two to carry, one on top of the other. The AB told us to put the 'duff' tray on the top. Together they weighed a fair bit; my bottom tray contained meat, extremely heavy potatoes, an intimidating pile of overcooked carrots and a mountain of unidentified green stuff. My upper tray contained a muscular suet-based monstrosity afloat in a sea of globular custard.

'Don't let the custard drip onto the meat, young 'un: blokes down the mess won't be best ferkin pleased if you do that,' explained the AB.

As I turned with my pair of trays *Petard* performed an acute turn to starboard. Everybody else in the queue adjusted their position: I didn't. Thankfully my full-bodied custard knew what was going on and didn't move at all. I slowly made my way down a ladder, hugging my trays close to my chest, and at the bottom bounced off a bulkhead-mounted fire extinguisher. My trays rattled. I staggered down the main passageway, rebounding from one side of the Burma Road to the other. The custard remained unmoved and uninterested. It was a Naval tradition apparently for those on the bridge to put the ship through a series of violent manoeuvres shortly after sending Cooks to the Galley. It took teamwork to squeeze all the trays through the small hatch leading to the mess without spilling anything, but eventually we managed it. The AB carried a small fanny full of something with a wrinkled brown skin on its upper surface, probably gravy.

In our absence the mess had been organised: chipped grey plates were stacked on the end of the table along with a pile of elderly, well-used cutlery that stood vertically in a large circular pot. Misty had been given the job of preventing the plates and cutlery from sliding off the table. We placed our trays on the end of the table. Those who were nominated to dish-out the food made sure that the few crew members received the best and most of everything ... in accordance with Ship's Standing Orders. The roast potatoes had to be chiselled off the base of the tray and the carrots had to be scraped free of a thick, glutinous brown substance. The unidentified green stuff smelled disgusting when it was disturbed. The custard wouldn't flow and the duff was difficult to slice, even with a couple of large rust-bladed seaman's knives. The ugliest and most fearful crew member was given the largest portion of duff.

The trays had to be cleaned before returning them to the galley. Thankfully that job was given to Lash and Blacky who hadn't done anything so far apart from consume some of the pudding. Most of the stains on the battered old trays looked as though they had been there since Valentine's Day 1942 and the burly, blackened remains of the potatoes looked as though they would be almost impossible to shift with normal hand-held equipment.

During and after dinner, some of 173 Class began to change colour. They were told the quickest way to the upper deck. 'Don't do it into the wind ... do it over the lee side!' was apparently sensible advice ... once it was explained which was the lee side. Spewing your guts up into the wind was a mistake you only made once. The worst thing we could do apparently was to 'Call for Hughie' in our neighbour's hammock. Up until then I had been OK but now that it had been mentioned, I began to wonder whether I was going to keep my dinner down or not. Spider had warned us not to believe any of the seasickness cures told to us by the crew.

As everybody drifted away from the mess table, someone poked their head down through the hatch and shouted 'Gash can be ditched for the next ten minutes ... gash can be ditched for the next ten minutes.' Tug and I didn't move quickly enough and we both got that job. Somewhat reluctantly, I grabbed the food-caked handle of one of the two battered mess buckets that was almost full to the brim with the uneaten remnants of dinner. With difficulty, I grappled my bucket up through the mess hatch, which took a bit of organisation as the bucket was slithery and the contents mobile in a thick gravy soup. I waited until *Petard* stopped rolling for a minute and set off on my zig-zagging way down the Burma Road, bouncing off each bulkhead alternately and eventually out of the after screen door and onto the Quarterdeck. A large rectangular shute stained with gravy and congealed pieces of fatty meat hanging tenaciously to its surface was fixed to the stern guardrails. There was a crop of the unidentified green stuff wrapped around one of the guardrails, flapping unceremoniously in the breeze. The bottom contents of my bucket took some banging to remove. The blokes on the bridge thought this was a good moment to put their foot down and *Petard*'s stern dipped and dug in to the grey waters of the North Sea. I was concerned about the amount of stuff clinging to the inside of my bucket, and I watched as a crew member washed his bucket by opening the valve on a nearby fire hydrant. Once he had finished, I tried it myself. It worked too well; I opened the valve too quickly and soaked myself, almost losing the bucket over the side in the process.

I eventually made it back to the mess with my empty, battered gash bucket, 'What happened to you then, young 'un?' asked a member of the ships company, pointing at my wet shirt and trousers.

'Ferkin ship moved, didn't it.'

It got a laugh. My spare pair of Number 8s were inside my hammock and I couldn't get to them until this evening so I had to suffer wet clothing, splattered with uneaten food, for the rest of the day.

Slinging our hammocks in the confined space of the messdeck wasn't as easy as it had been on the Long Covered Way. We crawled over and under each other and quickly realised that there was no space between hammocks; they touched and swung together. We got help from members of the crew who had the best slinging points, directly over the mess table. Once slung we had to demonstrate our skills in getting in: some did it, and some had to be pushed. Tug and I were in adjacent hammocks and on the other side of me was Muddy Waters, known for his snoring. Inches from my head was a large asbestos-covered pipe and a black-painted lever. Wrapped around the pipe was a piece of rope that I used as a hand-hold. I slept better than expected that first night. My hammock was surprisingly comfortable and the sound of machinery thankfully masked Muddy's snoring. We were assured that our hammock would eventually mould itself to the shape of our body.

During the following days we were given a variety of tasks. We were used as supervised lookouts on the wings of the bridge and on the Quarterdeck as Man Overboard Lookout (Lifebuoy Ghost). We kept ship's watches, with the exception of the middle watch (midnight to four in the morning) which we were not allowed to do at our age. We helped to anchor *Petard*, which was a frightening experience, watching all that chain rattle out. We all had a go on the wheel, that surprisingly wasn't located on the bridge but back aft and a few decks down. We washed down decks, spread awnings and took them down again. We hoisted and lowered boats by hand, learning some rather colourful sailors' terminology in the process. 'Marry Them Ferkin Ropes' meant to grip two ropes together. 'Two Six!' was a warning to pull or lift something. We were briefly shown the inside of a gun turret, shown round the Sonar Control Room and the darkened Operations Room. As Seamen we would be given one of these sub-specialisations to learn and this would determine which training establishment we would go to after *Ganges*. I was already inclined towards the Operations Room and the Radar Plotting option as this appeared to be the more comfortable and quieter of the available choices. Every day we had a fire-fighting exercise and every evening the mess was inspected by someone or other with a gold ring on his sleeve.

We made landfall on day two. On the western horizon appeared the craggy outline of Portland Bill. *Petard* gracefully negotiated the rough waters of the Portland Race and made her way north towards Portland harbour. Someone on the bridge with a megaphone instructed us to 'Close All Upper Deck Screen Doors And Scuttles. Assume Damage Control State One Condition Zulu Alpha. Special Sea Dutymen To Your Stations. Berthing Party Muster At Your Stations. Hands Out Of The Rig Of The Day Clear Off The Upper Deck. We Shall Remain Alongside To Store Ship. Special Sea Dutymen Remain Closed Up.' The crew moaned: apparently that meant we weren't staying overnight in Portland and there would be no run-ashore.

We berthed alongside an elderly wooden jetty.

'Clear Lower Deck. Clear Lower Deck. Store Ship!'

173 Class joined *Petard*'s crew to form a long, snaking line from a truck on the jetty, each of us a small link in a lengthy human chain. We man-handled boxes, bags, crates, jugs and jars over the gangway to a canvas shute rigged on the inside of an open screen door. It took about an hour to empty the truck. Once the last of the stores were safely down the shute, we heard the megaphoned instructions from the bridge wings, 'Hands Prepare For Leaving Harbour. Hands Out Of The Rig Of The Day Clear Off The Upper Deck. Assume Damage Control State One Condition Zulu Alpha. Close All Upper Deck Screen Doors And Scuttles. Special Sea Dutymen Close Up!'

Crikey! that was a lot to take in at one go, so I hid down the mess out of the way while *Petard* negotiated her way out of harbour.

That afternoon I was detailed off to act as Bosun's Mate. Because the ship had no Tannoy system, I had to walk the length of the Burma Road, blowing on a borrowed Bosun's Call and shouting 'Stand Easy!' Quarter of an hour later I had to repeat the process piping 'Out Pipes!' in other words, 'Back to work'. I doubt if anybody took much notice of me.

Later the same day we did more sea-boat launching and recovery exercises off the Isle of Wight. Tug said he could almost smell his Mum's cooking. He pointed out the Needles and the lighthouse and just stood there looking towards his home town of Cowes that was to the east somewhere. I felt sorry for him: if I'd been within sniffing distance of Pudsey I think I would have felt homesick as well. It would have been a miracle of seamanship however, as Pudsey is about 50 miles from the nearest sea.

A few days later, following a full-speed transit north we were off the mouth of the River Humber, a few miles south of Bridlington: my birthplace. It was a relatively calm day and a number of us were each given a paintbrush and a pot of Pusser's ships-side grey paint, and allocated something on the upper deck to paint. I was given the forward arm of the port sea-boat davit with strict instructions to wash it down with fresh, soapy water before painting. By the time I'd got myself a bucket full of warm water, some Tepol and a scrubbing brush it was Stand-Easy, so I stowed my paint pot and bucket of warm water round a corner and went below for a cup of something in the mess. As before, those on the bridge were delighted to perform ship manoeuvres while the crew were at rest and I was thrown sideways as *Petard* rolled to port. Those who knew what to expect grabbed and cradled their cups. The main gash bucket slid across the mess, stopped by the outstretched leg of a crew member. Those of us from Suffolk didn't react quickly enough and watched our cups of invigorating tea crash to the deck. *Petard* spent a brief moment on an even keel before being flung over to starboard. I no longer had a cup to worry about so I just clung onto a messdeck stanchion. When I went back to work, my pot of paint and bucket were gone, so I busied myself with nothing much for the remainder of the day.

A few days later *Petard* rounded the Felixstowe spit and I glimpsed the *Ganges* mast through the mist of a typical Suffolk morning. The guy on the bridge blew his Bosun's call, 'Close All Upper Deck Screen Doors And Scuttles. Special Sea Dutymen To Your Stations. Assume Damage control State One Condition Zulu Alpha. Forecastle Part Of Ship Muster On The Forecastle: Prepare For Anchoring. Hands Out Of The Rig Of The Day Clear Off The Upper Deck. We Shall Remain At Anchor For Approximately Thirty Minutes.'

173 Class were ushered up to the forecastle where we were again mustered behind the breakwater to watch the process of anchoring ship. A bloke wielding a large hammer took a swing at a clip and with an ear-splitting rattle the anchor chain clattered away amidst a cloud of brown rust-dust, plunging into the grey waters of the River Stour. We were back!

It wasn't imaginary salt that I was brushing off my shoulders as I waited to return the component parts of my hammock the following morning. Despite being back on solid ground I could still feel *Petard*'s rolling motion: according to Guns, it would take a few more days before our young bodies would readjust themselves.

At the end of September we were moved into Keppel 1 mess. It was exactly the same as Keppel 9 and we all selected beds that were in exactly the same place. The only difference was that our port side windows now faced directly onto the Quarterdeck. I doubt if there was any status in being in *Ganges*' Number 1 mess: it was just a number.

The Suffolk weather had been chilling for some weeks now, but it wasn't until the morning of the first day of October that we were instructed to replace our white fronts with our much warmer sea jerseys. My rolled-up and taped jerseys smelled as though they had been stowed in the back of my locker for the last five months and only brought out for kit musters, which was true. Sea jerseys were the most difficult piece of kit to wash and dry properly. On the plus side, our Stand-Easy Kye ration was restored. A cigarette and mug of strong brown sweet Kye was a brilliant Naval combination; much more restorative than the summer's cigarette and milk!

Spider reminded us that he had 'Put In More Sea Time On The Gosport Ferry Than You Lot Have Combined!'

I didn't quite know what he meant.

After dinner, and yet another mediocre Saturday morning mess inspection with no trophy awarded, we were all stood at the end of our bunk space having received a mess bollocking from our Assistant Divisional Officer. Spider took the deck space, consulted his clipboard and strode up the centre of the mess. 'Exped Weekend!' He pointed at the first six. 'You Six Are The Lucky Six, This Weekend You Will Be Going Back to Sea Onboard Our MFV For An Overseas Visit To Sahfend.'

Tug and I looked at each other: then the penny dropped ... he meant Southend.

Spider was opposite us now and Blacky was waiting expectantly. 'You Eight, My Academic Eight, Will Be Going To Cambridge To Inhale Some Of That Fine City's Learning.' Blacky smirked. He then ticked off the next 15 as he turned at the top of the mess and started to detail those on my side. He stopped in front of Tug. 'No Sailing For You My Lad.' He swiped three ticks on his clipboard paper. 'You Three Musketeers,' he looked from Tug to me, to Misty, 'Will Be Going To RAF Wattisham With Sub Lieutenant Casement This Weekend: The First Time That This Type Of Expedition Has Been Tried. You Are To Take With You Your Muffler And Your Gloves.'

Outside the Exped store, along with Tug, Misty and three Nozzers from Keppel 9 mess, I stood in front of a bespectacled Sub-Lieutenant dressed head to toe in camouflage clothing with a badly fitting beret on his head. He wrote our names on a sheet and told us to collect new camouflage clothing and an Ordnance Survey map of the Shotley Peninsular. He would explain what our task was once we were fully kitted out.

Our camouflage clothing was brand new and smelled strongly of mothballs. It was predominantly sand coloured, perfectly suited to camouflage us against the leafy green Suffolk countryside! Unfortunately, our rucksacks were olive green and un-camouflaged. At a separate counter, under the direction of our Sub-Lieutenant, we were each given a Ration Pack, a tin of dark green face-paint and a compass.

The Sub-Lieutenant, now known to us as 'Specky', gave us permission for a quick smoke whilst he went to organise our transport.

Our transport was a blue Naval utility vehicle, a small Bedford van with three rows of bench seats known as a 'Tilly'. Specky was the driver. We stowed our bags on the long back seat and fell-in alongside as instructed.

'My name is Sub Lieutenant Casement and I am an Instwuctional Officer at HMS Ganges. Some of you may have seen me about the school, my specialisation is geogwaphy. This weekend we are pwivileged to be the first gwoup to twy something completely diffewent ... something completely diffewent. We are going to twy and infiltwate Woyal Air Force station Wattisham. Our task will be to gain entwy to the camp ... gain entwy to the camp ... undetected. Their secuwity owganisation is not aware of our impending visit. Any questions?' We all shook our heads and smiled at each other: it all sounded great.

During our journey Specky gave us some more details; apparently he had already worked out a plan of attack. We were going to encamp in a barn in a place called Bonny Wood which was about thwee ... sorry, three miles from RAF Wattisham where our first task would be to pitch our tents, make a fire and have something to eat. We would try to infiltrate the camp at exactly three-o-clock in the morning when concentration levels were allegedly at their lowest.

The barn was in a sorry state. There were large gaps in the roof and it smelled of recent animals. Specky parked the Tilly in the corner under the largest hole in the roof and we pitched our tents in the opposite corner. Specky had an Officer's camouflaged tent all to himself and positioned it a discreet distance away from the rest of us. We Keppel 1 mess members had our own un-camouflaged tent and the Nozzers from 5 mess had theirs. The tents had that peculiar, well-used musty smell about them. After we had eaten a meal of beef stew, baked beans and processed cheese we formed a semi circle around Specky who explained some more of his plan. 'A thwee mile march should take us a little over an hour ... a little over an hour. We will allow ourselves a genewous two hours to work out how to gain entwy to the camp. So we will leave here at midnight ... twelve-o-clock midnight. I suggest that you gwab yourselves some sleep and I'll wake you all at about eleven ... about eleven.'

Sounded great to me, but I couldn't sleep. What would happen if we were caught? How were we to climb over large fences or walls or whatever? What was an RAF Station like? What were RAF people like? What was marching three miles at midnight like?

By two-o-clock in the morning most of my questions had been answered. Along with Misty and a Nozzer, I was squatting behind a dense hedge close to the southern wire mesh boundary fence of RAF Wattisham, greened-up with my scarf wrapped around my face. We had left the barn just before midnight and strolled the three miles or so along Lower Farm Road, keeping to the shadows. We had identified a couple of places in the southern perimeter of Wattisham's fence that were not overlooked by the sentries and had been split into two teams each with a specific section of wire fence to tackle. Specky and the rest of the team were to tackle an easier looking section of the fence about quarter of a mile to the north of us.

The only noise was Nozzer, who was noisily clacking chewing gum.

'Get rid of that stuff!' I said.

Surprisingly he did exactly as I told him. The first order I had ever given to anybody ... and it worked!

We had arranged with Specky that both teams would scale RAF Wattisham's wire mesh fence at exactly the same time. This, he said, could create misunderstanding amongst the sentwies. I checked my Timex, all three of us removed our boots, tied the laces together and hung them around our necks. I'd developed wire-mesh climbing skills as a schoolboy and knew that it was best done in bare feet or socks. At exactly three-o-clock Misty and Nozzer held the fence tight, to prevent it from swaying, as I scrambled up and over. The other two followed without mishap; it was surprisingly simple and apart from a few youthful farts, we did it in relative silence. The beans hadn't been a good supper choice. On the other side of the fence we crouched behind a large electrical junction box and checked the sentry to our right, who was still reading his book by torch light and totally unaware of us. In our socks we scampered across grass towards the shadowed side of the nearest building and squatted down behind some large dustbins. We put our boots back on. It took a while for us all to catch our breath.

'We're in!'

Two blackened faces, partially wrapped in scarves, nodded.

We heard a commotion back at the fence and assumed that it could be Tug whose fence-climbing skills probably weren't that good.

'Come on, let's try and find the Gatehouse,' I said. Someone had to take charge didn't they? I had this mental picture of the camp layout from my map, and we headed off in the direction I thought was approximately northeast.

We spent some time skipping from one building to another, avoiding the occasional car or wandering RAF bloke. At one point in our journey we were squatting at the back of a building beneath a dimly lit, slatted window of frosted glass. We had decided against having a cigarette, and were readying ourselves for a sprint over to the next building, when we heard a couple of female voices followed by the sound of a flushing toilet. I smiled beneath my scarf and signalled a halt. We made ourselves comfortable and those of us who needed a smoke lit a cupped cigarette. For the time it took to smoke a cigarette, we listened in fascinated silence as two women exchanged personal information about someone called Flight Lieutenant Wentworth. It was the first time I had ever heard a woman break wind.

We noted that at least two ex-members of Flight Lieutenant's Wentworth's fan club didn't wash their hands after toileting. We waited a few minutes, just in case there were any further developments, then ground our cigarette ends into the RAF grass and scampered away to an unlit area alongside another building about 20 yards away. All three of us were becoming pretty good at finding darkened areas where we could rest undetected for a few minutes. We had to find somewhere with sufficient light for us to read the map, as I reckoned we were getting close to the Main Gate: I could occasionally hear what sounded like the rasp of a barrier being raised and lowered. Eventually we found a small wall light at the back of a windowless building and huddled under the yellow beam. I reckoned that we were perfectly placed for a run on the Main Gate that I estimated was on the other side of an adjacent row of garages. We spread some more camouflage 'makeup' over our dampened foreheads and adjusted our scarves around our faces.

Round the other side of the garages, we strutted proudly towards the Main Gate, all three of us shoulder to shoulder. A couple of RAF types, with their backs to us, were facing the approach road to the camp, one on either side of a barrier. The Gatehouse itself looked empty.

I coughed.

One of the RAF types turned. 'Who are you ... the Black & White Effin Minstrels?'

I gave my name, rank, official number and 'HMS Ganges'.

'How did you get in?'

'Over your fence.'

'You didn't?'

'Did.'

'Impossible.'

'Did.'

'What, all three of you?'

'Yep.'

'Bollocks! How many of you all together?'

'Six and an Officer ... seven altogether,' splurted Misty

'Ah well ... we have the other four.' He waved his stick at the Gatehouse.

We all looked at each other and smirked.

'So you reckon you've breached our security then do you?' He smacked the end of his stick into the palm of his gloved hand.

We turned and ran. If our time at *Ganges* had taught us anything, it had taught us to recognise trouble. Neither of the Guards could leave the Main Gate barrier unattended and didn't follow us.

From the shadows of an RAF truck, conveniently parked to the right of a long windowless building, we watched as one of the Guards disappeared into the Gatehouse. The Nozzer discovered that the door to the truck was unlocked and we all three crawled inside. Misty and I squatted down on the floor well whilst the Nozzer, who was given the job of look-out, kept his eyes above the dashboard.

'A Jeep has just stopped inside the barrier.'

'What do you mean 'just' ... you're not one of the three just ferkin men are you?' I joked.

The Nozzer didn't get it.

'We don't have Jeeps,' said Misty.

'The RAF might,' I whispered.

'True,' conceded Misty.

'They've all got torches,' said the Nozzer.

'They'll be looking for us then,' I explained, a brilliant piece of deduction given the circumstances.

'Two more Jeeps have arrived, full of blokes in white caps.'

'Not the ferkin Navy?' said Misty

'No, these are RAF types,' said the Nozzer. 'They've got a dog!'

'What type?'

'Big ferkin thing. Don't know exactly.'

'Is he on a lead?'

'Yes.'

'That's OK then.'

It took the dog seconds to sniff us out. The spokesperson of the mob, who within seconds had surrounded the truck, explained the situation to us. 'You Navy Bastards Get Your Arses Out Of My Royal Air Force Truck!'

We remained silent. That was not the kind of invitation we expected.

'You've Got Exactly Thirty Effin Seconds Or The Dog ... Known Throughout RAF Station Wattisham As Senior Aircraftsman Bollock Ripper Will Be Paying You A Visit!'

Nozzer opened the door and we slowly clambered down. Pulling our scarves up to cover as much of our face as possible, we were confronted by a mob dressed in Wedgwood-blue greatcoats and holding white sticks. Senior Aircraftsman Bollock Ripper was lying down, wagging his tail.

'Follow Us!' ordered the biggest bloke.

At the back of the Gatehouse we came face to face with Specky and his team who were standing behind a series of barred gates shivering in their underwear and boots, each with a scarf draped nonchalantly over their shoulders. Tug smiled at us.

'Are These Pathetic Individuals The Other Members Of Your Team?' the big bloke asked me. He asked me because I was the tallest.

'Yes,' I admitted.

'You're not Flight Lieutenant Wentworth by any chance are you sir?' Misty asked the big bloke.

'I Most Certainly Am Not. Who Are You?'

'Junior Seaman First Class Melrose from Her Majesty's Ship Ganges.'

'And You Are?' The spokesman looked directly at the junior member of our team.

'He's a Nozzer,' I said.

'A Nozzer?'

'Yes,' I said. 'Junior Seaman Second Class Nozzer from her Majesty's Ship Ganges: the junior member of our team.'

'Foreigner Are You?' the spokesman asked.

Nozzer shook his head.

He turned his attention to me. 'And You Are?'

'I've already given my name and number to one of your blokes on the gate.'

I received a thwack on the shoulder with a long white stick for that.

All six of us were given a bed in an empty wooden hut around the back of the Gatehouse. Specky was escorted away to somewhere else, probably the Officer's mess.

We slept under guard and in the morning were watched as we bathed and removed the last of our 'make-up'.

Whilst we were enjoying a very nice cooked-to-order breakfast in a very swish and comfortable Dining Hall, a bloke in a well-cut blue uniform joined us at our table. 'I hear that one of you Navy lads was looking for me: I'm Flight Lieutenant Wentworth.'

We all shook our heads. 'No, not us ... sir.'

He stared at each of us in turn and smiled. 'My apologies. Sorry to disturb you, enjoy your breakfast.'

Nozzer, Misty and I just about managed to stifle our giggles until he had left the Dining Hall. Tug and his team looked at us inquiringly, until we explained what we had overheard the night before.

'So it was the girl's heads then?' asked a wide-eyed Tug.

'Women's,' I explained. 'They were definitely women.'

And they farted ... just like us,' said Nozzer.

We watched with mouths agape as a group of women, dressed in tight blue skirts and pale blue blouses, ordered breakfast, acknowledged a group of RAF blokes and sat at a table within smelling distance. They ignored us completely. Unshaven and dressed in camouflage gear, maybe they thought we were Special Forces ... yeah that was probably the reason ... deferential and a little intimidated perhaps!

Back in Keppel 1 mess on Sunday evening everybody had an Exped tale to tell. Blacky had been detained by the Cambridge Police as they thought he was an escaped Borstal boy. The team that had gone to Furze Hill told us about the Instructor's tent being trashed in the middle of the night by the team from somewhere else. Misty explained to everybody what a brilliant place RAF Wattisham was.

For a while we wallowed in the limelight: I was the accredited leader of the very first successful covert infiltration of an RAF camp by boys from *Ganges*.

The following morning we were all wide awake waiting for a 'Charlie' that never came. We were all washed and dressed when Spider arrived to get us out of our beds and explained to us that the rest of the United Kingdom and her Commonwealth had turned their clocks back an hour while we were sound asleep. If only we'd known.

I never saw Specky again. Those of us who had passed ETLR (Education Test for Leading Rate), whatever that meant, weren't spending much time on academic studies now that we were well into our final term.

I had been working on my excuse for not taking part in the first Inter Divisional cross-country race of the season for some weeks. I'd invented some slight damage to my instep whilst scaling RAF Wattisham's boundary fence and had convinced Guns that I needed a break from anything that might aggravate my weakened foot. He knew I was shamming, but excused me anyway.

The unfortunate participants assembled on football pitch number three to the right of the CMG at 14:15 for a 14:30 start on the second Saturday of October. It was a typical cross-country run type of day; cold, dull and drizzly. Guns had given me the job of standing by a small wooden bridge over a beck to ensure that all the runners ran through the water and not over the bridge. It was a nice relaxing job until the first of the runners started to arrive. Then it became impossible to ensure that everybody went through the water. I stood to one side whilst the competitive front section of the group pounded past, some going through the water, some over the bridge. My job became easier as the slower runners dribbled past, although by this time I was getting bored and was busying myself kicking clumps of vegetation. Tug was near the back, covered head to toe in Suffolk mud, beginning to stumble and unsmiling as he tackled the bridge. Overall, Keppel Division didn't do that well: coming in tenth out of 12 yet again. Blacky was the last to stumble over the bridge.

'You should have gone through the water,' I said.

Blacky stopped, turned and inhaled deeply as he staggered back over the bridge. He splashed through the water. 'That ferkin good enough for ya?'

'Perfect, thank you.'

'Piss off,' and he tottered away.

Considering the number of boys all living close together, fighting was rare and serious Junior-to-Junior problems were rare. However, tensions did spill over occasionally and it was during an unsupervised Stand-Easy that something aggravated a festering problem between two of our messmates. There was the sound of a scuffle and before we knew what was happening two of 173 class were rolling about on the Long Covered Way, with fists, spit, boots and obscenities flying. We stood and watched until the Class Instructor from the Communicator's mess opposite dived in to separate them – just as it was getting interesting.

'You shit!' the lad called Phil bellowed, spittle running down his chin.

'And you're a ferkin syphilitic arsehole!' replied Mucker, who was without doubt the best swearer in the mess ... maybe in the Division ... and probably in *Ganges*. If there were *Ganges* Colours for swearing, Mucker would have earned them.

'You're a brown hatter you shit faced arsehole,' replied Phil. That was a good rhythmic series of swear words.

'That's Enough!' bellowed the Instructor from the mess opposite. 'Calm Down ... NOW!'

Mucker spat out some blood and what looked like a tooth or two. 'Piss, bollocks and barrels of shit!'

Spider and Guns came around the corner at the double and immediately took over, with Spider getting a firm hold of a squirming Mucker.

Guns took charge of the rest of us. 'The Rest Of You Go And Clean Your Cups. Put Your Fags Out! Leading Junior, When They've Cleaned Their Cups Fall Them In By The Rubbish Bins And Keep Them Quiet!'

Mucker and Phil, each held firmly by an Instructor, were dragged still squirming up towards the Quarterdeck.

The rumours started as we fell-in. 'I heard 'em having a ferkin go at each other earlier.'

'Mucker's an argumentative sod.'

'They've been at it for ferkin ages.'

'I heard that 'Phil' called Mucker a Brown Hatter.'

'Wonder how many ferkin teeth Mucker lost.'

'Phil's a ferkin good rugby player, Phil is.'

'Did you see Mucker's shirt pocket was ripped?'

'Phil's got a ferkin short fuse you know.'

'Did anyone collect their cups?'

'Naah.'

'Naah.'

'Nor me.'

Our next period was seamanship, and we didn't see Mucker and Phil until after we'd finished dinner. They had been officially charged with something called 'affray'. They'd seen the Officer of the Day who had put them both on Commander's Report: this could result in both of them being given a stiff period of punishment, possibly 'cuts', and even back-classed which would mean an extra five weeks in *Ganges*.

As I looked at the rafters that evening, my new phrase was 'Brown Hatter'. The Arry boys in the mess, who knew about such things, had been quick to explain its meaning. It was a term used to identify anybody who was actively homosexual, something that was tolerated, but still officially illegal in Her Majesty's Royal Navy.

The following day, the Commander awarded Phil and Mucker 14 days' number 9s each. The class Instructors asked both to apologise to each other and shake hands, but neither would agree to do that, so a grudge-fight was organised. That evening a group of snorting, bent-nosed PTIs assembled in the mess with the Class Instructors to make the final arrangements for the fight that was to be held in the gymnasium the following evening after tea unless the two apologised to each other before then. Everybody hoped that they didn't ... we wanted a fight!

After tea the following evening, we were marched over to the gymnasium where a boxing ring and benches had been laid out at the far end, away from the dangling ropes. We all sat in excited contemplation of something violent and entertaining. A cauliflower-eared PTI clambered into the ring, stood in the centre and spouted, 'Her Majesty's Ship Ganges Is A Melting Pot For Boys Of Your Age. Boys Of Your Age Have Plenty Of What We Call Aggressive Testosterone Fizzing Around Their Bodies. This Is The Stuff That Makes You What You Are ... Boys With Lots Of Excess Energy.'

'Is that testoster-whatsit the stuff what keeps bits of me from going to sleep at nights sir?' someone interrupted. There were sniggers.

'Take His Name! Take His Name Someone! See Me Later Lad!' It silenced everybody for a while. The cauliflower-eared PTI took a deep breath and continued. 'Occasionally Differences Emerge Between Boys That Can Not Be Resolved In The Standard Naval Fashion. In These Instances The Royal Navy Can Authorise ... Under Strict Professional Supervision ... What We Call A Grudge-Fight. This Enables The Boys In Question To Vent Their Anger In A Controlled And Supervised Manner!'

I was losing interest in the verbals. All I wanted to see was Mucker and Phil knock ten-bells-of-shit out of each other. Normally, they were both relatively quiet individuals who kept themselves to themselves and didn't contribute much to the general mess banter. We all chose a favourite to support. I took the easy option and chose to support Mucker who was the larger of the two.

Chief Petty Officer PTI Ruffles, with a whistle firmly clamped in his mouth, took to the ring and signalled Mucker and Phil to enter the ring from opposite corners where they had been waiting surrounded by a small group of fussing PTIs. Both were wearing blue sports gear, plimsolls and tightly laced brown boxing gloves; they both stared at the canvas floor. Chief Petty Officer PTI Ruffles removed his whistle and invited them both to the centre of the ring and asked in a resounding tone if they would both apologise to each other. Both Mucker and Phil emphatically shook their heads. In stature Mucker was the taller of the two by about four inches and probably about a stone heavier, but Phil was the better Rugby player and moved faster. We all sat back, anticipating a real good fight.

'A bob on Phil to win. Anyone interested?' whispered someone behind me.

'Mucker will murder him.'

'No chance.'

'As long as we get blood!'

'Yeah!'

'Lots of ferkin blood.'

Apparently *Ganges* Grudge-fight rules dictated that the fight would continue for as long as the Referee considered it safe. Ruffles blew his whistle and Mucker and Phil came to the centre of the ring and emphatically refused to touch hands in the time-honoured fashion. We gave them an enthusiastic cheer, stamped our feet and slapped our bench.

If I'd blinked, I'd have missed it. Mucker caught Phil with almost the first punch of the fight, a swinging right arm that lifted him off his feet and dumped him against the ropes where he hung silently unmoving. Gasps of amazement buzzed as Chief

Petty Officer PTI Ruffles knelt over Phil and Mucker skipped around the ring like a demented fairy.

Eventually Phil was pulled back to his feet and was placed on the stool in his corner where a couple of PTIs fussed around him splashing water in his face, shouting at him and slapping his cheeks. When he was capable of yelling 'Piss off you Brown Hatter! Just a lucky punch' to Mucker, he was considered fully recovered.

At Stand-Easy the following day we realised that Mucker was nowhere to be seen. Guns explained that he had been back-classed, and that was the end of that. Phil always referred to Mucker as 'That Brown Hatter.' for the remainder of our time at *Ganges*.

Measuring us for our 'Sea Suit' was left as late as possible. During my ten months at *Ganges* my vital statistics had changed somewhat. I had grown two inches taller and my expanded chest was now a magnificent 35 inches. According to the man from Bernards, the Naval tailors from Harwich, the material of our new No 1 uniform would be much superior to our existing uniform suits and we would have zips on our trousers instead of flaps. We were assured that the suits would be ready in time for Christmas leave, providing we didn't eat too many duffs in the meantime.

We had the first foot-crunching frost of the winter on Bonfire Night. I remembered Bonfire Night at home and all the preparations that went into constructing a large burnable mass of trees and anything else that would burn. Chumping we called it; dragging large tree branches through the streets of Pudsey and raiding other bonfires for anything combustible. We even made 'dens' inside our fires in order to prevent others from stealing our material. Whole families would gather around once the fire was lit. There was always someone's dad in charge and our mothers used to bake potatoes and mushy peas in the embers. There were fireworks and sparklers for the younger ones and trays of brittle, black bonfire toffee for those of us with a sweet tooth. It was always great fun. I half expected something to commemorate the day at *Ganges* ... but there was nothing.

After tea, as we were all settling down to a quiet period of kit upkeep, the Communication Petty Officer from the mess opposite, known to us as Snotty because his nose was always dribbling, stormed into Keppel 1. 'Everybody Fall In Outside.'

Once outside and fallen in, we waited, looking a bit confused.

Snotty reappeared from his mess opposite with a couple of red and yellow flags tucked under his arm. 'Tin To The Left In Threes ... Left Tin!'

Shit! We'd obviously done something wrong.

'Double Maaarcha.'

We doubled all the way across a dark and deserted Parade-Ground and were brought to an undignified halt in the centre circle of football field number 1. It was pitch black.

Snotty unfurled his flags. 'An unscheduled lesson in communication using the ancient art of Semaphore.'

Semaphore ... in the ferkin dark?

Snotty had a torch.

To cut a boring lesson short, he showed us the semaphore alphabet then each of us had to spell out our name using our outstretched arms and his flags.

Frost was beginning to coat the grass by the time Lash, the last of us, spelled his name correctly at the third attempt.

My feet were freezing.

'Keppel one mess dismiss,' said Snotty as he switched off his torch and jammed his flags under his arm. 'Dismiss! Back To Your Mess In Your Own Time.'

As we passed the CMG Tug asked, 'What the ferk was that all about?'

I shrugged my shoulders.

'He was probably bored and wanted something to do.'

'I'm going to tell Guns in the morning.'

'You do that then.'

'I ferkin well will.'

To my knowledge nobody told Guns. Along with everybody else, I put the semaphore lesson down to experience.

I met up with Conkers again as we were both leaving the CMG at the same time after tea one day.

'Hiya Conkers.'

'Hiya Pete mate.'

'How are things going?'

'Great thanks. These ferkin sea jerseys are a pain aren't they?'

'Sure are. Everything going OK?'

'Yes thank you.

I hesitated to ask, but I had to know. 'How's the Homo thing going?' I whispered.

'Well,' he placed his hand over his mouth and looked around to make sure that we couldn't be overheard. 'When I was on summer leave ... and I was in my local park ...'

'Yeah?'

'Watching a mixed doubles game of tennis, you know one man and one woman.'

'I know what mixed doubles is.'

'Well, I suddenly realised that I was paying more attention to the women than I was to the men.'

'OK.'

'So, I've postponed the Homo thing for a while. Maybe when I leave *Ganges*, when I've got the time to think about it properly.'

'Sounds like a sensible option.'

'I'm a bit confused at the moment.'

Time for a subject change. 'What sub specialisation are you going for?'

'RP. Radar Plotter I hope.'

'Me too. Maybe I'll see you at *HMS Dryad* then.'

'That'll be good.' He took a half-smoked cigarette out of his back pocket, lit it and inhaled deeply.

'Spare a drag?' I asked.

'Sure,' he handed me his dampened filter-tipped cigarette. I'd forgotten that Conkers always dribbled over the end of his smokes.

I took a long drag regardless. 'Cheers mate.'

'Got to go. I've got Hornpipe Display Team practice tonight.'

'Bye then mate.' I watched as he skipped away. So the Hornpipe Display Team actually existed ... well shiver mi ferkin timbers!

Towards the end of our final term we were the designated Work Ship Class, which was a welcome change from the normal daily instructional routine. We were excused boots and gaiters and we swanned about wearing our shoes for five days feeling rather superior to those still under training.

The first day I was told to clean the inside of a small blue wooden shack at the top of Laundry Hill. It was the size of a garden shed and contained a desk, a swivel chair and a locked filing cabinet. I was given the door key, a dustpan, a hand brush, a deck cloth and a bucket with a small amount of Tepol in the bottom and told to 'Clean It From Top To Bottom.' It took me ages to figure out where I could get some hot water from: surprisingly, a deactivated gene kicked-in and I realised I was close to the Laundry. In my humble opinion, nothing much inside the small blue wooden shack needed washing, wiping or sweeping, so I didn't bother. But I gave the top of the desk, the window ledge and the filing cabinet a cosmetic wipe with a damp cloth to give the place a delicate aroma of freshly applied Tepol. I put my bucket of sudsy water in front of the door in case anyone walked in and sat myself down behind the desk. I couldn't resist fiddling with the desk drawers; they were all open and I discovered, secreted in the bottom drawer under a pile of typed sheets of paper, a pile of American *Playboy* magazines. I had no idea who used the small wooden blue shed, but I reckoned it was someone who could afford to buy such luxuries: an Officer probably.

I wiped another few surfaces with my damp cloth, closed the curtains, locked the door and immersed myself within the pages of what was a completely different world. 'Playboy: Entertainment For Men' it said on the front cover. The actress Stella Stevens, a well shaped and fair-of-face woman, was Playmate of the Month in the January issue. I grabbed February's issue, whose front cover was covered in red lips, and quickly flicked to the centre pages ... Jayne Mansfield: blimey! ... I wasn't prepared for her! Miss Mansfield had unsettled me; what a woman!

The following day I couldn't believe my luck: I was given the little blue wooden shack to clean again. It was exactly as I had left it the day before, so I locked up, drew the curtains and surveyed Jayne Mansfield again. April's Playmate of the Month was a woman called Linda Gamble, who was nice enough but not in the same league as Jayne. Once again, dinner time was an inconvenient interruption. However, as I was on Work Ship I was unofficially allowed to jump to near the front of the queue and I was quickly back behind my desk. April's issue had told me what to expect from the pages of May's issue. The afternoon flew by in the company of Ginger Young, pages 42 to 59 inclusive ... in gloriously revealing colour!

The wooden crucifix on the wall behind the desk should have given me a clue as to the occupant of the little blue shack, but I didn't notice it until I was locking up for the day.

It was back to reality on Wednesday. I was a part of a small group who were sent down to the Assault-Course to repair some netting that had been damaged. Supervised by Chief Petty Officer PTI Ruffles, I sat on my haunches, basking in the unseasonably warm sun and put my recently acquired net-making skills to practical use. It was a pleasant way to spend a day, but I was more than a little pissed off that I never had the opportunity of absorbing the delights of those *Playboys* I hadn't had the time to open.

The final day of Work Ship I spent in the Wardroom Galley washing, drying and putting away eating and drinking utensils. What a boring job that was. The Wardroom used a distinctly different grade of Tepol that still made my hands wrinkle, but smelled nicer.

That evening we all sat around discussing our Work Ship Week. I managed not to mention the *Playboy* stash, which was unusually secretive of me. During my few days enclosed within The Little Blue Wooden Shack I had learned when, why and how to keep schtum.

December. My Sea-suit was brilliant. Made from a beautifully smooth material, it fitted like a glove and, as promised, the trousers had a simple zip fastening. I was almost a sailor. Along with our suits, Bernards of Harwich presented us all with a bespoke plastic wallet for our Paybooks. It was only a cheap affair but it served its purpose and I used it until my Paybook was replaced by an ID card the following year.

The back-end of the winter term was taken up mostly with final tests and examinations. As members of the Seaman Branch, in addition to performing all the required seamanship duties, we had to learn a sub-specialisation. We were given some very basic instruction in our allocated duties, just to make sure that the selection process hadn't cocked-up and put a square peg in a round, oval or hexagonal hole. I was officially listed as a prospective member of the Radar Plotting branch and as such, was given some very basic instruction in what would be required of me in preparation for going to *HMS Dryad* for the second part of my training. For the first time I sat in front of a radar set and Spider taught me how to make sense of the various blips that covered the screen. We were told that we were the cream of the Seamanship branch, but I suppose the Sonar and Gunnery lads were told exactly the same.

The routine for Christmas leave followed the same pattern as before. We were herded into the gymnasium to watch the colourful VD film ... for the fourth time! Most of 173 class sat at the back and didn't pay too much attention; we'd seen all the gruesomely familiar bits before. We had lots of humorous comments to make about something we knew very little about ... and Spider quickly shut us up.

It was our third leave, so we were able to lord-it a bit. We enjoyed the respect that was automatically accorded to a class who sported an array of gold wire badges on their bespoke Sea Suits, tailored by Bernards of Harwich, Portsmouth, Plymouth, Chatham, Rosyth, Singapore and Hong Kong.

We tried to buy alcohol from the Pullman Dining car on the train from Kings Cross to Leeds, but as before, British Railway staff had been instructed not to serve *Ganges* boys. One lad changed his *Ganges* cap tally for one from *HMS Vanguard* and managed to buy himself three cans of beer which he drank himself.

Everything at home was the same. Mum was still hopping in and out of the shop whenever the shop doorbell rang. Tony was a typical 12-year-old, much too old to believe in Father Christmas but excited about what presents he would receive. Of course I had completely grown out of all that childish Christmas stuff. Mum, who knew a fair bit about cloth, was impressed with the quality and fit of my Sea Suit and settled herself once she had established exactly when I was going back. That evening Mum watched the very first transmitted episode of Coronation Street on television. During the course of my leave she watched all of the other episodes and became a lifelong fan. Me? I could take it or leave it.

I wore civvies for my visit to the large record shop in Leeds to buy some records; a Duane Eddy EP and The Shadows latest single *Man Of Mystery*. Gyrating girls occupied the listening booths, most of them listening to Elvis Presley's latest, *It's Now Or Never*, which was top of the Hit Parade and played regularly on Radio Luxemburg. The girl who had served me back in August wasn't there, so I had no-one to impress. As I walked over City Square towards my bus stop, the West Yorkshire light faded and the twinkly Leeds Christmas lights in City Square and the main City Centre roads were switched on.

On Christmas morning Tony and I awoke to find wrapped presents at the foot of our beds. Like she did every year, Mum had made the effort to sneak our presents into our bedroom while we were asleep. All of a sudden I was a little schoolboy again. Santa Claus had brought me a World Atlas (very appropriate) a Charles Buchan Football Annual, an *Eagle* annual, some chocolates and a large tube of Smarties. Tony had a few books, an Etch-a-Sketch and exactly the same amount of sweets. Secretly I would have preferred the December issue of *Playboy* magazine but I kept that one to myself. There were no photographs of Leeds United in the Football Annual ... again!

I watched my boss, the Queen, make her annual Christmas speech at 15:00. Sometime during the day my father came round with a couple of presents; mine was an Encyclopaedia.

I couldn't really avoid the attractive pony-tailed girl who lived up the road and we accidently found ourselves at the same bus stop one day. She couldn't wait to tell me that she'd been 'going steady' with a bloke called Barry, a trainee filing clerk in a building society, since early September. I didn't know him because he lived in Wakefield. They were extremely happy and Barry was going to start taking driving lessons soon. I crossed my fingers behind my back as I politely wished her all the best. I made a mental note to send her a postcard from the first exotic place I visited in the service of Queen and Country.

I went to Elland Road once, to watch my team draw 3-3 with Derby County the day after Boxing Day. It was a typical second division game. The heads were exactly as I remembered them. The entrance price was a few pence cheaper than the previous season but the yellow and blue match-day programme was still 4d, the same price as when we were in the first division.

Mum, Tony and I all saw the New Year in together. We all wished each other well for 1961 and wondered what it would bring. Little did I know, but within the year, the postcards I'd send to the pony-tailed girl and to Barbara, would be from the Island of Bermuda in the Caribbean ... after I'd quaffed a couple of ice-cold pints of beer in the Flying Angel Club, Hamilton.

D H Lawrence's book 'Lady Chatterley's Lover' was splashed all over the *Daily Mirror*. Apparently, the previous month an all-male jury had decided that, despite a number of unacceptable words, the book had literary merit and could be published. According to the *Daily Mirror* it was the story of the physical relationship between a working-class man and an aristocratic woman and contained explicit descriptions of SEX!

The following day I dog-eared the Encyclopaedia, tossed Charles Buchan's Football Annual into a corner cupboard and expectantly legged-it to my local bookshop to buy myself a copy of Lady Chatterley's Lover. According to the *Daily Mirror*, the publisher had purposefully priced the book at 3/6 which was the same price as a packet of fags.

I went to bed early that night and flicked through the first half of the book until I found something interesting. Some of the stuff this D H Lawrence character had written was rousing indeed. I had a mental picture of Lady Chatterley's physical attributes and her sexual preferences by the time I eventually fell into an unsettled sleep.

The following morning, sleepy eyed, I formulated a plan and went to Pudsey's other bookshop with the firm intention of buying four additional copies of 'Lady C', as it was known to the readers of the *Daily Mirror*.

The shop assistant, an elderly bespectacled lady, coughed into her hand before asking the obvious question. 'Why do require four copies, young man? We normally only sell single copies of this particular book.'

I'd anticipated this. 'I'm in the Navy and I'm buying them for friends who are abroad.'

She smiled, coloured a little and took four copies from the top of a tall Lady Chatterley pile. 'That will be fourteen shillings exactly then, young man.' She held her hand out, pouted and stared at a point over my left shoulder. I extracted a pound note from my wallet with a well practised peeling action, and handed it to her without a smile.

She handed me my six shillings change. 'Would you like your copies wrapped?' she asked fingering the end of a long roll of brown paper.

'Yes please.'

As I watched her expertly wrap the last of the four books and stack them up on the counter in front of me, I suddenly realised who she was. 'Excuse me, I hope you don't mind me asking, but are you Mrs Moorhouse ... Colin Moorhouse's mother?'

'Yes I am, young man.' She pushed my brown paper parcels towards me as she smiled in that strange way that old people do to naughty children.

Bugger! Colin was an ex-classmate of mine. It would be all round Pudsey by tomorrow that I had bought four copies of 'Lady C'.

8

PORTSMOUTH WELCOMES ME

Returning to Suffolk was no problem this time, because it was only three weeks to my final leaving day. Some things however, never change: the Petty Officer, who rifled through my Little Brown Case looking for contraband, waved my copy of Lady Chatterley's Lover in front of my face. 'And What Do We Have Here, Young Man?'

'A book sir.'

'Don't Come The Smart-Arse With Me, Laddie! I Know It's A Book!'

He sounded like a Scotsman. 'Right sir. Sorry sir.'

'What I Need Tae Know Is Why Yae Have A Copy Of This Particular Book?'

'I've read so much about it sir.'

'This Particular Book Is Banned. It's Confiscated!'

'But sir it's on sale in my local boo ...'

'I Don't Care, Laddie. It's Banned Onboard Her Majesty's Ship *Ganges*!' Then he homed in on one of my brown paper parcels. He tore at the paper to reveal ... 'Oh Oh Laddie, What Do We Have Here? Have I Uncovered An Attempt To Smuggle Multiple Copies Of Seditious And Disgusting Literature Onboard One Of Her Majesty's Ships In Contravention Of Queen's Regulations And Admiralty Instructions?'

'Not really sir no.' I didn't have a clue what seditious meant, but it sounded like trouble.

'I Take It That All Your Brown Paper Parcels Contain Copies Of The Same Book?'

'They do, yes sir.'

'Why Five Copies Of The Same Book?'

'One for me and I was going to sell the others to any of my messmates who couldn't find their own copy sir.'

'Proper Little Business Mogul Aren't We?'

I didn't know what a Business Mogul was, but I nodded anyway. I gave it one last try. 'I'm going on draft soon ... sir.'

He fixed me with his unsympathetic dark grey eyes and silently placed my five copies of Mr Lawrence's masterpiece on the table behind him. He slapped my Little Brown Case closed. 'Be Thankful That All I'm Doing Is Confiscating Your Books, Laddie. Be Grateful That You Are Not On A Charge Of Bringing Seditious And Disgusting Literature Onboard One Of Her Majesty's Vessels!'

'Yes sir. Thank you sir.'

'I'm Doing You A Favour, Laddie. When Do You Leave?'

'Before the end of the month sir.'

'And Where Are You Going?'

'*HMS Dryad* sir.'

He turned slightly and pointed to the spider's web badge on his left arm: 'Finest Branch In The Navy! Maybe We'll See Each Other There.'

'Maybe sir. Yes sir.'

'And These Are Not Allowed,' He held up my poker dice that I thought would be fun to play in the mess.

I swallowed. This guy was an out and out bastard. 'Right sir. Thank you.'

'Next!'

Back in the mess I told my mates about my copies of Lady 'C' being confiscated. About half a dozen other lads had also had their copies sequestered. Blacky, however, had hidden his copy inside his raincoat and had managed to sneak it through.

'After you with it then please, Blacky.'

'And can I have it after him please, Blacky?'

'Me next then please mate.'

'Then me.'

Then Tug joined the queue. 'Me after him please, Blacky.'

I explained, as well as I could, some of the things I remembered about the book to Tug who stared at me with his tongue hanging out and eyes bulging. 'Sounds ferkin great!'

I nodded, as someone who had read and memorised most of the best bits would. 'Great book: a great work of English literature!' I declared. 'The last half in particular. Nothing much happens in the first half.'

Back into the *Ganges* routine, I began to appreciate the benefits of the final weeks almost immediately. Basic Training classes such as Parade Instruction, School and Seamanship became less frequent; I appeared to have more spare time and, joy of joys, I was allowed to walk around some days wearing shoes instead of boots and gaiters. This alone distinguished us as one of the Senior Classes: nobody argued with us, and we didn't have to queue long for our food.

At the end of the first week back we had our Passing Out kit inspection. The threat was that failure would guarantee a back-classing and an extra five weeks at Shotley, but we had been here long enough to realise it was an idle threat. It was more than likely to be the final time we laid our kit out in *Ganges*, so that, along with the fact that it would be inspected by the Establishment's Commander, was sufficient incentive for us to make an effort. Those who had good kits helped those who still struggled. It worked and eventually we all stood by our beds with our kit displayed on a sparkly white sheet, with ironed creases, pulled tightly across our mattress.

The Commander gave the few kits at the bottom end of the mess a good going over, then gradually started to lose interest the further up the mess he travelled. By the time he got to inspect mine he was only concerned with the soles of one of my boots, my name-marking on my kit bag and the smell of one of my towels. Before passing onto the next kit he asked 'Where are you going when you leave HMS Ganges?'

'HMS Dryad sir.'

'You'll enjoy life there.'

'Yes sir, thank you sir.'

'Good kit.'

'Thank you sir.'

'But your boots will need new soles before long.'

'Yes sir, thank you sir.'

The Commander turned to Spider. 'And what has Junior Seaman Broadbent achieved during his time at Ganges?'

Spider consulted his clipboard. 'He was runner-up in the Annexe boxing competition, earned his Ganges colours as a member of the Establishment's swimming team and was an above average coxswain sir.'

'Well done,' said the Commander. 'Keep up the good work at HMS Dryad and on your future ships.'

'Thank you sir.'

'Was he any good at shooting?'

Spider consulted his clipboard again. 'Unfortunately not sir. Officially classified as rubbish sir. Not to be given a loaded firearm under any circumstances.'

The Commander smiled at my kit. 'Good job you didn't join the Army then.'

'Yes sir. Thank you sir.'

As Tug saluted the Commander and gave his name, rank and official number, Guns whispered in my ear. 'You Got Away With The Dirty Cap And Where Are Your Second Pair Of Blue Socks?'

'Don't know sir.'

'Scran Bag?'

'Probably sir.'

I began to stow all my kit back in my locker but kept one ear cocked to what was going on between the Commander and Tug. Surprisingly they discussed sailing and the possibility of Tug joining the Royal Navy sailing team. He never looked at his kit. It's not what you know, it's who you know in this man's Navy... that's plainly obvious!

The Commander asked Stumpy, who had the bed on the other side of Tug, if he was a marksman. When Guns replied that he wasn't, the Commander said, 'Good job you didn't joined the Army then!'

Stumpy and Guns both smiled dutifully ... again.

Our Passing-Out Parade took place on the morning of Saturday 21 January 1961 and those of us who had visiting family were given the opportunity to apply for overnight leave until 20:00 the following day. Mother couldn't make it but my father and brother accompanied by a dark-haired lady called Joyce, came down to watch me and the rest of my recruitment perform our final and possibly our best ever march-past.

After Divisions were finished, their Lords at the Admiralty had laid on a feast of beverages and buns in the NAAFI canteen for visiting families. The cuisine didn't overly impress Tony, Dad or Joyce, his dark-haired companion. If you couldn't impress people from West Yorkshire with your food, I doubted if you could make your mark in the catering trade.

After showing my guests around the mess and a number of other notable places, we went over to Felixstowe where we walked on the beach and had some photographs taken. Then Dad, who had occasional flashes of brilliance, drove us to London, where I changed into my civvies that I had asked Dad to bring with him. It was mine and Tony's first visit to the capital and we spent the remainder of the day touring all the sights that we had only read about or seen in pictures: the Tower of London, Trafalgar Square, Buckingham Palace etc. That evening we went to the London Palladium where we saw Cliff Richard and the Shadows top the bill.

On Monday morning we were told to remove all our *Ganges* badges from our uniform jackets and Number 8 shirts. Everybody else in the Establishment recognised that we were about to leave because they could see the slightly darker patches on our shirts where our badges had been.

Just before going to our last *Ganges* dinner, we were fallen-in outside the Divisional Office and subjected to the standard Divisional Officer's leaving speech. We were stood 'At Hease!' and waited for the pearls of wisdom to wash over us. Both our Mess Instructors were in attendance, unsmilingly scanning our faces for any sign of ... anything.

The Divisional Officer started. 'You Will Shortly Be Leaving HMS Ganges ...'

Yeah ... we know that.

'No longer will you be mollycoddled like you have been at Ganges: you will shortly be joining the real Navy where life will be tough, occasionally difficult ... but oft-times rewarding ...'

He'd lost me; what did he mean mollycoddled?

By the time he got round to telling us what a 'Well trained Class' we were and how proud he was to have known us all individually, most of us had lost interest and were staring into space. I'd only spoken to my Divisional Officer a couple of times in the last year ... and both of those had been a bollocking!

As the Divisional Officer nodded to indicate that his speech had ended. Spider stepped forward and thrust his chin out. 'Keppel 1 Mess ... Keppel 1 Mess ...Atten shun ...Three Cheers For The Division Officer ... Hip, Hip ...'

'Hooray!' We raised our caps in the prescribed Naval fashion.

'Hip, Hip ...'

'Hooray!'

'Hip, Hip ...'

'Hooray!'

Thank goodness that was over and we could now get on with the real business of leaving. Tonight we had to plan which mess we were going to trash the following day.

Guns' leaving words were much more specific. 'You've Been A Good Class. Not The Best, But Not The Worst. Work Hard, Concentrate On What You Are Being Told And Enjoy The Big World That's Out There.' That's what I wanted to hear about ... the big wide world that was out there!

Later the same day Spider explained to us that our Divisional Officer had served onboard the frigate *HMS Amethyst* during the Yangtze incident 11 years previously and had been awarded a serious gallantry medal. I wished I'd known about that earlier.

Our final full day was taken up with cramming our kit into our kit bags in the prescribed naval fashion: footwear in the centre, towels and sheets at the bottom, spare working dress and sports gear at the top. Tomorrow morning, at exactly 10:30, we would all be leaving to join Establishments in the Portsmouth area. Myself and the other potential Radar Plotters were going to *HMS Dryad* at a place called Southwick on the outskirts of Portsmouth. The Sonar specialists were going to *HMS Vernon* and the Gunners were going to *HMS Excellent* (also known as Whale Island), both of which were in Portsmouth.

We were given a copy of our individual pay sheet, a large complicated sheet with lots of columns containing hand-written notes and figures. Guns explained to us exactly where it showed what credit we had accrued during our time at *Ganges*. I was overwhelmed to see that I had 36 pounds 9 shillings and two pence. Apparently, when we did our joining routine at our next establishment we would be encouraged to use this money to open a Post Office Savings Account. My head said that was a sensible and mature thing to do, but my heart was yelling new civilian suit with a bright red lining, a new record player, an electric guitar and some money left over to impress a girl or two.

Our leaving uniform was ironed with razor-sharp creases, our shoes were clean and our best cap sparklingly white. I looked upon the mess rafters for the final time and wondered what the rafters would be like at *HMS Dryad*.

We had selected our target mess for the morning; we all had a specific task and knew how best to do it. In a break from *Ganges* tradition we had decided not to trash the Nozzers mess located almost directly opposite ours on the Long Covered Way, because they were expecting it. Instead, we had voted democratically to trash the Communicator's mess that regularly won the mess cleanliness trophy. Snotty was one of the Mess Instructors and we hadn't forgotten about the late night semaphore lesson.

On our last and final day, we waited until after morning Divisions (from which we were excused) until all the classes had been marched off to their first Instructional session of the day. Then Keppel 1 mess paid a visit to the Communicator's mess. Fully aware of what was about to happen, Guns and Spider tactfully found something else to do.

We turned over every bed and locker in the Communicator's mess, emptied every tin of Bluebell and a fresh bucket of Tepol over the deck, raftered the raincoats and piled the kit that was hanging in the Drying Room into washroom sinks and turned all the taps on, switching them off only when the sinks overflowed. We coated all the windows with Bluebell and Pusser's Hard. For good measure we also spiked a couple of the more disgustingly tatty caps on the pointed bit on the end of the beds. Other caps we threw out of the window into the spare ground.

Someone wrote on the mess blackboard 'STICK YOUR SEMERFORE FLAGS UP YOUR ARSE'. We reckoned it was Bogey who had written it because he was a notoriously bad speller. It was our final, satisfying act and the Communicators who couldn't sail or tie a decent knot would remember us of the Executive Branch for a while. We hadn't just trashed their mess ... we'd Trafalgared it!

Before we left I corrected SEMAPHORE: I didn't want the communicators to think that we seamen were an uneducated lot.

We cleaned ourselves up, stuffed our grubby number 8s into the top of our bulging kit bags and got into our Sea Suits. Everybody checked that their lockers were empty and, in their own way, said a silent farewell to Keppel 1 mess.

With our kit bags on our shoulders we staggered over to Nelson Hall to await our transport. My kit bag was unexpectedly cumbersome. Guns and Spider were both miraculously transformed into reasonable men and for the first time in almost a year we heard Spider laugh. They both had a joke and a friendly handshake for us, wishing us all 'Good luck lad!' They both tried to convince us that if we could make it through 386 days of *Ganges* training, we could handle anything the Navy could throw at us. It proved not to be true of course. Our final task was to pile our kit bags into the back of a three-ton truck before boarding our blue Naval bus to Ipswich ... and the world.

I suppose a few fingers were either physically or mentally raised as we passed through the Main Gate on the morning of

Tuesday 24 January and down Caledonia Road for the very last time. On reflection, every single day in *Ganges* had been a series of challenges from the time we dragged our reluctant teenage bodies out of bed in the morning until we crawled back in again many hours later.

We were accompanied on our journey to Portsmouth by three Petty Officers who made sure that we, and our associated kit-bags, were transported across London and onto the correct train at Waterloo station.

There was a fresh, salty, maritime fragrance breezing through Portsmouth Harbour station. On the platform was a small welcoming team who organised us into three groups: those who were going to *HMS Vernon*, those heading for *HMS Excellent* and my small group who were going up and over Portsdown Hill to the village of Southwick and *HMS Dryad*.

We didn't know if we would see any of our Keppel 1 messmates again and goodbyes were sincerely exchanged: we didn't appreciate it at the time but friendships formed at *Ganges* were lasting friendships. Some 30 years later I spotted someone from 173 class on the opposite side of a crowded room at the British Consulate in Jeddah, Saudi Arabia during the First Gulf War in January 1991. Both of us recognised each other immediately. Did we hug? ... of course we didn't, but we had a great time exchanging *Ganges* memories ... over a glass of iced orange juice of course!

On the platform, I waved a blokish farewell to Tug. With our kit bags on our shoulders the rest of us staggered down from the station towards a road called The Hard where a couple of blue RN buses were waiting. Directly facing us was a building with its first floor iron-railed balcony crowded with waving and whistling girls. It looked as though Portsmouth was going to be everything Guns had hinted at ... and probably more.

Was Portsmouth to be an enjoyable place? It most certainly was! But that's another story.

If you enjoyed *HMS Ganges Days,* then you will enjoy
Peter Broadbent's sequel

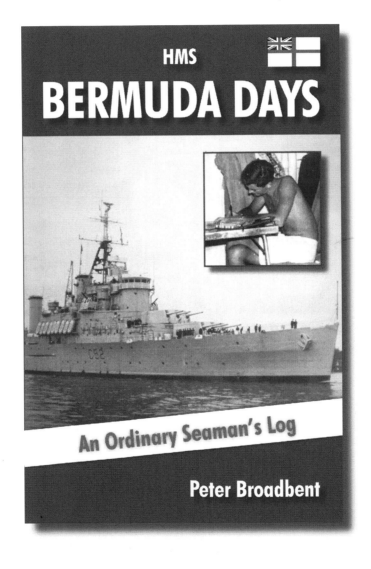

HMS
BERMUDA DAYS

An Ordinary Seaman's Log

Peter Broadbent

Published by Chaplin Books, October 2013